BETWEEN TWO WORLDS

BETWEEN TWO WORLDS

Great Summer

Translated by the author.

Laniakea Publishing

Revised Edition

Book design by Laura Boyle
Bookcover design by Ruby Kang

Paperback ISBN 979-8-9893981-5-7

The boundless love and unwavering support of my cherished family have profoundly shaped the creation of this book. To my beloved wife, YJ, the compass of my heart; to my dear daughter, MJ, the joy of my soul; and to my proud son, YW, who fills me with pride—this book owes its existence to you all. I lovingly dedicate this collection of stories to my parents, whose guiding spirits continue to watch over us from above, illuminating our paths with their enduring love.

CONTENTS

AUTHOR'S NOTE

THIS STORY DOES NOT INTEND TO DISCRIMINATE OR DISTIN-GUISH based on any political philosophy, religion, specific culture, race or gender, age, occupation, education, or nationality, either positively or negatively. The author disregards any correlation between them. The following names, listed alphabetically, are pseudonyms: Dohak, Hah, Heatya, HJ, Hyun, JM, KN, KR, MJ, MK, MM, Samuel, SJ, YJ, YM, and YW.

In this revised edition, the author changed the structure of the book, rearranged some articles in PART ONE, and changed the titles. The author significantly revised many details of the article. In this updated version, the section titled "BLACKPIN's in 2022 Comeback and Analysis," previously included in PART FOUR, has been removed. This article was very extensive, spanning almost 80 pages with 20,000 words. The author intends to publish a book in the future that will contain comprehensive content about BLACKPINK, which is why it has been excluded from this revised edition.

PREFACE

As I revisit and revise 'Between Two Worlds,' my narrative unfolds as a deeply personal journey that traverses diverse continents and cultures. Originally penned in Korean, this manuscript is a testament to my heritage and a conduit to reach wider audiences through its English translation.

Originating in South Korea, my tale spans the sea to the United States, navigating the intricate interplay between two unique cultures. This book isn't just about geographical transitions but delves deeper into the internal shifts that accompany them, exploring the tension between preserving one's cultural identity and embracing another.

Within these pages, you will encounter a tapestry of experiences—some distinctly Korean, others universally human. At its core, this narrative grapples with the allure and the trials of cultural adaptation, the perpetual ebb and flow of life's currents as they traverse borders.

'Between Two Worlds' is a chronicle of transformation and resilience, celebrating the human spirit's capacity to adapt and grow amidst changes. Through the stories shared, I hope to connect with those who have navigated similar paths and to offer others a window into the complex and vibrant interplay of life lived between cultures.

As you join me on this journey, let this book serve as a conduit of empathy and insight, a testament to the shared human experiences that transcend geographical and cultural boundaries. May it inspire understanding and a deeper appreciation for the nuanced mosaic of our interconnected world.

April 2024

PART ONE

GREAT SUMMER

Penned July 18, 2017

A NAME'S JOURNEY

Names are more than labels. They echo history, embody hopes, and reflect who we are. Each has a story to tell, and some even hold hidden layers of meaning. Let's explore this together, starting with a personal story that sparked a special conversation.

It was a sunny June 2017, not long after moving to a new home. My daughter and I, amidst the bustling routine of grocery shopping and making dinner, fell into a conversation about names.

"Dad, what would it be if you could name a town or country?" she asked.

Without hesitation, I replied, "Great Summer." It's unusual for me to decide so quickly, yet it seemed perfectly apt. In Korean, 'Great' translates to '위대한' (Widaehan), a term that can also serve as a given name. My daughter MJ offered a gentle smile to acknowledge the name's depth. She knew there was history behind my choice.

Caption: A card my daughter made for my 52nd birthday.

Happy Birthday!

Wow, Dad's already fifty-two? You've lived quite a while, huh? Gotta stay tough and live a long life ahead! Don't drive too fast! I wish you a fantastic birthday!

The animal that resembles Dad: Bunny.

Dad's many, many nicknames: M and ten others, including "Dad."

BE HAPPY, DON'T WORRY!

    On one of my birthdays, my daughter MJ, attending high school, made a card for me featuring a segment titled 'Dad's Countless Names,' in which she enumerated ten distinct names associated with me. Although MJ knew about my nicknames, Korean and English words, and titles, she was oblivious that I had additional monikers.

"But why did Grandfather name you 'Hah', meaning summer, when you were born in spring?" she asked.

Indeed, my birth in March coincided with the onset of spring, making 'Chun,' representing spring, a more suitable choice. This might appear odd, but I often think my life would have diverged significantly with a different name. My father once explained the reasoning behind my siblings' names and mine. He chose 'Hah' for summer, valuing the season's importance to a farmer for nurturing life, wishing to embed such aspirations within my name.

"Great Summer is a nice name. It's the season of growth," I told my daughter.

"Great Summer would be a good name... the season of growth," I told MJ. She was skeptical, as I'm often fixated on names. With her upcoming name change's application, she pondered changing her name — likely fueling her curiosity about the name. That reminded me of a formative experience.

IN MY LATE TEENS, I prepped for the GED at Geumjatap Academy, tucked in a Seoul alley near Kyobo Bookstore. It was an edgy area — infamous gangster Kim Doo-han (1918-1972) dominated the neighborhood during the Japanese occupation. It's where I met my lifelong best friend, Kwon Sunuk. Among that academy's staff was a talented Korean language teacher in his late twenties or early thirties who played a fateful role in inspiring the subtitle of this essay, "A Name's Journey."

One day, he decided to analyze the students' names, offering insightful comments on each. His observations often left the students in awe. For example, after a girl shared her name, he pinpointed a chronic ailment she suffered from, which left her and the class startled. His unique approach focused on the phonetic qualities of names, intentionally overlooking the literal meanings of the characters and sidestepping traditional forms of fortune-telling. We were captivated!

He also considered the stroke order of Hangeul characters. The teacher claimed some people develop a fist-sized mark somewhere on their bodies — entirely new, not an ordinary birthmark. He believed these marks held a special connection to the universe as indicators of a person's destiny to achieve greatness.

One summer in middle school, my mother washed my back by the faucet. Suddenly, she gasped. "What's this large spot on your side? When did this appear?" It was the first time I'd noticed it! The spot was in a place where I couldn't see it myself. At that time, boys used to take off their shirts in hot weather, so if the spot had been there before, my mother would have noticed it sooner.

The Korean language teacher's mention of such marks reignited this memory with a rush of excitement. It led me to embrace the name Wi Dae-han, symbolizing "Great," seeing it as a sign of my potential for significant achievements.

The teacher shared a story that chilled us to the bone: "Once, I was lecturing when a terrible premonition struck me. I ended class abruptly and raced home. Oddly, every traffic light was green, like fate cleared my path. I arrived just in time to see my young son leaning in a deep ditch trying to pick up his fallen shoe. I barely saved his life!"

His profound and unsettling story cemented our belief in his words. Following this revelation, he was no longer merely an educator to us but rather a wise sage deserving of a place of respect.

He shared that individuals whose names end with the Korean consonant 'ㅇ' might face challenging lives. This, he attributed to the phonetic characteristic of 'ㅇ,' which does not require closing the lips or tongue, leading to a metaphorical 'leakage' of energy. Consequently, such individuals may find seeing their endeavors to fruition hard. Besides phonetics, he also considered the number of strokes required to write the Hangul characters of a name, integrating these elements into his analysis. Hangul, composed of forty elements, including twenty-four consonants and sixteen vowels, varies in the number of strokes for each character. By aggregating these stroke counts with the consideration of the individual's surname, he provided a nuanced understanding of names and their impact on one's life trajectory.

In Korea, name analysis usually uses Chinese characters, not Hangeul. But this teacher was a Hangeul purist, and I respected that. Middle school Chinese class had been a nightmare of memorization for me! His reasoning made sense: "When people call your name, it's the sound that matters, not the written form."

That got me thinking deeply about names. I told these experiences with my daughter. Although I have yet to inquire about my own name, the teacher during those lessons. According to his theory, my name ends with "Ha," the sound that leaves the mouth open, letting energy leak out. It made me feel my name lacked strength. So, in my mind, I changed "Hah" to "Han," meaning solid and broad. Eventually, I decided my name was "Wi Dae-han" — the Great.

WI DAE-HAN

Wi Dae-han. That was the name I used when I got a waiter job at the "Queen," a fancy Western restaurant in Jegi-dong. Before enlisting in the military, I served as a waiter at a Western-style restaurant named 'Queen,' situated at the bustling intersection near Gyungdong Traditional Market in Seoul. The restaurant, known for its Western dishes and cocktail bar, boasted a luxurious interior that attracted a fashionable crowd. During my job interview, the manager, Huh In-ha, who was in his late twenties, inquired about my name. It was then that I introduced myself as Wi Dae-han for the first time, experiencing a twinge of guilt for not using my real name.

Manager Huh noticed my careful speech and dignified behavior, which set me apart from other young male staff. Our conversations revealed mutual respect; despite his position as my senior and superior, he treated me with genuine regard. He'd even shield me from the rowdy staff when I got lost in thought like he knew I needed the space.

One day, to my surprise, a young woman who had once been the object of my unrequited affection entered 'Queen,' now joining as a bartender. She moved with a grace that commanded the room, reminiscent of a queen herself. I recognized her immediately, but she didn't recognize me like she did before.

Before my military service, I worked at a quaint electronics company nestled in the basement of Sadang 3-dong, Seoul, with a friend from my hometown. This company produced FM radios and record players, primarily for Cheonggyecheon markets and OEM businesses. The president, a man in his mid-thirties, was intelligent and had a unique talent for designing circuits on printed circuit boards (PCBs) despite using a wheelchair due to polio. Our small team consisted of just four employees, including us, the newest and youngest members at seventeen or sixteen by Korean age standards.

Among us was an experienced individual in his late twenties, navigating life in a wheelchair, followed by a jovial man in his mid-twenties. My hometown friend stayed on, gaining significant expertise over the years, while I left after a few months.

Before my departure, a young woman joined the company, taking up the role of assembling electronic components onto PCBs alongside us. She was the epitome of beauty I had never encountered before, and her presence made my heart flutter with anticipation and dread at the prospect of confessing my feelings. Regrettably, her tenure was brief, disappearing from the workplace — and my life — within a week, leaving me with the lingering pain of unrequited love.

Years later, in a twist of fate, she reappeared as if conjured from my memories, this time stepping into the 'Queen' restaurant where I worked as Wi Dae-han. Despite the years that had passed and her mature appearance that made me question my recognition, the impact of our fleeting encounter at the electronics company remained. This moment of reconnection, albeit uncertain, stirred the embers of a love that had never entirely extinguished, challenging the notion of forgotten feelings and the paths our lives had taken since those days in the basement workshop.

DURING THIS PERIOD, my life was confined to the restaurant; I dined and slumbered there, finding rest on the long sofas designated for customers. And then, as quietly as she had re-entered my life, she vanished again after a few weeks. Subsequently, I, too, left, heading back to my hometown to gear up for military service, taking up temporary work as a field laborer on a school construction project.

Then, quite unexpectedly, I received a letter from Huh In-ha. It began with the salutation "The Great One Who Thought Greatly...!" which conveyed his deep respect for me, derived from our brief encounters. Yet, a misunderstanding formed the basis of this respect; my introspective nature at the time was not due to philosophical ponderings, but the woman primarily dominated the scene. My serious mien and evident concern for her might have projected a sense of depth and maturity not typically associated with someone my age. Mr. Huh's perception was undoubtedly shaped by the name 'Wi Dae-han,' meaning 'Great,' not realizing it wasn't my given name until after my departure when I informed him of my actual name through a letter. This incident prompts me to ponder over my actual name and the essence of my identity.

I remember conversing with my colleagues using my real name when I was at the electronics company I mentioned earlier. He was Kim Gyung-il, a mid-twenty man who always had a sense of humor, and one day, he threw a joke at me.

"A shrimp? A big shrimp?"

He laughed heartily, and I replied, "It's a great summer, not a big shrimp. The letter meaning is summer, not a shrimp." That was the first time I learned that my name's character also meant shrimp.

He told me that I would become significant and that he should remember my name, repeating it to himself several times. Then he complimented, "Your name is truly magnificent." I might have lived without worrying about my name if I had not met that peculiar language teacher at Geumjatap Academy. There is a saying, "Knowledge is poison."

While I served in the military, although I was a reservist commuting to the 22nd Division's engineering battalion in my hometown, I often ended my letters to a few friends in Seoul with 'From the Wi Dae-han.' Indeed, I wanted to be great. But I needed to figure out what I wanted to achieve greatness through. It always filled my heart with a vague passion. However, my expectations proved far removed from reality. Therefore, my heart was always oppressed and in pain.

MEMORIES OF HUH IN-HA FROM THE QUEEN

Even after 35 years, I haven't forgotten the 'Huh In-ha.' His handsome face, long hair, and long fingers made him appear like a protagonist from a Japanese manga. As I mentioned, he was the manager at the restaurant 'Queen' in Seoul, where I worked as a server before joining the military. To this day, I sometimes wonder how he is doing and wish to meet him again. I'm writing this because of a serendipitous event that happened today.

Caption: An envelope was sent to Kang Ha-neul by KR in Paris in September 1994.

While searching for an image to include in a piece titled 'My Father,' I was writing today on my blog, I stumbled upon an unexpected shot in my computer folder. It was an image I had scanned a long time ago. That image led me to reconnect with her on Facebook after 25 years. Her familiar name 'KR' appeared on a friend recommendation list, and I added her. It was a scanned image of an international mail envelope she had sent me. I scanned the letter, but the picture was too blurry to make out the details. Until then, I had no recollection of such a fact. However, judging from the September 14, 1994 postmark, KR sent it to me. She majored in French literature at Yonsei University, and I had met her and her friend several times around that time. The mail probably contained materials related to a documentary about Baek Un-chol, whom I oversaw producing then. I was planning the production in Korea for a French female director who was filming a documentary centered around Mr. Baek, an artist and photographer, the owner of "Tamna Mok-seokwon" in Jeju Island. In any case, I found the unexpected discovery very intriguing and delightful.

Prompted by nostalgia, I went down to the basement. Since moving into this house, I hadn't touched a particular cabinet until today, when I retrieved a bundle of letters and photographs from an old plastic bag. These were my items from before I married. I had checked the bag's content once or twice over the years but had yet to look through each item individually. Most of the things were letters exchanged with friends during my time in the military. I had lost my possessions on two separate occasions. Having lived away from home early in life, I frequently moved and sometimes even lacked a place to sleep. Once, after storing my belongings at a relative's house, I lost everything. Another time, I was storing my personal belongings in my office on the seventh floor (same address on the envelope sent by KR), and I lost them all.

I opened the plastic bag and examined each item. I exchanged most of the letters with my friends. Then, to my surprise, I found a letter from Mr. Huh In-ha. I had thought I had lost his letter, but it was still intact, along with the envelope.

Indeed, I used to think he possessed a traveler-like soul. Upon reading the letter, I discovered he described himself as a traveler. I guess I worked at the Queen for about a month, perhaps even less. I say this because I don't remember ever receiving a salary there. When I departed, I left without a word to the manager. The female bartender partly influenced my abrupt departure, though not by my desires.

ONE NIGHT, A FRIEND named Jeong Sun-il, who had never been of much help to me in my life, came to the restaurant where I worked. He was two years older than me, so we weren't real friends. However, that night, he confessed that we were the same age. Moreover, his birthday was twelve days later than mine. For years, I had respectfully addressed him as "hyung" (older brother), which is a title of respect reserved for older males in Korea. So, when I learned the truth, I felt a great sense of shock and betrayal. From that day on, we became awkward friends. He begged me to call him by name, which I found incredibly uncomfortable.

As you know, in Korean culture, calling someone older than you by their name is considered disrespectful. I still remember vividly at that moment how unpleasant it felt to call him "Sun-il" instead of "hyung," which I had used for years. I felt deeply uneasy at the time. The following day, confused by Sun-il's sudden appearance, I left the restaurant without saying goodbye or leaving a note for the manager, Mr. Huh In-ha, and went with him toward my hometown.

When I presented myself as 'Wi Dae-han' to Mr. Huh, he immediately adopted the name and addressed me without hesitation. I wonder where and how he lives now, as he must be in his mid-sixties. Perhaps, as he once said, he would become a bohemian and travel freely elsewhere. Will there be a day when we reunite?

Caption: During my military service, my friends from Seoul came to see me.
I was sitting at a coffee shop in a downtown area.

I was profoundly serious about my life when I shaved my head and enlisted in the military in the photograph. Someone took this photo during my military service, and I often lost myself in thought. That is probably why Mr. Huh described me as having "profound thoughts" in his letter.

MR. HUH'S LETTER

Caption: An envelope was sent by Huh In-ha from Korea in 1983 with a 60-won stamp. People wrote the recipient's address on the front, and the sender's information was on the back. It was on April 21, 1983.

The text below is a letter sent to me by Huh In-ha, and I translated it to reflect his wishes as much as possible.

To the Great One Who Thought Greatly...!

Like the great guy you are (just as you always said), you ruthlessly discarded our ties and hopes, leaving me all alone in the void. Yet, whenever I think of you, the image of Wi Dae-han, barely over 20 years old, still appears pure to me, In-ha, constantly contemplating and reflecting on each day with untarnished thoughts, fueled by the frustration of an undefined faith and always sparking flames in your eyes. QUEEN is still thriving.

In the place where your precious sweat and frustration briefly lingered, I, In-ha, still live a daily life where I have to run to answer the call. My heart is always empty, but no one else is there to share it. I'm still curled up in the corner of my heart's room, unable to chase away sleep.

Dae-han,

It seems that all humans are like that. With a seemingly plausible tongue, they lead lives that embrace others over trivial matters, just like I receive your precious letters on a non-particular topic without knowing it. When you left like that, I thought you were that kind of guy, and it turned out to be a precious gift for someone who never thought of you again. It's good to hear that you're healthy, Dae-han.

Suddenly, I picture you carrying pain in the manual labor frontlines, fueled by anger, as you move through the construction site. "I live on ambition and faith. I challenge pure, poetic literature and laugh at the corrupt, speculative world. Thus, my 20-year-old passion burns amid dust, pain, and hard labor. Come on, world. For the great ideas of the great, great Dae-han — " you shout, with sweat streaming down your face... That's the image I see, with your eyes full of burning curiosity.

Humans cannot easily live in this world because they lack the foundation of a life to share. That's why you, too, live in frustration. Amidst all this, there's a useless, incompetent bug called In-ha. But both In-ha and Dae-han were young and had tenacious strength, determination, and endurance. Even if we're stranded, we have the power to repair ourselves and enter the route again. We must be able to maintain our lives with that power. The same goes for you, and In-ha must also be the same. So even if our bodies experience fatigue and agony, our minds must not rot away.

A tree with deep roots does not fall in drought and wind; it always sprouts fresh branches, just like the situation, environment, and conditions we face cannot change our lives. In other words, a person with solid self-establishment will not have a rotten spirit. A person with an unspoiled heart will know how to smile in despair, laugh when abandoned, and rise when fallen.

Dae-han. We're still young, with ample time ahead to chase our dreams. We must wait while preparing (with our eyes always holding the unwavering light of progress). We can do it (the odds of winning and losing are fifty to a hundred).

As your enlistment in the military is drawing near, I know you must fill your heart with uneasiness. Despite this, you must focus on discovering the greatness within you (constantly engaging in deep thoughts, maintaining a simple life, and getting ample rest). Unfortunately, your lack of effort in writing letters has led me to write this one similarly carelessly. I don't care much about winning but don't want to lose. And as for the fountain pen, please try to return it when you can. This was a gift from my dear friend, just two days before he died. Though it's only worth 2,000 won, I cannot simply discard it.

You may not even know this story about the pen. If you don't wish to send it back, please keep it as a token of our friendship, and remember the name In-ha until the day you close your eyes for the last time. That pen has always been tucked in my vest pocket, breathing life into my heart as I lived my time-limited life alongside my 27-year-old friend, Hyung-seok.

Dae-han...!

During your short yet intense time at QUEEN in Seoul, you became a friend to In-ha, who always concealed his deep anguish and lived with a smile. The life of a traveler often reads like a sentimental tale of endless wandering and dying alone on the outskirts of an unknown city, not knowing where they belong. Draped in tattered clothes, they roam the world searching for their lost hometown (a longing they call homesickness in the traveler world), soaked in deep sorrow, and ultimately meeting their end. Fortune-telling songs with melancholic melodies and strange-looking stringed instruments are their companions, along with countless conversations and long, wandering journeys.

Yes, perhaps In-ha is a gypsy with gypsy blood cursing through his veins. Having become an outcast traveler in this land of Seoul, where seven million people with different personalities live entangled amid dry, polluted air and ruthless self-interest, In-ha is a traveler who roams today in search of truth, faith, and a lasting connection with others.

But I love poverty. That is why, and perhaps, I am suddenly thinking of you, who used to dwell deeply in your thoughts amidst anger and sorrow. Dae-han, thank you for your letter. Whenever you find the time, please keep sending me letters and poems. Let's get together and drink with this gypsy, powered by alcohol, before you enlist in the military. Adios.

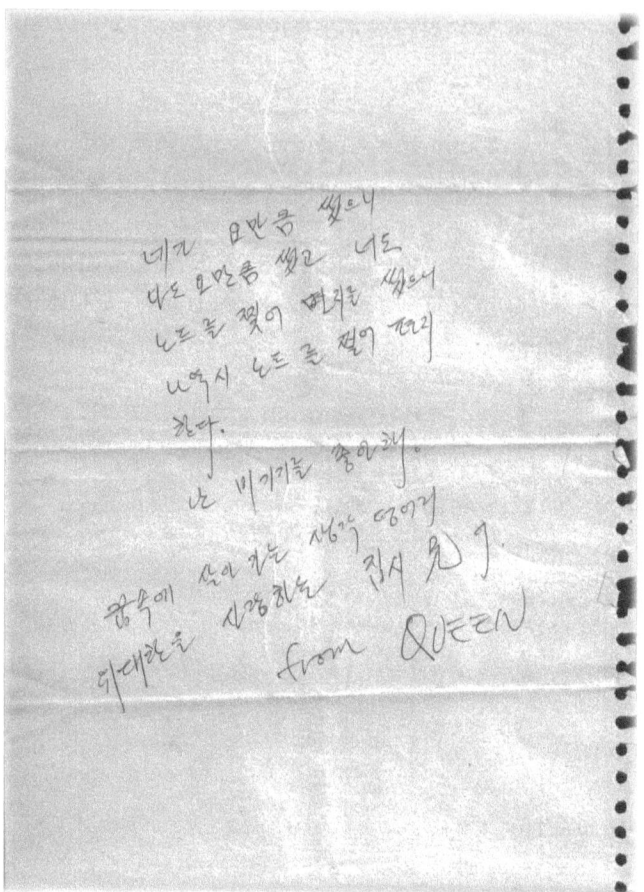

Since you wrote this much, I will write the same amount. In addition, you wrote your letter on a torn notebook page, so I will do the same. I do enjoy good competitions.

A brother who wanders, cherishing a life amidst dreams and reflections, In-ha, who admires the grandeur that lies within.

From QUEEN

THE ESSENCE OF NAMES AND THE WEBS THEY WEAVE

In reading Mr. Huh In Ha's touching letter to Dae-han, we traverse an emotive landscape that goes beyond the story of just two individuals. It epitomizes the complexity of human connections, ambitions, and yearnings, as intricate as the names we each bear. This narrative delves into the profound implications of names; they influence our social interactions, carry the weight of our familial legacies, and shape our personal identities in enigmatic ways. Mr. Huh's letter acts as a testament to the autonomous existence of names, emphasizing the significance we inherit and the significance we confer upon others.

Names are more than mere tags; they encapsulate histories, bonds, and aspirations. When Mr. Huh affectionately dubs Dae-han "the Great One," he encapsulates a spectrum of emotions and shared histories inherently linked to that name. Yet, as his letter unfolds the complexities of their relationship, it becomes evident that names can obscure truths, altering our perceptions of each other and even ourselves. In the interplay of darkness and light, names can reflect our deepest desires or greatest repulsions.

They bear our personal stories and collective memories — as seen in how the name "QUEEN," mentioned in Mr. Huh's letter, evokes nostalgia and fellowship. Names serve as beacons, uniting individuals across the expanse of time and space. "QUEEN" is not simply a name but a symbol of shared aspirations, trials, and a cherished epoch of youth for both Huh In Ha and Dae-han.

Nonetheless, the heritage of a name is both a gift and a burden, offering empowerment or imposing daunting expectations. The critical inquiry remains: Are our lives a reflection of our names, or do our names evolve to mirror us? Do we mold our identities to conform to a preconceived notion, or does the name transform and mature, enriched by each of our life's episodes?

The tapestry of existence, kinship, and self-exploration is as complex as the names we inherit and bestow. While the paths of Mr. Huh and Dae-han have diverged, their mutual narrative continues to leave indelible marks, both personally poignant and universally resonant. What lies within a name? The answer is as multifaceted as life itself — rich with subtlety, poetry, contradictions, and above all, steeped in the essence of the human spirit.

So, as we contemplate the name "Dae-han," laden with its lofty connotations, or "In-ha," imbued with its poetic somberness, let us acknowledge that names are dynamic entities. They evolve as we do, inscribed not merely on our official documents but within the hearts we touch and the correspondences we pen.

Echoing Mr. Huh's words, 'In-ha, who admires the grandeur that lies within,' the true worth of a name emerges from the life it encapsulates. Names, in their essence, embark on a journey and reach a destination, continually sculpted and marked by the narratives we live and the letters we draft, forging a legacy that extends beyond mere words to touch the core of our shared humanity.

FOOTPRINTS OF LOVE

Penned April 1, 2021

While wandering through the neighborhood today, I was greeted by the vibrant colors of beautiful spring flowers. As I climbed a small hill, a distant memory suddenly washed over me. It was of a time when my father had carried me on his back to visit a neighboring village. We crossed this very hill, my father humming a tune while I pressed my ear tightly against his broad back. The sound of the flowing river, the chirping birds from the mountains, and my father's humming, breathing, and racing heartbeats harmonized like an orchestra, creating a mesmerizing experience.

My parents' house sits in a secluded spot about five hundred meters away from the neighboring towns, making socializing with peers a lengthy endeavor and often leaving me feeling isolated. My father, who wasn't prone to openly displaying affection, nevertheless made efforts to spend time with us whenever he could. Despite his natural warmth, a stubborn patriarchal attitude made it hard for him to express these feelings to his family. That's why I remember him as a somewhat strict father.

My sole memory of being carried by my father is of him walking me across that hill. I must've been very young to need the help, and perhaps I drifted to sleep against his warm back, lulled by the rhythm of his steps, his humming, and the sounds of nature. Whenever I think of him, this memory is my touchstone — the feeling of safety, his gentle tune, and the warmth radiating from him as we talked. Sadly, I don't recall the words we shared.

Today, I took out a pair of shoes that my father had given me from the shoe rack and polished them. He passed these shoes down to me a few months before his passing. He also showed me his old electric razor, which he had cherished for many years. I brought it with me to the United States and used it until it no longer worked, but unfortunately, I lost it due to my negligence. Lastly, he gave me his compass, which he used during the Korean War. My son played with it when he was younger, and the glass cracked. These three items are the tangible legacies he left behind me before he passed away.

Caption: My father's shoes, gifted to me before he passed away.

AS I SIT HERE, feeling the weight of the shoes in my hands, memories of my father come flooding back. Moments like these make me miss him the most, yet there's comfort in knowing that his spirit lives on in these objects and my memories.

The soles of my father's shoes, marked with repairs, are still in good condition. They fit me perfectly. It is clear that he often wore these shoes when going out in the last years of his life.

On a visit back to my hometown, my father handed me these shoes, sensing his time was nearing. Despite his declining mobility, he insisted I take them, suggesting he had no further use for them. Yet, he might have also felt it wasteful for these cherished shoes to vanish after his passing. In Korean culture, it's customary to burn many of the deceased's personal items, so perhaps this was his way of leaving a piece of himself with me, a reminder always to remember him. Tears welled up in his eyes as we spoke, and though I held his hands, words of comfort escaped me; instead, I silently held his frail hand.

"I'm going to die like this, aren't I, son? I don't really want to, do I?"

Tears flowed from my father then, a sight of vulnerability I had never witnessed before. My father, once a beacon of strength both mentally and physically, showed the wear of life's final chapter. I gripped his thin hand, the gray hairs now unkempt.

"I had a dream. Beautiful pine trees. Two pines, standing tall on a sandy field, reaching towards the sky. How magnificent they were!"

My older sister, who became a monk in her 40s during the late 1990s and took the Buddhist name Hyejeong, recounted that these were our father's last words, spoken just days before his death. In 1998, as her mother lay severely ill, Hyejeong returned to our parents' home to care for her. She has served Buddhism and established 'Inyeonam.' 'Inyeon' is the meaning of fate. Gautama Buddha said, "Everything that exists is born through fate and disappears through fate," Koreans have an exceptional sensitivity to fate. After her mother passed away that year, Hyejeong stayed in her hometown to support her father, who was left alone. After our father's passing in 2004, she moved to a distant temple, adopting 'Inyeonam' as the temple's name, where she served as chief monk, praying for her parents' souls.

Near our parents' home, a large field fed our family of nine. Part of this land, known as "Sandy Field," was characterized by its high sand content. A majestic pine tree stood along its edge, not particularly tall or straight but beautiful and robust. Perhaps this was what my father saw in his dream, admiring its resilient beauty.

Those pines have become symbols for me: my father hoped for his grand-children, our family's future, to live strong, vibrant lives like evergreens. I wish my children will do the same, striving upwards, their spirit undimmed by the changing seasons. Before my father passed, I made him a silent promise to give my children that chance. I immigrated to the United States the following year and kept my word.

My father's gifts — the shoes, razor, compass — are more than objects; they hold his spirit. The shoes lived anonymously on our rack, and I felt guilty each time I saw them. Each move brought the same fear of loss, the same inaction. Now, they're a sanctuary, polished and proudly displayed on my bookshelf. His hummed tune often returns to me, and seeing the shoes every day will be like feeling the warmth of his hand on my shoulder, a re-minder of his love.

BRIQUETTES BRIDGING

A PENPAL AND HOPE

Penned July 27, 2017

In the summer of 1979, a few months after graduating from middle school, I started working at a factory in Seoul. I stayed in my hometown for the Chuseok holiday, then came to Goam-ri, Jecheon-si, Chungcheongbuk-do, and remained there until January 1981. Near Jangrak 3-geori in Jecheon-si, there was a high concentration of large coal briquette factories. In just one block, there were likely about five factories; among them was the Samhwa Briquette Company, run by my uncle. My eldest brother, Hyun, got a job at the company after completing mandatory military service in his hometown. After getting married, Hyun pursued self-employment over a modest salaried position. Hyun bought briquettes at factory prices and sold them retail with some markup, needing a truck. He acquired a 2.5-ton Titan from Kia Motors on installment. He sought my help. Fresh from middle school and at a factory job in Seoul, I was gearing up for my GED.

He considered my activities unproductive from his perspective. At that time, it was customary in Korea that the whole family, including younger siblings, would share in the fruits of the eldest son's success only when he succeeded. After that, he became the most financially secure among his siblings, but he wasn't wealthy enough to provide financial assistance to his siblings. Reluctant to sacrifice my future, I only agreed to help my brother after my mother's persuasion.

For over a year, I sold and delivered briquettes. During the summer, the off-season for briquette sales, my brother and I looked for alternative sources of income. Therefore, in the summer, which was the off-season, we bought old chickens (chickens that could not lay eggs) from poultry farms at a low price and sold them in rural areas. The briquette factory produced 16-hole and 32-hole coals, most of which were 16-hole coals. Workers loaded the hot briquettes into their trucks as they came off the conveyor belt. My brother's truck could usually carry 1,200 units. Every day, we sold briquettes to villages located tens to hundreds of kilometers away. We sold 30, 50, or 100 briquettes at a time, as customers wanted. If we could not sell it all in one day, we went to sell the rest of the stock the next day. Most roads were unpaved, and rough travel often resulted in dozens of briquettes breaking, rendering them unsellable on awful days. So, we brought them to the factory and returned them, but my brother lost money because they needed to receive the right price.

On the other hand, it was never easy to carry briquettes for hours, usually going up and down steep and high stairs, when telephone orders came from inns, restaurants, or private homes in downtown Jecheon. Despite its difficulty, the challenging work enabled Hyun to manage monthly car payments, living expenses, and even some savings. However, I didn't want a single penny of my salary for more than a year and a half despite the harsh manual labor I did for my brother's family. It was a time when families took for granted pure sacrifice, with no financial rewards exchanged. Besides learning to drive a car during that period, I wasted only my precious time. I went to the factory to take a bath, came home, and had dinner, always around 9 p.m. I would fall asleep after reading a little book because I was tired.

Caption: Overseas pen pal promotional materials in the 70s and 80s in South Korea.

DURING A PARTICULARLY exhausting time in the fall of 1980, I began corresponding with an overseas pen pal. It was a way to make friends abroad when there was no Internet. It was easy to find advertisements introducing overseas pen pals in inexpensive media such as weekly magazines. I bought a book by transferring money to a brokerage in Seoul, and those companies operated with that income. They gave me an A5 size thin booklet with information on everything from how to write an international mail envelope to pen pals abroad. The ads usually feature pictures of teenage boys and girls. They also provided a printed list of names and nationalities to choose a pen pal. I picked a pretty American girl from among the boys and girls featured in the catalog and sent my first letter to her agent. I had believed they delivered my letter to the pen pal of my choice. And when someone responds to my letter, we become pen pals.

Today, while sorting through old letters, I found letters from my pen pal back then. Unfortunately, I lost all my precious belongings while living alone in Seoul in my mid-20s. Although I have very few personal items from my teens and mid-twenties, I can keep these letters to this day because I left them at my parents' house.

Caption: Miss Kerri Hughes, my pen pal from Idaho.

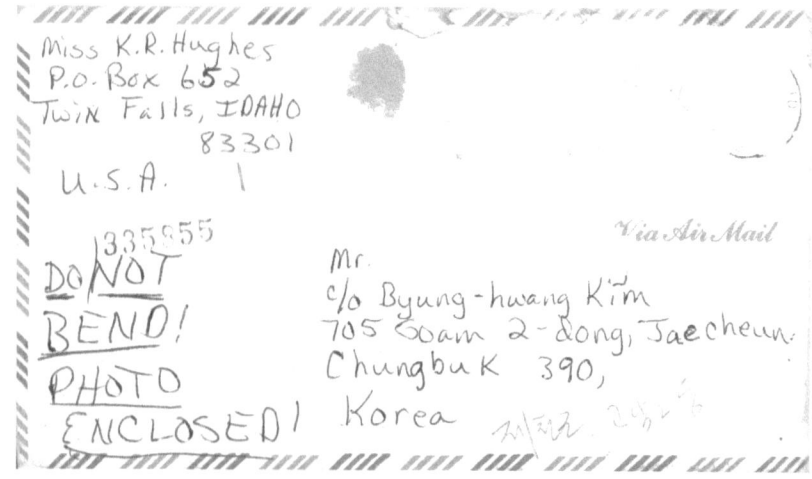

Caption: The envelope of Kerri's first letter. It reads, "DO NOT BEND! PHOTO ENCLOSED!"

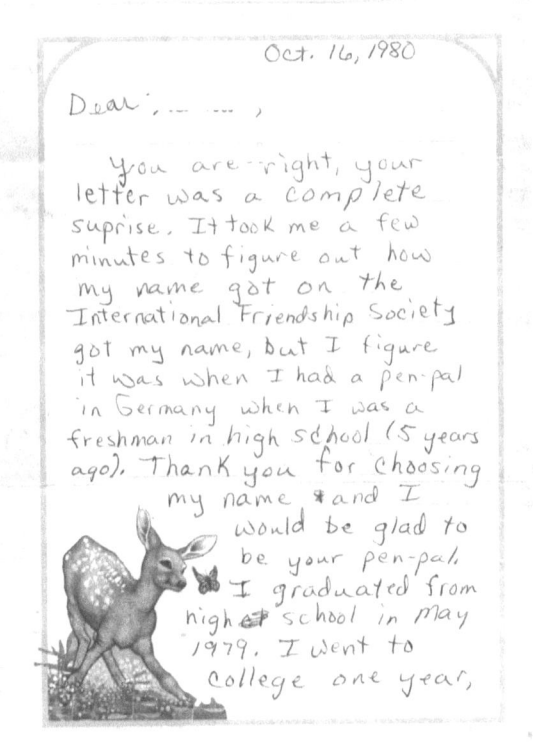

Oct. 16, 1980

Dear ,... ... ,

You are right, your letter was a complete suprise. It took me a few minutes to figure out how my name got on the International Friendship Society got my name, but I figure it was when I had a pen-pal in Germany when I was a freshman in high school (5 years ago). Thank you for choosing my name and I would be glad to be your pen-pal. I graduated from high school in May 1979. I went to College one year,

Caption: The first page of Kerri's letter dated October 16, 1980; the remaining pages were lost.

THE PEN PAL ads and brochures had featured many attractive girls, setting my expectations. Arriving home late one night, I discovered an international envelope addressed to me, and the excitement was palpable as I found a photo inside. However, the photo of Kerri caught me off guard; she was unlike anyone I'd seen before, noticeably overweight — a stark contrast to the slim figures commonly seen in Korea, both among my peers and adults. Additionally, she appeared more like a woman in her mid-twenties than a teenager, prompting me to swiftly hide the photo to avoid it when somebody sees it.

I was seventeen, and my whole world focused on other teens, on dating girls my age. The fact that Kerri was two years older and in college, while I had just completed middle school, felt like an insurmountable difference. My eagerness for our pen pal exchange might have remained unchecked if she had not included her photograph in her initial letter. Looking back, I recognize that age and physical appearance should not define our connections. However, my younger self's views were admittedly narrow and immature. Despite this, corresponding with Kerri offered a delightful escape from my daily routine.

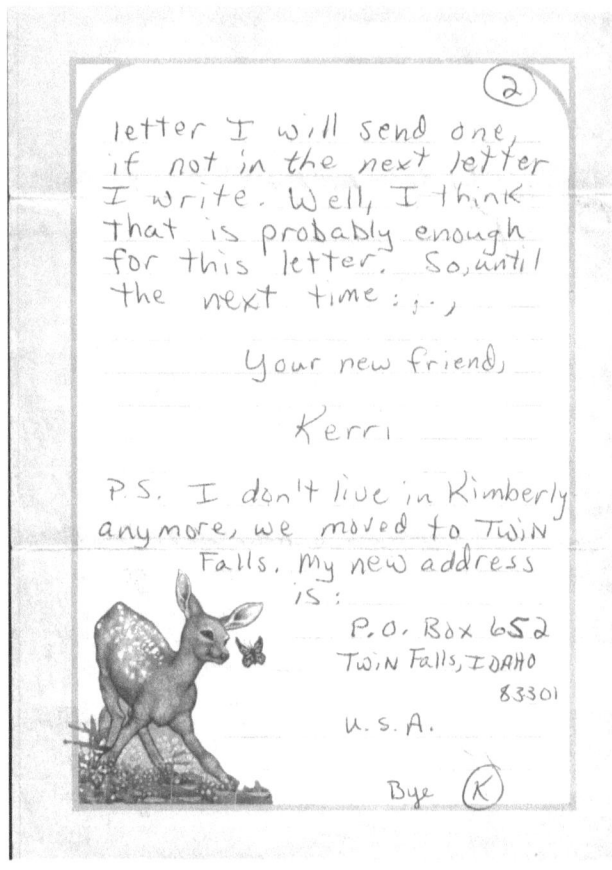

letter I will send one, if not in the next letter I write. Well, I think that is probably enough for this letter. So, until the next time :..)

Your new friend,

Kerri

P.S. I don't live in Kimberly anymore, we moved to Twin Falls. My new address is:

P.O. Box 652
Twin Falls, IDAHO
83301

U.S.A.

Bye (K)

Caption: On the second page of Kerri's one of her letters, the first page was missing.

and am now taking a year off
to save some money, get a car
and then go to a 4-year university
instead of the 2-year college I
went to last year. I don't mind
watching sports on T.V. most of
the time, but the only thing I
play is Frisbee. I really
like to read, listen to records,
make latch-hook rugs, and...my favorite,
Party. My birthday is November
7, 1961, I'm 18, almost 19. This
year is the first year I get
to vote (Nov. 2) I missed it by 4 days
last year; and, 19 is the drinking
age in Idaho (Had you ever heard of Idaho
before?), and I'm going to go
bar-hopping on my birthday. It
lands on a Friday this year.
Let's see... I work at Magic
Valley Memorial Hospital. I am
an insurance billing clerk. I have
two older brothers and one
younger brother. Yes, please send
a picture of you to me. If I
get it together before I mail this

Caption: The front and back of the letter pages were missing.

The date of the letter's arrival is unclear, but it is the second one from Kerri. There, she introduced herself further and asked for my photo. She must have been wondering for a while as I haven't written to her in a while. I mentioned moving to a new place but failed to provide her with my new address. Even today, I keep her photo, a snapshot of her at eighteen. Like Kerri's other pen pal, Mary, who lived in NYC, I'm an American now, with my own place there. I live surrounded by family, but sometimes, I wonder where Kerri is and if she remembers me.

Sherri Hughes
P.O. Box 652
Twin Falls, Idaho
U.S.A. 83301

Via Air Mail

835493

Mr.
c/o Byung-hwang Kim
705 Goam 2-dong, Tae cheun
Chungbuk 390, Korea

Nov. 11, 1980

Dear   -,

Hello! How's it going? Fine here.
I'm going to send Byeong-Soo's
address to my pen-pal in
New York City so she may be
writing to him soon. Thanks
so much for the picture.
Well, in all actuallity, my
daily life is rather boring.
I work at the hospital here
in Twin Falls. I bill patient's
accounts to their medical
insurance. I work from
8 until 4:30. But usually
I work overtime because
they changed computer's back
in May, + it's been nothing
but a pain ever since.
I started in June. After
work I come home and
either read, listen to records,
do my latch hook, or write letters.

On weekends, I usually ②
go to the bar, go to a party,
or go to a friend's house &
sit. All in all, not to
exciting. Idaho is a state
in the Pacific Northwest.
We are rather sparsely
populated. Almost half of
the state is National Forest
and Wilderness areas.
It's great to go backpacking
through. Most of the rich
people come here to live
when they retire. We are
known as the "Gem State"
because of an abundance of
Opals found here. The
eastern boundary of the state
is the Rocky Mtn. chain.
On the west most of it is
the Snake River, Idaho
used to be (on the southern
half) mostly sagebrush desert.
That was until the magic

Caption: Miss Kerri's letter of November 11, 1980.

At that time, I lived in a house rented by my elder brother's family, which we shared with the landlord's family. Among the residents was Kim Byeong-soo, two years my senior, who attended Jecheon High School while I was preparing for the high school qualification exam. One day, noticing Kerri's letter, Byeong-soo inquired if I comprehended its English content. "That's exactly why we're pen pals," I retorted, highlighting my understanding of her letters. Initially, he was skeptical and envious of my engaging in international penpal exchanges in English despite not having started high school yet. His curiosity was piqued, and he requested that I introduce him to another girl for pen pal correspondence, prompting me to reach out to Kerri on his behalf. Kerri and I exchanged inquiries about our daily routines and interests, allowing me a glimpse into Idaho and the life of an ordinary American girl through her eyes. Much of what she shared was alien to me, making it challenging to comprehend fully. The United States felt like a distant realm, far removed from my own experiences.

Jan. 1■, 1981

Dear   L,

Hello! How are you? What kind of movies are you favorite? What ~~so~~ kind of things do you like to read? Has Mary sent your friend a picture of herself yet? You will want to see it when she does, she's really pretty. Your form of government in Korea, what is it like? A Democracy? Do you have a president, King, or premier or what? At what age do your citizens get to vote? What kind of crops (besides rice) are grown in Korea? Yes, Korea is very interesting. No, I didn't see or hear anything about the accident at Kimp airport. What happened? Christmas in

②

these United States is
very commercialized. Lots
of people look mainly at
Christmas as the Day of
Jesus' birth. But, in
my opinion it is a time
to exchange presents and
get a day off from work.
I'm not religious, so
I generally don't really
consider that part of it.
Right after Thanksgiving,
all the stores bring out
their Christmas decorations.
The streets are ablaze
with all kinds of neon
of trees, wreaths, etc. Then
the sales start. Everybody
wants you to buy from them.
The thing I find most
entertaining is the children
going to see Santa Claus.
I like to watch them &

③

see their reactions. Some are very happy (usually the more older ones), some are curious, but most are downright petrified. No, I actually hate the snow. I also hate the cold & the wind. All of which are very common here in Idaho. Guess that maybe I should move. Somewhere where it is summer all or most of the time. It has only snowed here once & it was gone the next day. We didn't even have any snow on Christmas. It made my friend mad, but it suited me just fine. Well, enough is enough. Have a Happy New Year! Write back soon!

Your friend,

Caption: Miss Kerri's letter of January 1, 1981.

KERRI'S FASCINATION WITH Korea grew, leading her to request a map and a Korean language book. I had a chance to learn about her new culture from her. I always viewed Christmas as a joyous celebration, but her distinct perspective on the holiday was something I couldn't quite grasp at the time. That was the first time I realized that Christmas meant different things to different people. For her, Christmas meant exchanging gifts and not having to work for just one day. Then, I realized that the words Merry Christmas, which we ceremoniously share at the end of the year, mean nothing to people other than Christians. So, in America, most people use Happy Holidays instead of Merry Christmas. Justin Clark said it all started with the New York Herald and New York Daily Tribune's December 25, 1843, proposal to write "Happy Holidays."

I do not have any religious affiliations. For a long time in Korea, the Christmas season was when carol songs rang throughout December, regardless of a particular religion. People busied themselves by exchanging Christmas and New Year's cards. We strongly position it as an enjoyable event. Although the Christian population in Korea is less than 17% and non-religious people are over 60%, Christmas Day is one of the holidays that has settled well without resistance from people. And at the center, there was a white Christmas. But surprisingly, she hated snow and the Idaho winter. Perhaps she left Idaho forever to live in another milder state. I was amazed that there were so many views on the same subject then.

When I received this letter, I spent my last days in Jecheon. I was due to leave there in a month to stay with my parents. I decided to live my life and not help my brother sell briquettes anymore. I needed to obtain my high school diploma and pursue a college education. Still, while staying in Jecheon, I made no progress and had no hope for the future. It was just that my brother hired me without pay instead of employing his paid assistant. So, I decided not to do such a draining job anymore and stayed at my parent's house for a while before going to Seoul.

Feb. 20, 1981

Dear _____,

Hello! How are you? I'm okay, except I have a cough (from my last cold) that won't go away.

Sorry to hear about your car wreck. I hope you are alright. That's a long time to be in the hospital.

If Mary (my pen-pal from New York) hasn't written to him, then I can't help Byeong-Soo. She's the only one I know. Nobody I know here in Twin writes letters ~~with~~ with any enthusiasm. Sorry! Maybe he can get a name the same way you got my name.

Well, I'm glad ~~that~~ the hostages FINALLY got released,

②

& none too soon, either; but
I can't say as I'm too
thrilled about President
Reagan. I voted for Jimmy
Carter, myself.

No, no german pen-pal.
My best friend has one
in Austria, though.
I can count to ten in
German & say 'Sit
Down.' That's all I
remember from taking
one semester of it in
high school.

Nope, I've never heard of
Mt. Seolak & I can't find
it in my Atlas, either
The Rockies are near me.
They are beautiful, I
don't know what I would
do if I couldn't go camping
& fishing in the summer.
We sit in the front room

(3)

& watch T.V. while we eat. Well, I've got a date tonight, (& he's a special guy, so it will take me awhile to get ready), so I'll go for now. Take Care & thanks for sending me the book you are going to send. Write back soon.

Sincerely,

Kerri Hughes

P.S. Is there a book or
something you can send me
that I can learn to read and
write Korean from?
See ya,
(K)

Caption: Miss Kerri's letter of February 20, 1981.

The hostage issue Kerri referred to in this letter was the story of the hostage and death incident at the US Embassy in Tehran, Iran, on November 4, 1979. At the time, this case was the most critical topic worldwide. On January 20, 1981, Iran released the last fifty-two hostages, but Iran remains a revolutionary republic. I think I sent Kerri a book written in English that might be helpful about Korea, but I can't remember what kind.

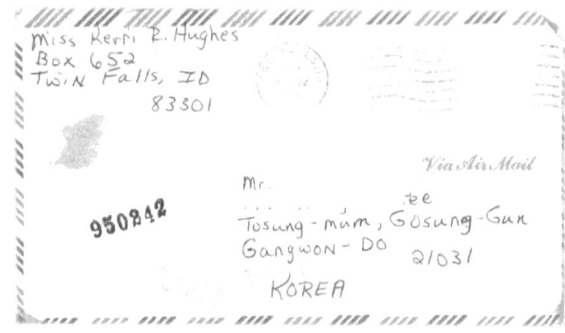

4-1-81

Dear _____ -)

　Hello! How is your cough? Mine finally went away, thank goodness! So, did you get all moved? Don't ~~forget~~ to give me your new address. Yes, please send me a map, because I've looked for your town ~~in~~ in my Atlas & I can't find it anywhere.
　Spring is <u>officially</u> here, but it is still cold as hell outside. I can't wait till summer, ~~because I do so hate the cold.~~ Good luck on those exams, or am I too late?, how did you do? Time to do the dishes. Sorry so short. Write back soon!

Your friend,
Kerri

Caption: Miss Kerri's last letter of April 1, 1981.

Judging from the content of this letter, I probably left my hometown again and went to Seoul. And I failed to give her my new address. I was busy and exhausted daily in Seoul, so I had no time to think about anything else. So, Kerri and I were pen pals for a brief period. Yet, this correspondence was a significant source of support during my difficult times.

The discovery of several unexpected pen pal letters made me think of the old days I could not usually remember. It's astounding to think that Korea, now among the world's top economies, was once struggling four decades ago in the early 1980s. The growth of Korea is as incredible as the fact that I, who left my hometown at the age of seventeen and sold briquettes in a small town in the provinces, became an entrepreneur, living in the United States and running companies in several countries. Exchanging letters with Kerri and living across the Pacific and the Rockies during my days of hardship inspired me to reach for broader horizons.

In those letters, each line was a promise of greater possibilities, a whisper from a world more significant than the one I knew. They taught me the power of connection, of shared humanity. They imbued me with a curiosity that would eventually lead me far from those provincial towns, across oceans, into the boardrooms and offices where my ideas could take flight. Looking back, the distance between then and now seems almost impossible, but individual steps make every journey — and mine started with a handwritten letter when I was seventeen.

ISU STATION: ECHOES OF THE PAST

Penned December 5, 2018

REMINISCENCE THROUGH POETRY

At Sadang Station

Poet: Hwang Young-ju
Translated by GS

The final station is warm,
Clutching the affectionate one,
Talking of the stop missed
while nodding off,
Life, at last, turns into laughter.

The first station waits,
Who is without mistakes?

Wandering and meandering,
Once barely managing to stand,
Life, each day, is a fresh step.

(Hwang, 2019. p. 80)

BROWSING MY SISTER'S KakaoTalk profile, I discovered a poem titled "At Sadang Station" by Hwang Young-ju. Her father was my mother's first cousin. In the 1980s, she and her family, including three younger sisters, resided near the Jongam Post Office in Seoul.

I only knew about her family once I visited Seoul; however, I remember meeting her father once in my hometown as a little kid. When I met her family in Seoul, I was suddenly surprised to have four younger sisters:
- Young-ju was in high school
- One in middle school
- Two in elementary school.

Visits to their home were always a delight, especially the engaging conversations with Young-ju, who had a remarkable talent for uplifting others.

Unfortunately, tragedy struck when her father suddenly died from leukemia, leaving Young-ju to care for the family without prior work experience. As a result, young-ju had to step up and take responsibility for the family's finances after graduating high school. Instead of attending college, she worked at the National Private Principals' Association. She worked for a long time in this non-profit organization while still being available to study.

Despite the many difficulties Young-ju faced in her youth, she found an unexpected turning point when she fell in love with a cadet from the Air Force Academy, with whom she had been exchanging letters since high school. Their love eventually led them to start their life together as companions at the Air Force Club in Boramae Park, which was a happy event. Despite the challenging circumstances she faced from an early age, Young-ju continued to care for her family and did not neglect her passions. Her unwavering dedication to household chores, her job, and her self-improvement are admirable.

Together with her husband, an ex-captain in the Korean Air Force, Young-ju raised two children. As a mother, wife, and professional, she dedicated herself tirelessly to her family's well-being. But she didn't stop there. She pursued her passion for writing and poetry, publishing a collection called "The Time of Verbal Rebirth" after earning her master's degree in Korean literature from the Graduate School of Hanyang University (Hwang, 2019). Her commitment to her passions and her community is an inspiration to us all.

Young-ju also devoted herself to helping others, volunteering for multi-cultural families in the area where she lived. Living outside Korea limits my knowledge of her present circumstances. Yet, her resilience and unwavering commitment to family, career, and community continue to inspire me.

Young-ju also devoted herself to helping others, volunteering for multicul-tural families in the area where she lived. Unfortunately, I don't live in Korea, so I know little about her current life. However, her resilience and dedication to her family, work, and community inspire me.

The poem "At Sadang Station" inspired me to pen "Memories of Isu Station: Echoes of the Past." It rekindled my appreciation for family bonds, the transformative power of poetry, and the life-defining connections we forge.

LOST LOVE AND LONGING AT ISU STATION

Seoul Subway Line 4 opened in 1985, and the Sanggye Station and Sadang Station were their starting and ending points, respectively. Isu Station was right next to Sadang Station. While its official name is "Chongshin University Entrance Station," it's a mystery to many why it bears that name, considering the university is 1.7 km away. In 1996, Seoul City opened Line 7. Isu Station evolved into a transfer point for Lines 4 and 7, commonly known as the Isu Intersection. However, it will always be just Isu Station, which holds special significance.

The Jeonggeum neighborhood encircling the station was once quaint, with tiny houses closely clustered on a gentle incline. But now, all that remains are large apartment complexes that have taken over the area. Once, a woman lived in this village, and I harbored feelings for her, but to SJ, I was merely a friend. I remember standing on her small, pretty balcony one foggy day, looking at the town below. Across the main road, Seomun Girls' High School stood prominently, with Gyeongmun High School's playground peeking out from beneath. Her modest single-room dwelling, perched halfway up the hillside, in a place that will always hold a special place in my heart.

The name "Jeonggeum Village" is lovely and has a friendly pronunciation to Koreans. Adjacent to the station was a village called Pear Tree Valley. People rumored that numerous gorgeous and sizable pear trees had stood for centuries. Whenever I pass by that station, I think of the Jeonggeum Village where she once lived, and the memories of that time come flooding back. At twenty-two, those moments now seem like distant echoes from another lifetime. I think of Isu Station and Jeonggeum Village, and some memories come to mind.

Many years ago, when I was seventeen, I worked for a small electronics company located in the basement of a nearby house in the area. It was a humble company that made FM radios and record players with two cassette tape players. I spent my days soldering and plugging electronic components into PCB boards. Evenings often found me wandering through the nearby Sadang Market, lost in thought.

At that time, Seoul's subway system had only a single line, and my workplace was near what is nowadays Namseong Station on Line 7. There, I met a girl whose presence immediately enchanted me. From the moment she entered our basement workspace, I was utterly smitten. Yet, after merely a week, she departed from the company. I realized I had not even exchanged words with her, let alone secured a way to contact her again.

A profound yearning for her engulfed me; even my boss, a man in his mid-thirties, played Kim Jung-ho's "Unknown Girl" during cassette player inspections. With every note of that song, my heart ached with increased intensity, pining for the girl whose name remained unknown to me.

A MISSED OPPORTUNITY ON THE ROAD NOT TAKEN

Over the years, Seoul's subway system has evolved, with Isu Station changing from a tiny stop on Line 4 to a bustling transfer point for Lines 4 and 7, now known as the Isu Intersection. Yet, Isu Station is more than just a mere subway stop. It's a place that holds memories of lost love and a longing that I can't seem to shake off. Whenever I pass through, my mind fills with shaky stories from the past, reminding me of a moment when I had to make a choice that still haunts me.

The year was 1994, and I owned an entertainment company called Shinmyung Communications, located near Bangbang Intersection in Yeoksam-dong, close to Gangnam Station in Seoul. I still vividly remember the day I transferred from subway line 2 to line 4 after receiving a print box from a factory in Euljiro Printing Alley. The box contained flyers crucial for our company's income, aimed at recruiting members for new movie preview screenings. Along with my colleagues, I handed out these flyers on the streets of areas with many offices, like Yeouido, ultimately recruiting over 2,000 paid members. We also used telephone voice mailboxes at that time to share news and information about preview screenings of new movies, with the voice mailbox number being 1588 — FILM (3456). So, the box held that much importance.

As the train passed Ichon Station, crossing the Dongjak Bridge, I drew my attention to a woman beside me. Though I didn't dare look at her face, we prolonged eye contact as the subway entered the long tunnel after Dongjak Station. I could feel she was preparing to disembark at the next stop, Isu Station, leaving me torn over how to act. The subway had long luggage compartments near the ceiling above the windows where people used to put their bags. I placed the heavy print box on it and looked at it, knowing that if I left the box and followed the woman, I would have to request another leaflet.

As the train approached Isu Station, I faced a decision that would later haunt me with regret. I opted to stay with the box, leaving the woman behind, convinced that prioritizing my company duties was the responsible choice. I was also afraid of appearing low-ranking if I carried the print box with yellow paper. Though I should have abandoned the box and followed her, my heart screamed at me to do so. She vanished into the crowd with a fleeting glance back at me as the train pulled away. I felt a sharp pang of regret, regretting not following the echo of my heart. Standing next to her for that fleeting time was enough to set my heart on fire, filling me with the ecstasy of meeting my heavenly lover. Looking back, I should have followed her, but I never heard the voice of my heart.

Though I caught only a fleeting glimpse, I knew she was my destined match. I didn't understand her age or whether she was my ideal type, but I could feel her atmosphere well. Unfortunately, I only saw her face reflected in the window under the fluorescent light as the subway entered the long tunnel. However, it was enough to make my heart race. She looked back at me as she got off at Isu Station, her regretful face etched in my memory. I still regret not following her to this day. The memory of that missed opportunity still lingers, reminding me of Robert Frost's poem, "The Road Not Taken."

POETIC MEMORIES AT ISU STATION

Isu Station is where I met SJ, whom I once had a crush on, and a girl who made me heartbroken and disappeared without a sound in only a few days. And it was where I foolishly bumped into a woman who might have been my match made in heaven. In her poem "At Sadang Station," Hwang Young-ju called Sadang Station "the final stop" and "the first stop," which is a perfect expression (Hwang, 2019. p. 80). How would my life have been different if Isu Station had been "the last station" at the time? We may have become lovers after getting out of the carriage.

After that, I got into the habit of looking closely at passengers on the subway every time I passed through the Isu station. But the girl who set my heart fluttering never crossed my path again. That made me even sadder. Because of that experience, I knew what I would do if I had that opportunity again. However, a few months later, a similar encounter occurred on Seoul's Jungang Line. An exchange of glances happened with a lady sitting opposite me. Our gazes lingered for a moment, silently communicating. She wasn't my type, and I didn't feel any emotions conveyed to me, but I stared straight into her eyes. Perhaps I was expecting some kind of feeling for myself. But that did not happen.

Reaching Ichon Station, she exited. Compelled, I followed despite it not being my stop. Ichon Station then had just a flat platform, needing more shelter. I approached, suggesting coffee. She declined, leaving abruptly. I have a very muscular upper body. So, when sitting down, people often think I'm a tall man with a heavy build. This experience taught me that mutual glances don't guarantee attraction. Genuine connection requires more than just a look; it requires the heart to resonate first.

Reflecting on Young-ju's poem transported me back to the events tied to Isu Station, memories anchored in a distant past. Her words demonstrate the profound power of poetry to transcend time and space, resurrecting forgotten moments with vivid clarity.

A TUTOR'S TALE OF HOPE AND RESILIENCE

Pinned October 22, 2019

Amidst the bright sunlight of a mid-1980s afternoon, clutching my basic study materials, I entered a lavish apartment in Seoul's Seocho-gu. As I held the address in my hand, I could immediately sense the opulence of the place. I rang the doorbell, and a high school boy opened the door. The fact that he was alone struck me as unusual. Usually, when tutors arrive for their first session, the student's parents are present to greet them without fail. Elevated expectations accompany parents when they employ a new tutor, hoping their child's academic performance will soar and their tutor will positively influence them.

Remember that teachers from Korea's top universities are in high demand and receive higher salaries. As a result, parents meticulously scrutinize the background and achievements of applicants during interviews before hiring them.

Parents paid in cash monthly, with verbal agreements lasting for the same duration. If either party wishes to terminate the contract, they can express their intention during the salary transaction. For example, a parent might hand over a paycheck envelope and say, "I apologize, but we must conclude our sessions today due to unforeseen circumstances." The same applies to the tutor: "I am deeply sorry, but personal matters prevent me from continuing to tutor your child." While the market gives neither party the upper hand, prestigious universities often disadvantage those who graduate from them. This dynamic further illustrates why many Koreans are eager to attend elite universities like Seoul National University.

Koreans readily understand this scenario, yet it might necessitate some explanation for those less acquainted with the culture. This aspiration resonated with the desires of Korean parents. Since A.D. 958 (during the Goryeo Dynasty), Korea has had a system for selecting officials through Gwageo, the highest-level state examination. The Yangban, or ruling class, would participate in these exams. If they failed repeatedly, their families would lose their status and become commoners. This system persisted for 950 years, spanning the Goryeo and Joseon Dynasties. Despite a challenging history marked by Japanese rule and the Korean War, South Korea's success in diverse fields stems from a longstanding focus on high educational standards.

Koreans widely consider education essential for a fulfilling life. To this day, the country's passion for teaching remains unparalleled worldwide, boasting the lowest illiteracy rate and highest university entrance rates. Consequently, parents are willing to pay a premium for their children's college education. In the 1980s, when South Korea's economic development was still nascent, there were few desirable job opportunities, and graduates of prestigious universities often dominated these positions. As a result, parents were eager for their children to attend top universities at any cost. Moreover, if their children could receive additional tutoring outside of school, they would have a better chance of excelling in college entrance exams. Consequently, the private tutoring market in South Korea flourished early on.

However, the agreements between parents and tutors were often verbal. These agreements, terminable at any moment, fostered a vibrant free market. According to a report by Economy21.co.kr on September 19, 2001, the Korean private education market was estimated to be worth around 30 trillion won ($2.363 billion), approximately 7% of the gross national product. The Korean Ministry of Education estimated the market to be worth around 14 trillion won ($1.102 billion) annually. While editing this article, I researched recent private education expenses; it was 26 trillion won in 2022. Son (2023) reported through the Chosun Ilbo that the Ministry of Education decided to announce measures in the first half of the year, saying that private education expenses were 26 trillion won, the largest ever for two consecutive years (Son, 2023). The actual figures are challenging to ascertain due to the secretive nature of these private transactions. Recently, a new law required individuals to report their income from private tutoring, making the market more transparent than in the past. A 2014 study by the Ministry of Employment and Labor in Korea said the Korean private education market was worth about 40.43 trillion won ($3.184 billion) in 2010.

MY NARRATIVE TAKES place during the early to mid-1980s when I was in my early twenties. From the 1980s to the early to mid-1990s in Korea, most private tutoring market workers were impoverished college students (undergraduates, master's, and doctoral candidates) who needed to cover their tuition and living expenses. As demand grew, professional groups specializing in private or group tutoring emerged, including full-time teachers from private academies and adults.

According to a study titled "Investigation of the Status of Job Introductions for Occupations Other than Workers, such as Private Tutors, and Legal Application Plans," published by the Ministry of Employment and Labor of South Korea in 2014, the size of the South Korean private education market was approximately 40 trillion 4 thousand 3 hundred 13 billion won, based on 2010 data (Sim et al., 2014).

Additionally, various forms of private tutoring markets connect to meet the needs of adults. Depending on the situation, private tutoring exists in numerous formats, ranging from 1:1 to 1:4. Tuition fees for private tutoring are much more expensive than those for institutes. As a result, households with higher incomes not only preferred 1:1 lessons but could also hire teachers for all subjects, maximizing the effectiveness of learning. In contrast, lower-income families had no choice but to select group tutoring, like 1:4, and limit themselves to specific subjects such as English or math. Consequently, the parent's financial situation directly influenced their children's college admissions.

A sense of peculiarity shrouded my visit to the high school boy's home. I had never met his parents before, and I had agreed to tutor the boy at the request of a man who worked as a manager at a workbook company. Still, I had expected the boy's parents to wait for me. Contrary to my expectations, however, the student was waiting for me alone. This unusual situation unfolded due to the following events.

"Shall we touch?"

I received a call from a 'Sunbae.' It had been a while since I last saw Mr. Kim. When I first met him, he was a theater directing major at Chung-Ang University and led the Arirang theater company. At the time, Chung-Ang University was Korea's top school for film and theater departments and graduate schools. He took pride in being a college graduate and leading a theater company. However, sitting before me, he held the manager position at a new work-study company based in Gangnam. I had never seen him in a suit before.

As I recall, he used to brush his long hair aside or shake his head to tidy it up. He had always worn loose clothing and seemed unconcerned with his appearance. However, the sunbae had neatly trimmed hair and a cleanly shaven beard. He had transformed into a typical office worker. His sudden metamorphosis was a shock to me.

However, he had transformed into a typical office worker. His sudden metamorphosis was a shock to me. Despite his perfect transformation, I could see that he had given up on his dreams of making a living — inevitable loneliness filled his eyes. Life as a struggling theater director was tough and lonely in those days, as Korea was still economically and culturally underdeveloped. The minimal audience in the theater industry made the lives of many artists challenging, including him. Therefore, I could understand why he might have left the theater world and entered the workbook industry. His transformation might have eventually made him wealthy.

When we first met, I handed him my business card as a magazine reporter in 1985, and he gave me his. I remember his surname was Kim, and he represented the Arirang troupe. He was over 180 centimeters tall and looked as if he could have played the role of Jesus Christ. If a performance of 'Jesus Christ' had taken place during his college days, he would have been the main character. He had a prominent nose, a slender and long face, and deep-set eyes like a Westerner. His ancestors may have had Western blood. In short, his face resembled a Westerner's. As his transformation slightly took me aback, he said,

"I got a job. It is a study-book company, and it is popular in Gangnam among wealthy people. Would you like to collaborate with me?" Mr. Kim asked, his voice tinged with loneliness. I shook my head. It seemed as if he had already anticipated my answer, and he explained the purpose of our meeting.

"Can you take care of him? He is a junior in high school, and his father is a pastor." Mr. Kim briefly explained the situation.

The student was one of Mr. Kim's team's clients. He explained that once his teammates had instructed the student once, everyone would give up teaching him. The company he worked for published and sold study materials. However, it also supported individual private tutoring according to customer needs. If all his teammates had abandoned guiding the boy, it was evident that he would be challenging to handle. Mr. Kim approached me because he knew I had a wealth of successful tutoring experience. I was curious about the high school junior. Though failure seemed likely, I was determined to take the risk myself. The high tuition also played a part in my decision. I told Kim, "I will take on that difficult student."

It was so long ago that it's hard to remember the exact workbook brand. It might have been Kyowon — the company famous for Red Pen. They've gotten huge since then. Of course, my memory could be off. I haven't lived in Korea for a while, so those details get a bit fuzzy.

I could see a refreshing green park through the living room window. I sat facing him across the desk in the living room.

"What about your parents?" I asked.

"They went out," the boy replied bluntly.

It must have been a Sunday. Christians go to church every Sunday for worship. Moreover, the student's father was a pastor and must have been at church with his wife. But perhaps his parents deliberately avoided me, growing weary of changing tutors every time. They may have expected that the next tutor would soon quit. But, on the other hand, it did not matter if I didn't meet his parents. After all, I wouldn't receive my tuition from them, but the workbook company would pay me.

Opening my textbook, meticulously prepared by Mr. Kim, I began the lesson, only to find the boy uncooperative. The boy was uncooperative. His complete disregard for the tutors must have led many to abandon their posts. He was indeed a stubborn, arrogant young man. Instead of blaming the child, I cursed his parents inwardly. How had the boy's parents raised him? I needed help understanding their approach. Long after I began my lecture, he grew restless. He could not bear sitting in his chair. He was not able to concentrate during class. As I ignored him and continued the lesson, he finally got up, headed for the window, and screamed as if frustrated.

HIS OUTBURST BROUGHT to mind a memory of tutoring another child amidst opening a new apartment complex in Nowon-gu, Seoul. He was a boy in the third grade of elementary school with a fifth-grade older sister who excelled in school and did not need tutoring. However, the boy struggled academically, so I took him under my wing. His mother, a beautiful and kind woman in her late thirties, always greeted me warmly with excellent orange juice during the early summer days before the summer break. She maintained a bright smile and held onto the hope that I could help her son. Yet, the boy could not concentrate on his studies at all. He grew restless as the class progressed, and one day, he even threw his pencil on the floor. "Min-sung, you will improve little by little if you study," I gently appeased him. Reflecting on my past, I have always been gentle with my students.

My teenage dream was to become an exceptional teacher and create my high school, providing quality education to children. With such a clear goal, I skipped high school and took the GED (high school equivalency) test. I attended four private academies in Korea, called "Hagwon," to prepare for the exam. Navigating various academies, I faced financial difficulties and searched for one that met my standards. However, I ultimately passed the GED test two months after leaving my last academy.

The influence of a teacher I met at my final Hagwon solidified my desire to become a high school teacher. His name was Oh Sang-gi, and he taught English while majoring in law. He commutes daily by subway from Incheon.

Whenever I think of him, it reminds me of Simon & Garfunkel's song "Bridge Over Troubled Water." One day, he sang that song in front of his students, tears streaming down his cheeks. The memory remains vivid, and the song became one of my favorites, whose lyrics I still know by heart. Mr. Oh Sang-gi passionately instructed his underprivileged students who, for distinct reasons, could not attend regular high schools. By the end of each class, his passion manifested through his voice, which often cracked with emotion.

My friend Kwon Sunuk studied with me at the same academy. He met Jeong Soon-il and Song Myeong-sun, whom I had known from delivering newspapers for several years. Another student, Kang Chun-hee, was inspired by Mr. Oh Sang-gi and went on to study English Language and Literature at Kyunghee University in Seoul. Sunuk and I spent a lot of time together, ultimately deciding to open a private high school in the future. We wanted to tutor students well, just like Mr. Oh Sang-gi. I then realized how profoundly one person could influence young people in such an abbreviated time.

As I continued tutoring, I always did my best to ensure my students genuinely respected me. Then, one day, Min-sung confided in me:

"I want to die, sir. I really want to die. I'm sick of studying."

He looked straight at me as he spoke. When I gazed into his eyes, I saw they were brimming with unshed tears. His expression was not one of annoyance but rather a plea for help. I felt a sudden chill run down my spine. 'Oh, this child is struggling so much that he genuinely wants to die!' Compassion for him filled me. 'How difficult must his life be?'

I gently grasped Min-sung's hands and asked,

"Min-sung, would you like to go out with me?"

After discussing with Min-sung's mother, I spent half a day out with him. Then, we traveled by bus to a nearby location. Nowon-gu had several apartment complexes surrounded by single-story houses and vinyl greenhouses scattered throughout the area. Many people were farming, and orchards were easy to find. Min-sung and I spent hours together, enjoying each other's company.

Upon returning, I spoke with his mother:

"Min-sung is having a hard time. Your son is brilliant and pure. However, we must reconsider sending him to so many after-school classes. Each child has unique characteristics and abilities to manage such a schedule. Min-sung needs more time for himself. It would be best for him to quit my lessons first so that I will step down."

The words were heavy, but I knew it was the right thing to do for Min-sung's well-being.

I remember Min-sung's mother's expression, a mix of emotions. She bit her pink lips, lost in thought. She knew that all the parents around her sent their children to private academies after school and arranged for additional private tutoring. In an apartment complex, sensing this competitive atmosphere was effortless. At that time, apartment complexes rapidly expanded in Seoul, Korea. The private education market was booming, centered around these new developments. Min-sung's mother could not ignore the educational phenomenon surrounding her, and her feelings must have been incredibly conflicted.

I said to her, "Min-sung is sending a signal now. How desperate must he be to say to me, 'I want to die?'"

I was deeply shocked by the boy's words. Each encounter found him playful and carefree. He would goof around before sitting down to study, a beautiful smile lighting up his face, much like his mother's. At first, I thought he wanted to play rather than learn, so I wasn't serious. When I heard such shocking words from such a young boy, I initially thought he was joking. Maybe he had also sent these signals to his parents, and they had been too preoccupied with appeasing him each time. I told her about my conversation with Min-sung, how he had described it as "deathly hard," and that we should let him rest for a while. She quietly wiped away her tears.

As I looked at the high school student standing before me, his drooping shoulders reminded me of Min-sung, who would now be in the 6th or 7th grade.

"Are we going to have class outside today?" I suggested to the young man.

"Really?" he asked incredulously.

"Yeah, let's go to Sinchon and get some fresh air instead of class today."

The young man's eyes lit up as if he had never experienced anything like this before. It recalled a younger Min-sung, who had once cried out for help years ago. Everywhere I looked, I saw children longing for a reprieve from their circumstances, whether in elementary or high school. What was truly frightening was that their parents pushed them toward the edge of a cliff instead of understanding their situation. They refused to listen to their child's sincere words, not even once.

The young man standing before me could not find a way out. His parents had trapped him in a suffocatingly dense web woven by his life and environment. He could not break free from the intricate tangle. Eager to give him a temporary escape, I took him to Sinchon, where we spent several hours playing games at a computer arcade before returning to his home. But, of course, that marked the end of my relationship with the unfortunate young boy.

My relationship with Mr. Kim, the representative of Arirang Theater who later joined the study-workbook company, ended. After that, I no longer worked in after-school tutoring. I continued my path, running hard, without connection to Mr. Kim. I reminded myself of him because I mentioned him in another article a few days ago.

Frequent visits to his room bring to mind the unique decoration of one wall adorned with bookshelves. He creatively employed blunt, thick wooden planks for shelves, skillfully interspersed with red bricks to create a rustic pedestal. He filled this makeshift bookshelf, which covered the entire wall, with books he loved. His bookshelf inspired me, and I decided to decorate my living room someday similarly. At the time, I was running an international film festival and a film school for teenagers, so I had many video materials from all over the world that needed storage. So, I built wooden frames large enough to cover one living room wall, and my father-in-law, who was quite handy, helped me.

I EARNED MY livelihood primarily through teaching. Post my stint in after-school tutoring, I ventured into running a video and film camp for the youth. Countless students, now likely in their 30s and 50s, must have gleaned valuable insights from my programs. By now, they must be in their 30s and 50s. It has been so long that we probably wouldn't recognize each other, but I would love to meet some of my former students if given a chance. One of them is Min-sung, whom I mentioned earlier in this article. I do not think he chose death; instead, I believe he overcame the difficulties of those days and is now living well somewhere.

Another student I would like to meet is a girl I tutored privately in a neighborhood near Min-snug's district. She lived in a single-story house with her parents; we shared the same last name. As a freshman in high school, standing at 168 cm, she was, without a doubt, the most captivating person I'd ever encountered. In our initial session, I focused on the periodic table, aiming to bolster her confidence across her subjects.

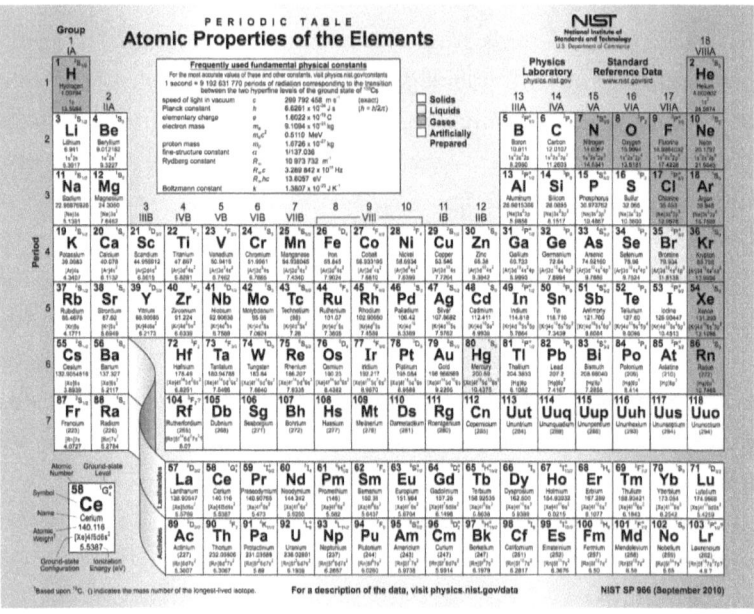

Image credit: nist.gov.

Do you remember the chemical standard periodic table? I graduated from Jongro Academy, which maintained an overwhelming reputation as a college entrance exam preparatory academy in Korea. A chemistry teacher taught my chemistry class, and I always enjoyed his lessons because he explained chemistry so clearly and effectively. I had only learned compulsory subjects since I came from a GED background. However, there were many compulsory subjects I had never studied before for university entrance exams. All the other students had already learned chemistry during their first year of high school, but I encountered it for the first time. The teacher, a professor of chemistry at Seoul National University, was full of confidence. He encouraged us, telling us that if we trusted him and did our best, we could score perfectly on the chemistry test. In addition, he taught us the secrets of memorizing the complex periodic table quickly and easily.

Years later, I still remembered the content, so I taught the girl the secret to mastering the periodic table. When I returned to her home for our second lesson, her face lit up with joy as soon as she saw me. After learning chemistry from me, she took exams at her school and scored remarkably well. She was thrilled. Unfortunately, as chemistry progressed, it became more challenging for students who disliked math because of the numerous calculations, much like math itself. Complex chemical formulas and calculations gradually emerged, and the girl struggled, eventually losing her motivation. It hurt me to see her like that.

Our lessons unfolded in her room, always prefaced by her mother's thoughtful provision of drinks and snacks. When the class began, her door closed, and I taught her several subjects she needed for her school classes. Regrettably, she seemed more suited for a career in the entertainment field than the academic realm. Had she pursued that path, she might have found remarkable success. However, in Korean society at the time, parents did not encourage their children to work in the entertainment field. Instead, they hoped their child could land a job at a large company or hold one of the most sought-after professional positions (lawyers, prosecutors, judges, doctors, or professors).

When studying became tiresome, she would chat with me. Some of her stories still linger in my memory. She had a best friend who had gone to America to study. The girl recounted when her friend returned to Seoul for summer vacation. As they had always done, the girl held her friend's hand while walking down the street, only for her friend to pull away gently. With wide, incredulous eyes, she told me she could not believe it. "Inquiring 'What's wrong?' my friend explained, 'In America girls holding hands suggests they're dating,'" she said, her beautiful eyes still wide with disbelief. She found it unjust, a sentiment I couldn't fully comprehend at the time, as I often walked hand in hand with my male friends. However, suppose Americans had seen such a thing in Korea. In that case, they might have misunderstood it as evidence of numerous "homosexual relationships" in the country. We shared a laugh as we talked about cultural differences.

We studied together as we sat beside each other at the girl's desk, which was against the wall. It was early summer, so we both wore short sleeves. Our adjacent arms, hers right and mine left, often brushed against each other significantly as our sessions progressed, and her attempts at contact became frequent. The subtle sensation of her soft hair brushing against mine was thrilling. Each time, I quickly pulled my arm away from her forearm. She increasingly attempted to engage me in conversations about topics that piqued the interest of men and women. Once, she even playfully tried to kiss me. With only a five or six-year age difference between us, it would not have been strange for us to be curious about each other as members of a different sex. However, given my moral standards, I had to make a tough decision. I informed her mother that I would cease tutoring the girl. Of course, I provided a reasonable excuse.

When I look back at my difficult youth in my teens and twenties, I often think of that girl. After graduating from Jeongeui Girls' Middle School in Ssangmun-dong, Dobong-gu, she attended Jeongeui Girls' High School. Although not particularly interested in her studies, she was cheerful and beautiful. I sincerely hope that, with fortune on her side, she finds her aptitude and talent, leading a happy life.

Min-sung was a third-grade elementary school student in Nowon-gu; the girl from Jeongeui Girls' High School was in Dobong-gu, and the pastor's son was a sophomore in Seocho-gu. These young people and children joined me in navigating the challenges of youth. I hope that, like me, they can one day smile and look back on their past with fondness. We should strive to usher in the sunrise amidst life's complex labyrinth. Suppose the maze is too complex and profound for sunlight to find its way in. In that case, we must initiate a revolution that turns our circumstances upside down with unrelenting force. Please do not wait for the sun to rise; boldly stepping out is the key to unlocking new possibilities for us.

Throughout my life, I have turned my circumstances upside-down many times. Sometimes, things get worse, but they have improved slightly at other times. Nevertheless, I do not regret my choices; they were my decisions. It is better to feel excitement while dreaming than to harbor regrets when looking back. I did much tutoring to make a living but gave my all in those moments. Even when delivering study materials like the 'Janghaggyosil' door to door, I did my best for my students. These daily workbooks greatly benefited Korean low-income households who could not afford the expensive private tutoring market. The study papers were affordable, allowing students to receive them at home, solve the problems independently, and check their answers the following day. As a delivery man, I would visit over 100 households, stopping door to door to provide answer keys and explain incorrect responses. Although my time at each home was brief, I endeavored to be an excellent teacher for them even now. As a private tutor, I hoped that even one person would benefit from my influence.

SURVIVING TOXIC

WORKPLACES

Penned October 18, 2019

CHONJI

In 1986, I dedicated significant effort to crafting a feature article on a Seoul-based corporation. Following publication, I delivered some newspapers to the company. Upon arriving, I handed the newspapers to someone in the company and waited in the guest room.

During previous visits for coverage, I noticed a marked increase in the respect they accorded me compared to earlier interactions. During the 1980s, individuals typically extended courtesy only to reporters from major press outlets (Wikipedia contributors, 2022a). Seoul's six major daily newspapers, two economic daily newspapers, and two broadcasters were considered the most significant media. The press I worked for was also a daily newspaper. However, it was a shabby, third-class newspaper that needed to be more well-known to the public. In addition, it primarily relied on industrial companies as its primary sources, so it needed to make its presence known. When I worked there, I had just heard the newspaper's name.

Despite their affiliations with lesser-known media, certain journalists exploited their perceived privileges. They imitated the unhealthy habits of reporters from major media companies. In Korea, there were power groups that consisted of political, judicial, and media circles, which held the highest power. It might be a characteristic of politically backward countries. In the early 1980s, a military force that came into power through a coup d'état forcibly abolished and integrated existing media outlets to control and tame the press. As a result, it was almost impossible to register recent publications, such as newspapers and magazines, during that time. As a result, existing media outlets struggled to survive unless they cooperated with the political world. At this particular time, people intricately connected with the political community and the media world, forming a deep bond that influenced one another. They created enormous power in the judicial world, such as the courts, prosecutors, and police ruling Korea. Thus, it became natural for companies and influential individuals to fear harmful exposure to the media. Consequently, journalists from the more effective press were more authoritative and intimidating to the political groups of the time. Even third-party journalists functioned as if they had great power.

After waiting for some time, a seemingly senior executive approached and handed me a thick white envelope. He gave a white envelope to MM (I'll call him MM in this writing), who was in charge of photography when I was covering the article. MM entered our newspaper about a week before me, and we were colleagues. Handing me the 'Chonji,' the executive bowed respectfully and expressed gratitude for the company feature I wrote. Perhaps the company's President and other officials liked my article. They shocked me when I opened the envelope from the company on my way. Astonishingly, the sum inside amounted to a staggering 500,000 won. 500,000 Korean Won in 1986 equals 1,658,082.56 in 2019, about $1,430. In 1986, the monthly salary of a ninth-level civil servant was only 140,000 won. According to the Dong-A Ilbo, on December 18, 1986, it announced the wages of public officials in Korea. The President's highest salary was KRW 1,470,500 in 1987. How much was the 500,000 won I received in return for the gift?

It was the first time I experienced Chonji while working as a journalist. I felt the thrilling taste of Chonji. It was the story of my young chicks who did not know that such Chonji was daily life. When working for some magazines, I never dared to dream of receiving such a Chonji. So why would an interview attendee give Chonji to a reporter? When we work for a poor magazine, we cannot get an opportunity to interview famous people efficiently. First, we can't directly access celebrities, so we must go through an assistant. However, persuading a secretary who manages such tasks is even more challenging. Interviewing celebrities like this takes work. So, who among them would pay a petty journalist like me a bribe?

Of course, even journalists from the same weekly or monthly magazine were treated differently by people as journalists from major media. They must have quickly received Chonji by pressing the neck of their target, stiffening their necks, like a reporter for an influential press. Even in such a third-class world, first-class, second-class, and third-class always existed. I didn't know Chonji's world, as I worked for an unnamed weekly and monthly magazine before working for that daily. However, even though it was a third-rate daily newspaper, the world was a unique ecosystem when I reached the bottom. MM, who has had one or two years of experience on the floor, was familiar with receiving the Chonji. Perhaps he was waiting for that moment in his mind the whole time he talked with me in the company's waiting room. I never imagined receiving an envelope of money from that company, even hoping for it.

When I returned to my workplace, my mentor, the deputy editor-in-chief, asked how much Chonji I had received. He had expected in advance that I would receive Chonji. Hearing my reply, he gave me a light pat on the shoulder, saying with a bright smile, "You got it pretty well." He seemed proud as my mentor. At that moment, I thought the envelope's thickness judged the article's quality. I almost fell in love with Chonji's exhilaration, so I nearly became a pseudo-reporter for the rest of my life. What would my life be like if the accident hadn't happened at my workplace? Life's journey often diverges based on a mere step or two.

I wrote about Oriental Electronics Co., Ltd. (Allimex, n.d.), which produced and supplied CCTV installed on Subway Line 1 in Seoul. It was a product promotion article. However, I authored an article that went beyond just product promotion and put much weight on the company's brief history and future development potential. I was interested in CCTV high-tech equipment and wrote the ending emotionally and powerfully. For example, I remember getting a hint from the company's name and finishing it as a promising mid-sized company with the potential for future development of the CCTV industry and leading the global market beyond the East. It was the first article I had written for the newspaper I had just joined, and it was a full-page, heavily planned feature article. When I first drafted the article and handed it over to the editorial desk, the company's President, who read my manuscript, said to the editor-in-chief, "He writes well. Support him well," I heard. I could feel that my mentor and several reporters from the editorial department in the office heard it and looked at me with wide eyes. I caught my boss's eye at once.

If a good article appeared in the newspaper, it would be the best way of publicity for the company to increase its public reputation. Unfortunately, influential newspapers in Seoul seldom featured small businesses in a way that served promotional purposes. Even if they wrote about small businesses accidentally, most were brief articles on a few lines. Small companies could not use newspaper articles with high marketing effectiveness, so they had no choice but to rely on expensive advertisements. The five major daily newspapers and two TV channels were the most influential. Therefore, Oriental Electronics Co., Ltd. must actively use my article for marketing. After the company published my writing, the advertising sales department threatened to visit the company and place an advertisement. They used that kind of coercive advertising sales in all daily newspapers and media outlets nationwide. Nothing is free in the world.

It touched my heart when I received Chonji. 'Uh, what is this?' Initially surprised, I quickly grasped the significance of the gesture. 'Oh, I'm finally in the position to receive Chonji.' That's 500,000 won! It was equivalent to one person's monthly salary. It was 1986 when I was only twenty-three. At that age, a man working as a daily newspaper reporter was a rare case in Korea, perhaps the only one I had. At such an early age, I experienced the world of Chonji.

Unfortunately, they fired me after an incident. So, I could only show my skills partially. So, I couldn't taste Chonji anymore. One day, about two weeks after I was at work, it was payday. All employees, in turn, received their payroll envelopes, packed their bags, and left. However, I need help remembering his name in that neat suit, and MM still needs to receive a pay envelope. On the original payday, even if you worked for a week, it was customary to calculate and pay for that day. However, MM, who started working about a week before me, did not receive a salary. Of course, I didn't get it either, but I had no complaints.

MM, a chemical engineering major, faced the scarcity of jobs in his field upon graduation. So those from top universities occupied those few jobs. MM, who is tall, was much older than me, probably over twenty-eight. In Korea, it's typical for men to fulfill their military service during their university years. Therefore, when men returned to their colleges after completing their military service and graduated, they would have been around twenty-seven to twenty-nine. While MM's name eludes me, his distinct face remains clear in my memory. Given his career-driven nature, I assume he was considerably older. Although there was a significant age difference, we respected each other. Though we frequently lunched together, like classmates, our relationship lacked depth, leaving much unknown about him. And our time together was too short for an intimate conversation.

We didn't get paid that day, so we became a team. The next day, when I was about to file an objection to the company, my mentor, the 'deputy chief,' who brought me to the company, stopped me.

RELATIONSHIP WITH THREE PEOPLE

Before joining this company, I formed a brief yet profound bond with my mentor, whom I'll refer to as the 'deputy editor-in-chief.' After that, I joined a newspaper called the Dokseosinmun in Yeouido, founded in 1970 (RN, n.d.). I had many circulations up to that time. As I write this, I checked the company's website and found that it has not disappeared and is still alive. It's like a weekly newspaper with a pretty tough vitality. A glance at the company's online history shows a notable achievement: in 2014, its publisher was honored with an award from President Obama. In the mid-1980s, I accidentally saw an advertisement for a reporter. I entered the newspaper after passing a written test and an interview. I couldn't understand what kind of test I had to get into a company. During my time there, I formed strong relationships with three individuals.

The first was a female reporter my age. Long before I joined that company, when I was working for a monthly magazine, I became familiar with the head of the Arirang theater company. One day, he said, "There is a gathering of theater people in Cheonan, and if you are a journalist for a cultural magazine, you must attend." After following him, I met YM for the first time. I enjoyed drinking and talking with local theater people late at night at a tavern. It was Cheonan Samgeori! They also mentioned the lyrics of the famous willow tree. YM, then a fresh face in the theater scene, was also present at this vibrant gathering. Perhaps she was a third-year college student. Memories sometimes disappear, distort, and become blurred. Fate led me to reunite with YM later at the newspaper. Our connection was profound. YM's striking beauty was unforgettable, leaving a lasting impression in my memory. Sharing the same age facilitated our quick rapport. I found myself enamored by her, particularly when her smile broadened beautifully.

Another colleague was HJ, three years my senior and a seasoned journalist at the time. Years later, she married and had a son a year older than my daughter. Whenever her son met my daughter, he would playfully touch her face and kiss her. It always bothered my daughter, who would try to escape from the pesky boy. If he persisted, she would cry and plead with me to intervene. Watching the video clips of these moments always makes me smile. In the pictures mentioned, you can see my daughter's expression just before she bursts into tears. But beneath the surface, everyone carries one or two secrets in their heart. HJ, someone I deeply care about, has her own secrets. We lost touch in the mid-'90s over a minor misunderstanding. I have been waiting to reconnect with her and her family since then. All this while, I have been keeping her secret.

And my third and final relationship with that company was with that guy in his early to mid-forties, whom I call 'deputy chief' or my 'mentor' in this article. He was the deputy editor-in-chief of the newspaper, directly below the editor-in-chief. He was probably Lee or Kim. No wonder I can't remember his name. If there was only one person in a specific position in an organization, we did not add the last character before the job title when calling that person. However, when two or more people were in the same position, putting their surnames in front of them was expected to avoid confusion. For example, there was only one editor-in-chief and one deputy editor-in-chief, so when subordinates called him "deputy chief," everyone knew who he was. In Korean culture, it's customary for younger individuals to address elders by their titles or a combination of their last names and job positions rather than by their first or full names. That is Korea's unique culture.

It's not surprising that I can't remember the full name of the deputy editor-in-chief. However, it's worth noting that I was not obliged to remember their name, especially given that they have a common surname. Thinking about the man's age now, he may have been in his early forties or late thirties. He confused me about the person's age because it was so long ago; it happened 33 years ago. Since I was young, I may have thought I was too old for the other person. In general, younger people view older adults as older than they are.

I vividly recall the face of the deputy chief back then. Distinctive sideburns framed his stern expression. The cleanly shaved areas around them had a blueish tint, noticeable every time I saw him. By late afternoon, those blue-tinged sideburns darkened, with short stubble sprouting from under his ears to his chin. He also had dark, thick hair styled like a model's, and his eyebrows were long and dense. His figure was slender, and he spoke clearly, commandingly. He would easily pass for a model or an actor in today's world. Reflecting on it now, he might have been in his early to mid-forties or possibly in his late thirties. It's tough to be sure about his age since it was 33 years ago, a significant period. Also, being relatively young then, I might have perceived him as older than he was. However, my budding relationships with these three colleagues soon became complicated following an incident just as I adapted to my role at Dokseosinmun and the company culture.

UNINTENTIONALLY JOINED THE COUP D'ÉTAT

One day, an unexpected announcement rippled through the office: an emergency meeting of the editorial board reporters was imminent. Reporters began to gather in a murmur. Thinking it had nothing to do with me, I was about to leave the office when someone said, "Mr. Kang, sit down too." Since I had almost no presence in the company, no one would have objected if I had just opened the door and walked out. However, someone called me, so I approached the big table at the round table. The meeting room was tense, filled with stern-faced men. No female reporters were present.

As the deputy editor-in-chief began to speak, the audience subtly shifted their upper bodies. The overall atmosphere was full of accusations against the editor-in-chief of 'Crazy Guy.' Most of the criticism was about how absurd the editor-in-chief was and how much it ruined the editorial desk because of that guy. But, of course, it was the deputy chief who led it. He explained that the newspaper was in crisis because of the editor-in-chief. It appeared as though a unanimous agreement resonated among the attendees. Eventually, organized action would drive out the editor-in-chief.

The deputy chief, who was leading the meeting, asked me to say a word and sat there without speaking until the end of the session. "What are your thoughts, Reporter Kang?" he inquired. I needed more basic information about why the editor-in-chief had to step down. Unfortunately, I had no choice but to rely entirely on what the people there had to say. I had only been in the company for about two weeks, so I needed help to figure out the editor's problem.

Moreover, that was not my concern at all. When I thought YM was my destiny, I fell for her and floundered. I constantly spent time together with her, went to interview places, and helped her like her exclusive photojournalist. Until then, I had no interest in anything other than her. I was so obsessed with her that as soon as I joined the company, I did not know what was wrong with the media or what I was supposed to do there. YM had just joined the company a few months ago, so she didn't know the most profound circumstances of the company like I did. I had never heard from her about our company's issues.

"Yes, I agree," was my simple, albeit uninformed, response. The confident deputy chief smiled at me. And the meeting was over. The next-ranking deputy chief would take over the desk if the editor-in-chief resigned. Eventually, They would take collective action to carry out their will to the President, who oversees personnel authority. But, unfortunately, the editor-in-chief in his mid-fifties had the impression that he was hiding a lot of greed or something rather than his skills. Rather than that person, it would be better if a young and good-looking deputy chief took the desk. I wondered if I was about to witness a metaphorical coup d'état unfold within the confines of this small company, so with a mix of intrigue and anticipation, I departed, the day's events replaying in my mind.

Koreans are remarkably familiar with Kudeta, which comes from the French term coup d'état [ku deta]. It refers to the sudden use of force for political purposes. In other words, Kudeta suddenly raised the power to over-throw the state. Although it's funny to apply such a word to a small company, it's weird, but "Coup d'état" isn't all that awkward because people's fates can change even in such a small world. It was Saturday, so if I had gone to work on Monday, I would have known how things were going. As a newbie, I couldn't take responsibility or comprehend the company's direction. My only focus was on YM, my fateful woman with alluring beauty.

AN INVESTIGATION

A palpable chill permeated the office atmosphere upon arriving at work on Monday. The editor-in-chief, who had never said a word to me before, called me directly to his office on my way to work. No, it's been a few hours since I started working. I still vaguely remember that the editor-in-chief individually called those who rebelled into their office. The editor-in-chief had turned into an interrogating detective in his suffocating space with the tightly closed door. He always looked like an urgent person because his eyes bulged like a frog's, with red veins threatening to burst at any moment. His face was flushed red from the excitement of one of his previous meetings.

He spoke to me, pretending to be calm. On his desk was my resume. Through it, he would have known information about me in advance. When I entered his room, he encouraged me to take a seat. He told me he was from the same Gangwon Province as me, and he grew up in Samcheok and knew my father indirectly. He strained to draw connections between us based on my resume. And he let me know he could exert pressure on my father at any time. I laughed at him inwardly. How could he harm my father? And I won-dered how he could threaten my father, who is more vital than anyone else. It was my first time conversing with him, and I wouldn't say I liked his style. This interaction echoed the sentiments of disdain expressed at the emergency conference. And he convinced me he was a very sneaky person. A traitor had relayed the meeting details to him. Otherwise, how could he quickly turn the company upside down on Monday? He would have personally interviewed several reporters on Sunday as well. Failing to extract the pivotal confession he sought, he resorted to questioning even a newcomer like myself. The man, talking about various things, finally asked me a question.

"Reporter Kang. Who led the meeting?"

"I do not know." I answered firmly.

"Think carefully before you answer. If you want to continue working here, be honest!"

He pressed me for an answer, but I chose silence over betrayal. Finally, he realized he had nothing more to gain from me and asked straightforwardly.

"What did you say at the meeting?"

I might have moderately flattered him if YM came to mind at that moment. But, of course, if I get fired from there, it will be difficult for me to meet her adequately. Curiously, thoughts of 'My YM,' usually consumed my mind, were absent in that tense moment.

"I know little because I'm a newbie, but I said that I agree with the core argument of the meeting."

That was the end. The company kicked out the deputy chief and me, whether that day or the next. The others made moderate compromises with the chief, prioritizing their livelihoods. Although many had aligned with the deputy editor-in-chief, they ultimately retreated.

Ironically, as a small fish who barely interacted with the deputy chief, I shared his doomed fate. The bitter aftertaste of the failed coup lingered. But, of course, there were only male reporters at the emergency meeting, so there was no harm to HJ, who had always shown me kindness, and YM, as innocent to the company's machinations as I was, both played crucial roles in helping me navigate the complex dynamics of our workplace.

HER RENTAL ROOM

Time away from Korea has dimmed my memories. YM must have lived in one of Mapo-gu's Daeheung-dong, Gongdeok-dong, or Yeomni-dong. I still remember the house and street where she rented out. She lived alone in a modest room in a slate house on the first floor, nestled in a Mapo-gu neighborhood in Seoul. The space was compact, with a small kitchen blending uneasily with the modest living space. When I first visited her, her room was sparsely furnished, lacking essentials. A flimsy plastic closet teetered against the wall in one corner as if a gentle nudge could topple it. A small round Korean dining table, meant for floor seating, occupied the center of the room, adorned with a new book atop it.

Standing in the corner of her room was a small luggage bag she might have used when she came to Seoul from her hometown of Cheonan. She rolled up a thin blanket next to the closet. There was no bed. There was a small window made of opaque glass toward the street.

Fortunately, black iron fences protected the outside of the window horizontally and vertically, preventing the thief from intrusion. I had time left because they fired me from the company. So, I accompanied YM's interviews and helped, sometimes editing her articles for her. One night, we lay side by side, talking about her writing until she drifted to sleep beside me just before dawn. My heart would often burn with a mix of love and yearning as I gazed at her. I was very moral in that respect. As we were too young for marriage, our time together was innocent. We never even shared a kiss. Had I foreseen the ordeal that awaited her, I might have chosen marriage, intertwining our fates. I often wonder if choosing her would have shielded her from future misfortunes. I sometimes regret that I didn't choose her then. The unpredictability of life left us navigating a path fraught with insecurity.

BRINGING UP LABOR LAW

After a few weeks like that, I got a message from the deputy chief. Thinking about it now, it's fascinating. I am curious to know how we communicated back then. At that time, there were no cell phones or e-mails. Moreover, there were only a few cases of meeting someone personally since there was no pager. It is the easiest way for a company to contact a working person. Just find a public phone booth on the street and make a call. If you can't reach someone like that, you can write a note or letter and contact the person. If it is inconvenient to send and receive messages, or if you need to get them quickly, you can pick up the address and go to them. It's nice to have the person at home or the workplace, but if that person is unfortunately out, the only option is to wait all day or leave a note. Of course, people who rented didn't have a phone at home.

So, with the landlord's permission, the tenant gave the landlord's phone number to an essential person, such as their parents. They were fortunate cases. It was common for many people to move out every few months or a year because there was no fixed place for them to stay. Therefore, knowing the address made it possible to find a person. In some cases, the address and the actual residence site were different.

I was also unstable because my fixed address or place of stay fluctuated. Then, in my vague memory, I got a message from HJ, a senior at the Dokseosinmun. When I met the deputy editor-in-chief, he offered me a job at a company he had been working for in his career. He said the company was much more extensive and livelier than the previous one. It must have been somewhere in Cheongpa-dong, Yongsan-gu. It was called the Daily Industrial Newspaper, which mainly deals with industrial companies. I had never heard of it before. What kind of industrial newspaper? There is a newspaper with the same name in Japan, and the boss of the Daily Industrial Newspaper must have copied the model. The Nikkan Kogyo Shimbun is over 100 years old and is the same medium as Korea's economic newspapers, such as the Maeil Business News Korea or Hankyung Daily (TNKS, n.d.). At that time, Korea copied Japan into most fields and borrowed many ideas from them.

The deputy chief who gave me a job at the company felt sorry for being fired from the previous company because of him. "You were the only one who didn't betray me. So, I am proud of you, and at the same time, I feel sorry for you," he told me. "I'll lead you well in a new place, so let's do it together," he said, holding my hand tightly.

I was fired immediately from my new job due to a triggering event. The company should have paid me for working for half a month. When I was about to complain to the company, the deputy chief told me to hold on for a second. He explained, "It's been less than a month since you started working, so they don't seem to have paid you, but you will receive payment together next month." I always had no money in my pocket to survive without a paycheck. Moreover, didn't you even get Chonji?

But the man MM, whom I should call my colleague, grabbed me and pretended to die. He complained that he had to get paid and that his situation was too difficult. People who dare not take the lead tell others about their tricky situations and hope others act on their behalf. Unfortunately, MM's behavior meant that he asked for a gun on his behalf. Ultimately, I should have done more justice and gone to the Accounting Department to discuss salary. Then, a person who seemed to be the head of the company's HR department asked me for an interview. "We're just going to fire MM, so you wait for your next paycheck," he persuaded. The company's boss recognized me initially, so if I had to wait a while, I would manage to make a living there.

However, they soon cut the incompetent MM from the company. It was worth paying at least a paycheck to get him out. I couldn't understand the position of the company. In the end, I knocked on the boss's office. I still need to figure out why I acted like that on behalf of MM, which has nothing to do with me.

"Come in," said the boss. I opened the boss's office door and entered, bowing my head to him. In his late forties or early fifties, wearing gilded glasses, the man had worked as a reporter for the Hankook Ilbo, one of Korea's five major media outlets. In short, he was a well-trained journalist; he seemed pretty proud of himself. Moreover, he was a person who had the authority of the editor-in-chief, such as screens for the direction and contents of articles. But, looking at him up closely, I thought his impression was that he was a strict man. He looked like a typical person who wouldn't expect a drop of blood from a needle in his forehead.

His face remains etched in my memory. I've often seen employees freeze in front of him. We shared a few casual conversations, and then I told him why I had come. A colleague of mine had to leave the company without getting paid, and I argued that this was not right under the labor law. When the word 'labor law' came out of me, he shouted more angrily than expected.

"You dare to invoke the Labor Law?" he exclaimed incredulously.

He shouted at me, saying the same thing twice as if it was ridiculous. Onlookers quickly gathered, peering through the transparent glass wall into the boss' office. I stood my ground, adding a few more words, though our conversation promptly reached a stalemate.

When I exited the President's office, people stared at me momentarily. At that moment, I felt a surge of courage and pride. An incredibly young newcomer has entered the boss's office, where everyone in the company is afraid of their boss. Perhaps because there was no one there who could be vital against their boss except me, I could feel those thoughts in people's eyes. I left a powerful impression there in a brief period. However, like a clumsy newcomer, I did something without measure.

LABELED AS AN OUTCAST

When I went to work the next day, someone who seemed to be a go-between there called me and said, "You can't go to work anymore." Of course, I knew I couldn't go there in that situation. So, my mentor took me to a nearby coffee shop. "Our boss ordered his secretary to register with the Korean Newspaper Association as a blacklist." He gave me the information. "If they registered your name there as a person of impure ideology, you probably wouldn't be able to get a job in that field anymore," he said. After getting hired by a media company undercover, I became a perceived threat for causing strife through involvement in labor movements. I want to remember the conversation with the deputy editor precisely. One thing is for sure: His face had a hint of impatience. That was the last meeting with him.

The person who vouched for me at the company also found himself in a precarious position. He genuinely mentored me, often bringing me to interviews and imparting valuable lessons. In those days, the more fake journalists were, the more they tried to show off their power. Therefore, each department head always carried two or three of his subordinates whenever he went out. His several staff trailed behind him, lugging large camera bags. When visiting a company for advertising sales, such a boss acted like a king, and his subordinates pretended to be embarrassed. It was a directing to show off their power. These pitiful figures orchestrated such facades, masking their lack of journalistic skills.

However, in those days, such childish pressures often worked, and they were psychologically intimidating enough to their corrupt counterparts. Moreover, most companies need to improve, including tax issues.

Therefore, only some companies can avoid defects when reporters dig deep. Thus, for large companies, it was the primary task of the corporate PR office to hand over money bags when reporters appeared to dig up their weaknesses. Doing so protected the company by making reporters stop at the proper line. Failure to do so could expose the company's corruption and lead to tax investigations.

However, even if they gave some money to a reporter, the guy had to author articles. Hence, the reporter often inserted vague nuances about the company. After that, the advertising sales department took advantage of it and demanded that the company publish advertisements. If the deal was successful, the head of the advertising department asked the reporter who drafted the article to issue a correction article. It was a typical habit of fake journalists and low-quality media outlets to do it like a meal.

Among the newspaper staff I had been with for a few weeks, a man still vividly recalls my memory. People called him the manager. He was in the advertising sales department. He ate so much in his late forties that his belly popped up. So, his protruding belly pushed his tie askew, never quite aligning at the center. Each time he tried so hard to center his necktie, I struggled to hold back my laughter whenever I witnessed his outrageous behavior. The man always had a high voice in the company. The belly guy used to show people the advertising sales figures he had won by threatening companies. He was always full of confidence, and his laughter was thunderous. He liked to show off his achievements, mainly where journalists worked. Perhaps he was trying to emphasize that the incompetent people who spend the company's money are journalists. Still, unlike them, he attempted to be a capable person who contributed enormously to the company's finances.

He used to argue that the good news is reporting the weaknesses of companies so that his team has time to make money for our company. His values were typically poor journalists. He's not a journalist, but he takes a few of his underlings whenever he goes out. They carried excellent cameras, just like photojournalists. How they will behave in front of their prey is all too obvious, even if we don't witness it.

On the other hand, my mentor's deputy chief was gentle. I don't know how he survived such a hostile press, but he was the only one who got expelled during the attempted coup to change the toxic environment. Ah, now I remember. I remember a particular part of the conversation with my mentor at the coffee shop the day I left the company. He tells me he ordered his secretary after the boss got mad at me. And the secretary had contacted the Dokseosinmun and found out about me. Hence, I'm still piecing together the subsequent fate of the deputy chief position. He seemingly aimed to guide my actions early on, but I brushed off his counsel, leading to significant disruptions. Like me, he may have faced a ban from the Korea Newspaper Center (now Korea Press Foundation). Consequently, he probably severed ties with the company and left the industry permanently.

The last time I saw him was then. Perhaps he also became an impure worker proudly because of his relationship with me. So, he would have cut ties with such a cruel and fake journalism world and walked a new path worth him.

SICK YOUTH

1986 unveiled life's bitterness, mainly through my experiences with YM. The most heartbreaking was because of YM, whom I once fell in love with. Since leaving my job at the daily newspaper, I've been hustling to earn a living. It's been over half a year since I saw YM.

Then, one day, I met HJ and heard the terrible news about YM. HJ graduated from the Creative Arts Department at Seoul Arts College. She knew how to author her articles with dignity. Her appearance swiftly garnered admiration from men. After Miss HJ left the company, she was a freelancer providing reports and articles. She knew that I once loved YM. When I asked her what she was doing at her YM, she hesitated for a moment and then told me,

"YM has transformed; she's not the person I once knew. There are rumors she's using her body to sell the newspapers."

It was. Among the criticisms poured out on the day of the emergency press conference in Dokseosinmun, the biggest complaint was that the SOB, the editor-in-chief, forced reporters to make money by selling newspapers.

The newspaper's profit structure functioned in this manner. There were a few advertisements in the newspaper. If it is a tabloid version with about 64 or 128 pages, six or eight full-color promotions and six or ten black-and-white full-page advertisements should fit in the newspaper. Besides the other reasonably expensive title protruding ads, the five columns of ads need to reach dozens of pages to make a little profit.

However, the newspaper's advertisements were almost black-and-white for books with five or seven columns. The company must operate on a scale of advertising sales. Thus, journalists mainly relied on sales bonuses instead of regular salaries. The basic salary must have been minimal, but they have not paid. I need to find out the details. The compensation will vary depending on how many monthly newspapers each reporter sells to their clients. When I was there, in the conversations I heard occasionally, I overheard a few times that someone had sold tens of thousands of copies. But, of course, I was obsessed with YM, so I didn't grasp those profound meanings!

Therefore, there is only one criterion for a reporter to select a potential interviewee. How many newspaper copies can they sell after publishing the interview article? This newspaper will be the only one where reporters get paid by selling newspapers! This newspaper received positive reviews from external sources due to its dignified and valuable information. Editors compose a primary newspaper by editing trending news in the publishing and reading world based on each publisher's book reviews and press releases. Therefore, they skillfully packaged it so that it wouldn't appear fake or third-rate on the surface.

On the other hand, field reporters focus on interviewing famous and wealthy people who can buy many newspapers. The size and position of the page occupied by the article are determined entirely by the number of copies sold. At the end of the interview, the reporter asks the interviewee how many copies of the newspaper to purchase. The reporter then reports it to the editor-in-chief. The editor-in-chief determines the layout and quantity of pages in the order of the most purchase promises. Usually, some people buy from a few thousand copies to tens of thousands of documents. After they bought the newspaper, they would have used it for promotional purposes.

There are bound to be people who want to take advantage of such an opportunity, even if they spend PR money to get their attention in a popular newspaper. People who have never been in the spotlight in the general media are more likely to respond to these deals. The newspaper's core strategy was to sell as many newspapers as possible to pretentious customers. Field reporters were often a source of fear for people. Using that, Dokseoshimun deliberately set a low basic salary for reporters and created a system so that the rest receive a certain percentage of the sales as a bonus. So, the company's reporters essentially became salespeople rather than traditional journalists. They had a structure in which the better the sales performance, the higher the salary; if not, it took more work to make a living. As a result, the company's system cornered its reporters into a dead-end situation.

The company knew the total number of copies for each production, so it could reduce production costs by preventing wastage. After printing, the company distributes the allotted newspapers to each reporter. Therefore, each reporter must deliver the newspaper to the customer. The company does not need to use the cost of delivering newspapers. The company only needs to receive the amount promised in advance from each reporter. In other words, the field reporter was responsible for interview recruitment, article writing, photo shoots, sales, delivery, and money collection. Above all, there were cases where some people did not pay money even though they promised. In that case, the reporter in charge had to spend the money instead of the company. As a result, some reporters had more money to repay than they would receive, but they could only leave the company once they paid off their debts to the company.

THEREFORE, THEY HAD no economic freedom or human rights. In the 1980s, there were few legal mechanisms to protect workers' rights in Korea. Therefore, legally excluded workers did not have the proper, lawful means to request protection of their rights even if they suffered harm.

Using such a unique system, the company did not rely on advertising revenue. Instead, they could save money and make high profits by cheapening reporters. There was no need for advertising sales personnel, which is essential for a media company. It lowered the cost of newspaper production and solved the inventory problem. Crucially, dozens of reporters engaged in newspaper sales and published hundreds of thousands of newspapers every time, increasing the newspaper's reputation. It was the first time I'd heard of any media company with that business model before or after. It is the only business model among all the media outlets worldwide. Whoever designed such a model in the first place was so innovative that only the owners benefited.

In the 1980s, Dokseosinmun had the highest avid reading rate and recognition among weekly magazines (probably biweekly) in Korea. They forcibly sold it by systematically mobilizing dozens of reporters, issuing and distributing hundreds of thousands of copies weekly. As a result, the newspaper was extremely popular with the public. In addition, all national and private libraries and schools at all levels across the country subscribed to the newspaper for a fee. I remember reading the newspaper regularly in the early and mid-1970s, even at a small elementary school in the mountains where I attended. Unfortunately, they registered the reading newspaper as a periodical in 1970. Recording a new periodical was almost impossible just in time since the enactment of the Yushin Constitution in Korea in 1972.

Moreover, in the 1980s, when the dictatorial military regime came to power, the Korean government controlled publishing and media more strongly. Therefore, there were no new competitors from existing operators. Despite people's limited freedom of press publishing, many media companies, including Dokseosinmun, benefited the most and formed a strong power group to protect undemocratic regimes.

So the company owner could live comfortably and make much money. And since there were few advertisements on the paper, it had the effect of enhancing the dignity of the newspaper. Therefore, the outside world, completely unaware of the internal situation of the newspaper, evaluated that the newspaper's number of subscribers was equivalent to the number of circulations of any national daily newspaper. When poor female journalists made a living by selling their bodies, the evil owner would have lived in luxury in his palace-like house with high walls. He likely amassed considerable luxury and wealth, enjoying external accolades as a media owner and publisher.

MY HEART ACHED when I heard about YM's situation from senior Choi. Her eyes, as large and innocent as a deer's, carried a pure and beautiful expression. Usually, she was afraid that even the slightest noise would startle her. But I was just sad about how she walked such a wrong path. According to senior Choi, YM sent money to her mother in the countryside every month to support her family. However, YM's monthly income was so low that it invariably caused her trouble. But then, her income suddenly increased dramatically from some point on, and HJ told me those with a keen eye could figure out what it meant. HJ added that there are several such reporters in the company.

Therefore, if YM eventually chose that path, it would be difficult for her to escape again, Miss HJ regretted. It seemed YM interviewed affluent corporate presidents, allegedly trading intimacy for their substantial newspaper purchases. At least HJ noticed that. The company spends the money on publicity even if corporate presidents buy newspapers. Moreover, it was a tremendous advantage for greedy bosses because they could distribute the purchased newspapers for free for their advertising around them. And since they can use a pretty young girl like YM as a sexual toy, it must have been a good deal. It would have been more critical for female journalists like YM to make as much money as possible from greedy older adults. Therefore, they did not differ from prostitutes.

From then on, I put aside her sweet future with her, who could not return to her former place. I forgot about her after that. Then, after drinking quite late at night, I unknowingly walked into her rented house. No matter how much I called her name outside, the light in her room wouldn't turn on. In desperation, I gently tossed a pebble at her window, breaking the stillness of the night. "Clap!" The sound of sharply hitting the window ripped the still night sky. Soon, the lights in her room turned on. She opened the window with a sleepy face. Her face, which I yearned to see again, remains etched in my memory with vivid clarity.

When she found me, she had a surprised look. "Reporter Kang, why are you here at this hour?" she asked, a mix of surprise and annoyance in her tone. I said a few words then, but she didn't respond to me anymore and just closed her window. Suddenly, her room went dark. I don't remember what I said to her (maybe my brain deleted it because I didn't want to place myself).

Anyway, I ended our relationship with her; we were not friends anymore. I am too fragile to drink alcohol, so I rarely drink alcohol. However, several years earlier, I had ended a relationship in similar circumstances. So, I don't like alcohol anymore.

Did she later become a theater artist? One perpetrator became most famous for the #MeToo movement in Korea. Lee Youn-taek is a tycoon in the Korean theater industry and was one of the vicious sexual assault victims of theatrical versions in the 80s and 90s (Ryu, 2018). Countless women endure suffering due to the sexual misuse of power by influential figures. If YM later went to the theater to pursue her dreams, she might have been another victim.

We were the afflicted youth of the 1980s, battered by life's relentless storms. However, I was reluctant to use the word 'Sick Youth' as the subtitle of this article because the title of the essay collection 'I am Sick Youth' came to mind in Korea. I hadn't even read the book, but I searched and found that the author was from Seoul. His father was a prosecutor at the height of power in Korean society. Thus, it's likely that his parents raised him in a very affluent way. And he studied at an American university, where only a few were available then. Moreover, he is a professor at Seoul National University, another powerful institution with the most considerable influence in various fields, including academic areas in Korea.

He is the same age as me, born in 1963. However, this person's 'sick youth' will differ from the 'sick youth' I have experienced and felt. I know at least that it will have nothing to do with the youth of YM and me in that era and the countless stragglers and losers who did not pass the social standards. Therefore, I don't feel remorse for the sub-title of 'Sick Youth.'

FAKES DO NOT GO AWAY

A sudden rush of memories brought me back, painting a vivid picture of modern journalists — a mix of gangster-like cults, fabrications, absurdities, and zealotry. This realization spurred me to write this article. In Korea, the term 'pseudo reporter' is commonly used to describe such inept journalists, but it's a misnomer. Nevertheless, Korean media and government agencies always use it in press releases.

To be more precise, it is correct to write 'good-looking,' politely, 'poor quality.' However, adding the word 'pseudo' gives a mysterious feeling and makes you look more vulgar or like a counterfeit. Anyway, as a pseudo-reporter, I only received Chonji once. But I assure you, my writing about the company wasn't motivated by the expectation of rewards. Instead, the company complimented me for drafting an article that helped their company image. Yet, by accepting the Chonji without returning it, I unwittingly stepped into the role of a counterfeit journalist.

Since then, I've frequently observed journalists brazenly soliciting monetary gifts. When you go to the movie reporter premiere, the organizers receive business cards from reporters who attended the premiere. That is, to check whether they are on their invitation list. It is to prevent their secrets from leaking out. Let's see what happens after that. Public relations workers at film distribution companies select media companies and reporters to be invited according to their criteria and ask them to attend the premiere. And prepare a press release envelope for each reporter on the spot. They carefully calculate Chonji according to the influence of each press, then place it in the envelope. When the movie ended, the PR staff handed them thick envelopes, and the reporters were about to go home. Journalists are well aware of what's in it. It's all in the same boat. Distributors are bribing them to author good articles to promote the movie. Reporters who readily accept money, even though they know it is a bribe, and distributors who give money all the same ratings.

I discovered that secret because I've been to a few premieres only reporters attend, just because I am associated with the film's distributor. And I know the case of a reporter in a specific position with tremendous media influence. The reporter doesn't even attend premieres with other reporters. And he demands "Premier Alone" from the distributor. Naturally, the demands of fake reporters who talk like that are always acceptable. The newspaper's influence is comparable to that of the entire Korean media combined. The thickness of the money envelope delivered to the reporter must have been different. If people expected a Hollywood movie to be a significant hit at the time, it would have received tens of millions of won. I saw that Chonji culture had disappeared when I left Korea. But, of course, now such funny Chonji culture will no longer exist. The properties of the media channel have entirely changed now.

I ALSO RECEIVED much help from media reporters while running a film-related agency, video education institution, and international film festival. But I never gave them Chonji. As a private, not-for-profit organization, it lacked sufficient funding and could not promote itself that way. Above all, I wouldn't say I liked Chonji culture. So, most film reporters still need to look at the press releases I gave them. Even when I earnestly asked for publicity, they almost turned away from press releases that had nothing to do with Chonji. But even then, some reporters were utterly different from those people.

Representatives were reporter Oh Dong-jin of YTN and reporter Lee Seong-bok, the head of the Digital Chosun Ilbo's video division. On the other hand, when I was active in the film industry, reporter John Doe would have been the deputy director of Chosun Ilbo's film department. However, he was so influential in the film world that he did not attend press previews jointly with film reporters from other newspapers and broadcasters. Instead, under the rumors, he requested a premiere just for himself. However, I unintentionally and appropriately felt out his eyes. He had tremendous power in the film industry. After that, I received no help from him through the news.

In 1995, I held a press conference to announce the establishment of the first international film festival in Korea (although I founded the International Environmental Film Festival in 1994). Director Kim Soo-yong, a respected elder in Korea, held a press conference as the executive chair. Many Korean media reporters attended the event. But one evening before the press conference, a swindler called me, a film reporter for the Hankook Ilbo. "Can you fax me the press release? Just for reference," he urged. I declined because there was a press conference the next day so that I would distribute the press release on the spot. But he kept drowsing at me, saying it was just for reference. So, ultimately, I had to fax the material to the scammer. And, of course, the scammer beat me on the head.

After the press conference, I went into the office. I received a call from reporter John Joe of the Chosun Ilbo. He was furious but said in a cold, forcibly subdued voice that the Hankook Ilbo had published an article about it first. He got angry at me, stating that he had known the reporter of Hankook must get information from you in advance. Then he declared he would not cooperate with us in the future. He hung up the phone unilaterally without listening to my explanation.

My head went blank. I ruined the press conference. When I found the article in the Hankook Ilbo and checked it, there were traces of the scammer hastily handing over his manuscript to the desk. They crookedly printed his film festival-related pieces as if they hurriedly inserted the printed film in the middle. It was also a slightly longer article than a short, brief article! He was a cunning reporter who struck me in the head. How can he do such a terrible thing, knowing it held a joint press conference? Is that any scoop?

Because of that, Hankook Ilbo reported it, so most media companies avoided writing about Korea's first international film festival. Only a few people, including reporter Ahn Jung-sook of the Hankyoreh, dealt with it alone. After that, it took several more years to get help from Korea's most influential newspaper, the Chosun Ilbo. Finally, as his successor, this random reporter oversaw the film, and only then could he get support little by little. However, as this person also learned from his mentor, his stiffness was like a lump of stone. Chosun Ilbo's two John Doe combinations were like an immense mountain that was unavoidable in the film industry. This guy has become famous on the floor now.

GRATEFUL FOR THE PEOPLE OF THAT YEAR

I admit that I inadvertently became part of the pseudo-journalism circle to conclude this article. Chonji, I received 500,000 won in the mid-1980s, which is 1,637,500 won (about USD 1,385.34) as of 2019, according to the monetary value calculation of the Korean National Statistical Office. So, it's a lot of money. And I had no expectations or demands from the company from the start. I did my best to research and draft the article. It was then that I first discovered the existence of the Chonji culture. But obviously, I was part of the pseudo-fake journalism circle. I can't deny that instead of confirming and returning Chonji, it thrilled me with the thick Chonji.

Many pseudo-media companies, including these two places I have experienced, quickly attracted failures who failed to pass the media exam. Such cheap companies have created journalists for young people, forcing them to sell their sham newspapers and blackmail advertisers. Even such low-quality media has plunged the YM I once had in my heart into a hopeless place.

At that time, the greatest hope of the Journalism and Broadcasting Department graduates was to get a job as a reporter for a major daily newspaper in Seoul or as a reporter or producer for a broadcasting station. The media outlets were one institution of power, so the competition for employment was exceedingly high. That's why it's called a press exam. It was when people considered it essential to pass the press examination, including the administrative test and bar examination, to become a career in Korean society. In the case of the bar exam, the country selects only a limited number every year. Hence, it was typical for them not to pass, even if they had tried dozens of times. Once they passed the bar exam, they monopolized the judges, prosecutors, and lawyers. They formed a class of power while seizing control of the Korean judiciary. In the press' case examination, there is an age limit for employment so that men could try twice or thrice. Still, if they failed, they lowered their expectations and entered a local press or a large-scale publishing house in Seoul. Those who could not seize even that opportunity had no choice but to look around for monthly or weekly magazines, where wages and treatment were much poorer. Large media companies or corporations treated the magazines they published well. Still, most of the rest were economically small companies. Some places were closed without notice, and often needed to pay wages promptly. In short, it impoverished the working environment compared to those working at major media companies.

In addition, as I am accusing them in this article if they get jobs at fake media companies with no luck, it will completely change their lives. Instead of just journalists, they eventually turned into fraudulent salespeople who practice fraud and intimidation. Young people with cheap journalist IDs had to hunt for suitable prey to sell magazines or recruit advertisers to get a paycheck. I needed the proper academic background, one prerequisite for the press examination. So, I could not enter a media company with great power. It was not the path I wanted. I never liked to be a journalist. I got into a B-level media company by chance to make a living.

Fortunately, it was a coincidence that I ceased to be such a gangster journalist. I can't remember his name, but it's thanks to MM, who joined the

Daily Industrial Newspaper around the same time as me. I am grateful to him. Before I wrote this, I only thought of his pathetic and incompetent side whenever I accidentally recalled MM. But as I was writing this, I finally realized that MM had caused me to quit that hellish company. After that, I never thought of getting a job at such a B-level media company again. So, I should feel grateful to him. If he hadn't complained about not getting paid, I wouldn't have done anything dangerous for him. He wasn't even my friend, and I was in a dry relationship, knowing little about him. I wouldn't have argued against the terrifying boss by stating the labor law for such an MM.

Before that, as soon as I entered the company, my boss recognized my skills, so I guaranteed my future. But why would I do such a reckless thing? So, it wasn't for MM. In that case, I might have been a scammer, enjoying the sweetness while dipping my feet deep into the disgusting ecosystems, even at the young twenty-three. Choosing that path would have led my life in a completely different direction. Two years after that, I would have participated in something other than the founding of the Hankyoreh, which presented a new press spirit utterly different from the existing press system. And I would have walked on a completely different axis from the path I had walked. Sometimes, even scammers transform themselves into entirely new people, so my luck may have steered me in the right direction. Therefore, if we look carefully at the lives of people pointed out as B-class reporters, they are not so different from ours. In any case, it's apparent that they, too, are working tirelessly to sustain their family members. Living as a human being is so sad and heartbreaking at the same time.

IN OUR LIFE, there are roads we haven't traveled yet. Like a spider's web, among the streets in all directions, there are the roads we walked on in the past and the roads we are walking on in the present. There may have been countless thinner and lighter ties than a piece of paper before such roads. We realize how important it is to cherish the people around us as we go through life. The deputy editor-in-chief, my mentor, will remember me. When I thought of MM, my mentor might feel I was a kid who ran wild like an animal, knowing nothing about the world. Thus, he may have remembered his past. He endured many hardships, unable to set foot in the media again because of his foolish behavior. But then, as I authored this article, I became grateful to MM so my mentor may also value my memories. I don't know forever, but he must have forgiven me long ago. Reflecting on it, he was a decent man at that time. He would now be in his seventies. I want to meet him once.

Despite our painful memories, we don't have to focus solely on the agony. Even during tough times, moments of beauty are always present. And because it drenched us in sorrow, isn't our present and future bright?

I used my real name without filtering at first while writing this article. My post is not a public blog, and I reject the search engines, so it does not set it to be searched on the Internet so that I can change it anytime. So, I tend to write in a diary because I don't have to look at anyone when I write. If, as soon as my writing goes up, many search engines stick together and index it, I won't be able to write freely. A search engine permanently preserves published books in a digital library once it exposes them, similar to how a physical library would store them. Therefore, mentioning the actual name even 33 years ago is not good if it is not a diary.

If I see my writing among the people who have seen their faults in this article, I don't know what sad things will do to me. Moreover, suppose YM, one of the essential characters in this article, saw this in my story. How painful would she be to remember the hellish memories of that time? Among the things I have learned from my extensive experience is that words and writing are different. Although there is a saying that "your words cannot be taken back," we can correct misrepresented comments if we don't miss the right time. However, writing is only practicable sometimes.

We can control sufficient words while detecting subtle changes in other people's emotions. However, it's impossible to maintain the writing due to the structure of unilaterally sending or disclosing the text to the other person. Words are conversations, so you can control them while talking to others. On the other hand, since the article is one-sided, it is a cold message sent or announced, resulting in itself. Words contain the tone of my voice, breathing, and emotions in three dimensions, making room for the other person to think more broadly. However, writing is straightforward and cold because we use it only in letters. That's why letters are sometimes called hard letters.

I have witnessed several cases where written communication resulted in misunderstandings and rigidity, leading to severed relationships. As I write this, realization strikes me. Converting my ideas to others in writing instead of meeting and talking can turn into a sharp dagger, inflicting deep wounds on the other person. The relationship with WS, a lawyer, was the same this spring. He had been my business partner for over 13 years. However, I struggled due to business issues and finally broke our relationship. The last cold words I sent him must have hurt him deeply. Because of this incident, I decided to become a lawyer in the U.S. that summer.

However, I flew across the Atlantic in September 2019 to see him again, and we restored our relationship through sincere conversation. If I had been younger, I would have severed the connection with such a person even if we had reconciled. But having lived a little longer in the world, I realized that it is not a human's duty to wrap up relationships with people so quickly.

It's often better to speak directly, even if it's more cumbersome, for significant decisions, than to write. However, it would be best if you did not drink alcohol. We are still determining when the words that stick the dagger in the opponent will pop out. As I live, I should refrain from wielding harsh words like a sword, regardless of my disdain for the adversary. Recognizing the finite nature of life, I've come to value the preciousness of fate and connections.

A FILM FESTIVAL

DIRECTOR

Pinned December 12, 2016

Within cinema's sprawling expanse, filmmakers, festival directors, and audiences form a distinct nexus. It's a meeting point where art and curation converge, personal histories blend with shared experiences, and storytelling becomes a broader narrative of the human condition. As I navigate these converging paths — from personal identity shaped by cinematic culture to serendipitous encounters that have enriched my life and career to the distinct yet interconnected roles of filmmaker and festival director — I'm reminded that our stories do not just live on screen. They exist in the unseen spaces between us, thriving in the bonds we create and the communities we nurture, stretching across continents and decades. It is a tale of not just films or festivals but life itself.

"Sometimes, at my work, I meet someone who just shines so brightly I am really dazzled. Sayaka Suzuki is such a person. I'm incredibly lucky that, despite the vast distances between us, fate allowed us to meet and forge a deep, rapid friendship. Sayaka is talented, beautiful, and smart, and her spirit is filled with generosity and fun. Knowing her has enriched my life and made my days brighter. Thank you, Sayaka, for shining your light on me, and thank you, KINEKO International Children's Film Festival, for bringing us together!" by Liz Shepherd on November 11, 2016, on Facebook.

In response to Liz's post above, I left a comment that day as follows:

"My journey into the world of film festivals began with a pivotal discovery. It all began after reading a book that was a directory of over 1,000 international film festivals. Around 1992, I studied filmmaking and had just completed my first short film, "Piano, 15 min., 16mm." But that book, AIVF Guide to International Film & Video Festivals, changed my future (Bowser, 1991).

Inspired by the festival director, Liz Shepherd, I decided to pursue a career as a festival director instead of a film director. I envisioned creating my own international film festival and sharing it with others globally. And I'm proud to say that I made it happen! Between 1994 and 1999 (or 2001), I had the honor of serving in several film festivals in Korea.

Liz even visited South Korea twice to lend her support and expertise. I remain deeply grateful for her invaluable help and guidance during those formative years. Looking back on it now, it was such an incredible and fulfilling journey." — Great Summer on November 11, 2016.

The passage above describes Liz's experience attending the KINEKO International Children's Film Festival in Tokyo, where she met Sayaka, a staff member (KINEKO International Film Festival, 2023). Their grateful friendship blossomed, and upon seeing Liz's Facebook post, I couldn't help but reminisce about my challenges in establishing an international film festival. I left a comment on her post, and now I am compelled to recount those past experiences in writing.

In Korea, the term' 감독 (Gamdok)' is commonly used across various fields to mean 'director.' The National Institute of the Korean Language's standard Korean language dictionary provides six different definitions for the term director (감독 監督). For instance, the first definition is "Supervisor (001) (noun): The act of overseeing and controlling work or people to ensure that they do not make mistakes. Also, the act of directing the overall course of an operation." The second definition is "Director (002) (noun): The individual responsible for the overall direction and supervision of a film, play, sports event, or similar, taking on practical responsibility for its execution."

The second definition is the focus of my article, which centers on my experiences with film festivals. This article delves into my journey into the film industry and how I became a film festival director in Korea for the first time.

MY INSPIRATION FOR creating an international film festival struck me while working at Kumi, a trading company near Bangbae Station in Gangnam, Seoul. Kumi primarily imported foreign books, annually bringing in hundreds of thousands of specialized volumes and tens of thousands of magazines. University libraries, national research institutes, and corporate research facilities in Korea purchased these materials through open bidding or individual sales.

Leading the product management department, I managed thousands of new titles, with prices ranging from tens to hundreds of dollars per volume. Our team would load the books ordered by the import department onto trucks and transport them to the company. We meticulously entered and maintained bibliographic information for all books in a database, identifying each new book's content and displaying each subject's assigned code and price.

Accurate inventory management was crucial, and one of our primary tasks involved publishing the managed directory, either as a booklet for sales purposes or as a booklet for bidding. My tenure at the company spanned from the spring of 1990 to the spring of 1992, lasting approximately two years.

In the product management department I led, we also managed the company's computer room tasks. Our chief executive graduated with an information and library science degree from Yonsei University. Since Seoul National University, Korea's top-ranked institution, did not offer this program, Yonsei University graduates dominated the industry's academic sphere. Consequently, our company held a competitive edge in book management and professionalism.

We managed and processed all book data using the Book Management System (BOOMS) developed within our department's computer room, making us the sole company in Korea to employ such technology within the related industries. Professor JM of the Department of Information and Library Science at Chonnam National University created BOOMS. After completing his degree at Yonsei University, he went to the United States. He later earned his master's and doctoral degrees from Case Western Reserve University's School of Information and Library Science, renowned for its expertise in information philology. I have maintained a connection with the professor, and we meet whenever opportunities arise. His son, who completed middle and high school in the United States, majored in computer science at the University of California, Berkeley. He now works at a high-paying job in an American company.

When I joined Kumi, there was only one IBM XT 86 computer. The IBM Personal Computer XT had 128 KB RAM, a 10 MB HDD, and a 360 KB double-sided five¼ inch floppy disk. The CPU speed was a mere 4.77 MHz, which is unimaginable today. Modern mobile phones boast CPU speeds of around 4 GHz, demonstrating a difference of nearly 1,000 times in speed alone. Nevertheless, taking such incremental steps forward can only achieve advancements in technology and science.

Using an XT-class personal computer to check the program's results was time-consuming. I stayed up many nights on the phone with Professor JM, receiving instructions on modifying the program source. However, I knew nothing about that field then. Remember, there was no Internet at that time! After finishing the program edits, I would issue commands to obtain the executable and then head home, only to return to work the following day to review the results. Considering the computer's limited hard disk capacity, people had to store most of the data on floppy disks. As I look back, nostalgia fills me for that era — a time of learning and growth that brought me new adventures, self-discoveries, and a deeper understanding of the world around me. Aside from my department, the rest of the employees used electric typewriters for document creation and correspondence.

My company adopted the ISBN (International Standard Book Number) and ISSN (International Standard Serial Number) systems. However, Korea still needed to fully implement these as basic indexing processing algorithms, which significantly sped up book processing. Additionally, we implemented a library management system, enhancing search functionality and precision.

Shortly after joining the company, I had already mastered my job duties. I proposed investing in computer facilities to the company's top management and received approval. I boldly upgraded the system and provided daily computer training to all employees. By establishing a Direct Link Network System, employees on every floor — from the basement to the fourth floor — could access the upgraded central computer in my department for book searches, inventory management, and sales activities. Additionally, I built an affordable intranet by installing monitors, keyboards, and printers on employees' desks, allowing sales staff to print out needed lists at any time. As a result, the company rose to the top spot in the foreign book import and supply industry, outperforming around two hundred Korean competitors during my tenure.

During that period, I enjoyed the most leisurely time of my life. Despite my youth, I received a generous monthly salary. I oversaw a department, so I did not need direct supervision. New employees who had recently graduated from college were my age or older. While we could be friends outside the company, they had to follow my direction within its walls. Then, my passion for music, which I had briefly dreamt of pursuing in middle school, was rekindled. I spent a month's salary to purchase a cello.

SIMULTANEOUSLY, I ASPIRED to become a film director. I devoted my evenings to studying film at various underground film circles and informal film schools. I had gained the trust of my workplace's top management and, without a direct supervisor, enjoyed the freedom to step out during work hours. Through this balance, I directed the short film 'Piano, 15 min. 16mm,' with aspirations of becoming a film director.

One day, an unexpected event altered the trajectory of my life. One caught my attention as I was sorting through new books. That book was a monograph titled "AIVF Guide to International Film & Video Festivals, 1991." Leafing through its pages, I was astounded to learn about the numerous film festivals held around the world. Before this, I was only aware of the four major international film festivals frequently mentioned in Korean news: the Cannes International Film Festival, the Berlin International Film Festival, the Moscow International Film Festival, and the Venice International Film Festival.

However, the book revealed many more film festivals focused on diverse and intricate themes, such as the environment, children, animation, tourism, PR, documentaries, human rights, LGBTQ+ issues, sports, music, science, marine life, and agriculture. Depending on their nature, the book introduced over 1,000 international film festivals, distinguishing between competitive and non-competitive events. This revelation entirely transformed my perspective on the world.

Upon later meeting with Korean government officials and film industry professionals, I shared that over 1,000 film festivals take place annually across the globe. Without exception, everyone was astonished and speechless for a moment. Unfortunately, Korea did not host any international film festivals then, and people were generally only familiar with major events like the Cannes International Film Festival. Therefore, the mere idea of organizing such a festival in Korea required significant support.

Naturally, Koreans were familiar with many other film festivals. Anyone with even a slight interest in cinema could learn about lesser-known international film festivals, such as the Montreal International Film Festival, the Rotterdam International Film Festival, the Locarno International Film Festival, and the Tokyo International Film Festival. Occasionally, stories would circulate about renowned Korean actors receiving awards at these festivals. Again, however, this information was primarily accessible to those genuinely interested in movies.

Even individuals working in the film industry estimated that seventy international film festivals were held outside Korea yearly. Therefore, clarification was essential during that period. However, everyone seemed shocked when I revealed the number of film festivals introduced in the book, including those who claimed to be film experts after earning doctorates in film studies from prestigious institutions in England, France, and the United States.

I EVENTUALLY LEFT Kumi Trading Co., Ltd. I became involved in creating and producing "The Cinema Journal," a weekly film publication. Due to my planning and efforts, the journal's readership quickly rose to fourth place among all weekly magazines, according to Lee's PR (a survey research corporation), within just a few months of its launch. This remarkable achievement led to a subscription frenzy among junior college students. Even though it was free, subscribers deposited the subscription fee into their bank account in my name. Advertisement orders were abundant, and I gained a deep understanding of the Chungmuro (Korean Hollywood) film industry at that time.

Even then, I harbored dreams of becoming a film director. However, the inner workings of the Korean film industry appeared to be an endless, dark, labyrinthine path. Consequently, I reluctantly abandoned my aspirations to become a film director, a decision that weighed heavily on me. Instead, I focused on creating and organizing Korea's first international film festival. Among my staff were two women from Ewha Womans University, a junior from Yonsei University who had collaborated with me at Kumi, and other friends. Together, we began planning an international film festival.

I registered with a professional committee called the Korea International Film Festival Organizing Committee to establish the international film festival. My team and I translated and analyzed the AIVF book I had acquired from my previous company. However, we required more information than the book could provide. Without the Internet, we relied on books and magazines for data. Nevertheless, the AIVF book remained the only source of information about film festivals. One day, I purchased an updated version of the book from someone on a business trip to New York. AIVF, the Association of Independent Video and Filmmakers, was the only New York-based organization that published a book on international film festivals. While drafting this article, I searched for the book's title on Amazon and found that it required more information. Instead, someone was selling bound copies of books that were available then. I was pleased to learn that on June 14, 2006, issue of Indiewire. com, Anthony Kaufman reported the association's closure (Kaufman, 2006).

My team meticulously constructed a database using the analyzed data. We then utilized this information to develop a plan for a new film festival in Korea, which we presented to various individuals, ranging from high-ranking government officials to executives in large corporations' video industries and film industry directors, producers, critics, and reporters. I advocated for establishing an international film festival representing Korea each time I met them. I then owned a costly white LG Electronics 486 laptop, priced at about two million Won ($2,000). I carried this laptop with me everywhere, using it to demonstrate the need for an international film festival by showing the 1,000 festivals I had organized, opening their eyes to new possibilities.

With the increasing prevalence of the Internet, film festivals began launching websites dedicated to providing information about them. People remember Filmfestivals.com as one of the first professional sites in this field. According to the site, there are now approximately 4,000 film festivals worldwide. Although I have since forgotten much of my early involvement in film festivals, writing about it now brings back memories of a time that feels long ago.

Caption: Liz Shepherd and YJ in Seoul, South Korea 1997.

Liz Shepherd, festival director of the Chicago International Children's Film Festival, inspired me to run my own film festival better. Liz provided invaluable support and inspiration, and I would like to take this opportunity to express my gratitude to her once again. Liz once visited my home when my daughter MJ was less than a year old. The child she met is now attending university in the United States. Liz Shephard herself gave birth to twins when she was around forty. My wife visited Liz's home in Vashon, an island south of Seattle when her children were still young. In 1997, I had the pleasure of inviting Liz to Seoul twice: first for my film festival's pre-promotion and then as the head juror for the event. I remain eternally grateful for her unwavering support and dedication.

Since relocating with her husband, Tom, from Chicago to Vashon, an island south of Seattle, Liz has been serving as the longtime director of children's film festivals at the Northwest Film Forum (https://www.nwfilmforum.org). Suppose someone were to ask Liz how many film festivals she has attended. She might pause, considering her extensive participation in numerous film festivals worldwide. Yet, despite her 60th birthday approaching, her expertise remains in high demand among multiple film festivals.

A FILM FESTIVAL Director's role is all-encompassing, from orchestrating the festival's blueprint to spotlighting and promoting resonant cinematic works that align with the themes of each festival segment. The most crucial aspect is ensuring that audiences engage with the films in a way that fulfills the intended purpose of the festival. It was also the case when I transitioned from film director to film festival director. Directing a film is channeling life's musing through cinema, aiming to resonate with viewers. It's less a pursuit of profit and more an expression of profound philosophies through cinematic arts.

In contrast, a film festival director reflects on contemporary issues and seeks solutions within global cinematic works. By identifying films that embody the essence and tone of the festival they are curating, they can recognize emerging trends while encountering various positions and individuals. The film festival process brings together diverse languages and styles from multiple countries, with the festival itself serving as a window to the world. The selected work could then engage with audiences. Consequently, film directors and film festival directors share the common goal of connecting with audiences, albeit from different perspectives. Moreover, each film festival possesses its unique colors and tones.

Suppose a film festival was to emphasize the personal tastes of the individual leading it solely. In that case, it may only attract a limited audience. However, in such instances, it is possible to cultivate close relationships with regular attendees and filmmakers, even if the festival does not achieve commercial success. Such festivals often require financial assistance. On the other hand, some film festivals cater exclusively to the public's preferences, selecting works and organizing events in line with current trends rather than maintaining the unique characteristics of the festival. While this approach may yield commercial success, it risks diminishing the festival's original identity and voice.

Influential film festivals adeptly navigate their mission, selected films, and target audience, harmonizing these three pivotal components. One of my favorite Korean novelists, Ha Il-ji, offers an interesting parallel. After graduating from the Department of Creative Writing at Chung-Ang University in Korea, he pursued further studies in France, earning a master's degree from Poitiers University and a doctorate from the University of Limoges. His dissertation, "Theory of Distance in Novels," posited that the writing distance varies according to the distance between the author, the work, and the reader. He applied this theory to his "Racetrack Series," which includes The Road to Racetracks (1990), Racetracks at Crossroads (1991), For Racetracks (1991), An Alder Tree at the Racetracks (1992), and What Happened at the Racetracks (1993), all of which I thoroughly enjoyed reading. Similarly, a film festival should maintain an appropriate distance in line with Ha Il-ji's novel theory.

I decided to become a film festival director, a role that did not exist in Korea then. I was 28 years old. Eventually, when I was thirty-one, I founded the first international film festival in Korea with my own hands. Although I did not continue working in international film festivals for my entire career like Liz, I was the first person in Korea to have the title of Festival Director printed on my business card. This achievement fulfilled my vague dream when I first encountered the position of Festival Director in the 1991 publication "AIVF Guide to International Film & Video Festivals." In Korea, it is rare for individuals to display such a title on their business cards, as people prefer more authoritative designations like executive or organizing committee chairperson. I take immense pride in having once been a Festival Director, Creator, Organizer, and Innovator.

PART TWO

OVERCOMING FEAR

Penned January 13, 2009

I read several books in the New Year, some seemingly mismatched with the festive atmosphere. One standout was 'Life Lessons,' a book elegantly translated into Korean. The author, who passed away in 2004, is also a pioneer in the hospice movement and is one of the most outstanding psychiatrists of the 20th century; Elizabeth Kubler-Ross was the last book she left in bed. Yet, it is only a story of death and the book that shows how we should live through the desperate stories of countless patients facing death. So, while it could have depressed me to read this New Year, it was, ironically, a feeling that made my heart lighter than any other New Year.

인생 수업

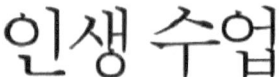

엘리자베스 퀴블러 로스 · 데이비드 케슬러
류시화 옮김

Caption: Korean edition cover of the book 'Life Lessons.'

Put this book in one sentence: "Start right now, what you will desperately want ahead of death." It is surprisingly easy. My parents have already passed away, but my heart still aches when I think of them sometimes, significantly when I feel about my mother, who died at age 64. The thought of my mother dying so prematurely was unimaginable to us. She radiated vitality and robust health. So, I just put off the precious times I had to do with my mother. However, everything changed when my mother was suddenly diagnosed with pancreatic cancer, facing her mortality. Completely unprepared, she faced the prospect of leaving this world. But I did not know what was most important to her, as a patient, and I was in my daily grief.

Caption: Kubler-Ross, Virginia Farm, 1987, No tabloids. Picture credit: missfoundation.org.

My mother lived by the northern shores of the East Sea, a distance too far from Seoul for frequent visits. So, my older sister oversaw her mother's care. In my naivety, I regretfully never asked my mother about her wishes and desires, most like the author of this book. My mother had many desires for her remaining time: meeting friends and sharing her thoughts. My mother would have never expected her death to come so abruptly. So, she must have felt a lot about the futility of her life. So how much regret does she have for the things she rarely did and put off for her later days? I knew nothing about my mother's precious things, like her son. Each recollection brings a surge of profound guilt, echoing in my heart. So, I decided to write about my mother's life when I wrote one day. It will probably be a novel. My mother knows everything about me from the moment she conceived me, but I know little about her life.

AS SUCH, DEATH is not so far away for us, but an object right next to us, and it becomes our immediate problem someday. Then, and only before death, do many people finally regret it and try to escape it, even at the last moment. As co-authors, Ross and her student David Kessler urgently convey the need for readers to grasp these truths, learn from them, and act promptly. If we always want to be aware of what value is valuable to us in life, and if we put that into practice right away, there will be no regrets.

Death is an inevitable part of life, looming over our uncertain present where the future is unknown. But in fact, we find that the accidents or events we fear are very weak compared to the total number of cases. Despite the daily operation of countless vehicles in the United States, fatalities remain a rarity. Considering the relatively low crime rate in Metropolitan Seoul, with 136 reported cases in a population of twenty-six million in 2019, nighttime walks downtown seem safe. We lose a lot because of fear. Because we are afraid, we can't feel deep love. We can't meet strangers because we're so scared and can't challenge new things because of fear. Shying away from fear might keep us safe but at the cost of invaluable experiences. The authors poignantly state, 'Fear doesn't stave off death; it stifles life.'

Our fears loom large, even when their realization is unlikely. Insurance companies make a lot of money because things we worry about rarely happen. People who are afraid to go out to social gatherings fear they may end up feeling bad. However, most of them indeed have happy memories of good meetings. In climbing, the joy and health benefits gained from companionship far outweigh the risks of a fall. When we escape fear, we get more value for joy and happiness.

Therefore, overcoming fear changes our way of life. For example, some families have never had a dog at home for life because of one who fears dogs biting people. So many worries have given us up, bypassed, or brought us to our knees. However, it is dangerous to ignore fear itself because the sign of fear warns of a threat to life. However, petty fears or worries not related to life persistently hinder our lives.

This book convinces us in that respect. Through the authentic voices of patients about to die, we can gain the wisdom of life that is conveyed intensely to our hearts. Our lives shine brighter when we push aside our worries and fears. This book is constantly ringing with messages to challenge what you want without fear. If we've made many mistakes, it's better than we've lived doing nothing, and if we have a lot of sense of loss, that means we've tried that much.

Caption: In the spring of 2017, I traveled to Lanzarote Island in Spain with my two children.

That's right. In life's fleeting journey, embracing challenges, even at the risk of failure, holds more meaning than the hesitation that comes with inaction. The most profound lesson from those at life's end is to embrace each day to its fullest, savoring every moment. If you miss someone, wait to put it off until tomorrow and see the person right now. When you conceive an excellent plan, pursue it, undeterred by the scrutiny of others. Act on anything that excites you now without any hesitation. To live a life that is not just complete but one that pulses with passion and vitality!

A QUEST FOR RESPECT

Penned November 18, 2010

"Moments of sadness shake me awake no matter when or where." — Great Summer.

Caption: A scene from the Thanksgiving school festival at Willard Elementary School in N.J., which my children attended.

My family and I set off on a thrilling road trip to North Carolina, brimming with the allure of adventure and discovery. We journeyed through several cities and six states, taking in the stunning scenery. Finally, we arrived in Raleigh. We enjoyed experiencing the unique southern culture and delicious cuisine at the State Farmer's Market restaurant. Our trip also took us to Durham, where we visited the prestigious Duke University. This iconic landmark left us in awe. With so much breathtaking scenery and new experiences, this road trip was an unforgettable journey that energized and inspired us.

Caption: The Washington Monument stands majestically, bathed in the red hues of sunset, symbolizing Washington DC's grandeur.

YET, ALONGSIDE THESE tangible journeys, we can traverse the globe through Google Earth from our couches. This virtual exploration instills a deep sense of awe for the planet's vastness and intricacy. Each mouse click rotates the globe, revealing multiple layers of information and life. It is a humbling experience that fills me with a sense of purpose of living meaningfully as part of this fantastic planet. The breathtaking natural beauty around us is a poignant reminder of our duty to preserve this planet for future generations.

Caption: A view of the State Farmer's Market in Raleigh, North Carolina.

AS I DROVE THROUGH the beautiful countryside, I thought about the fantastic experiences I had on my travels. Every destination offered fresh perspectives and renewed hopes. It's incredible how much beauty there is in this world and how much we haven't discovered yet. Travel captivates me primarily for engaging with people from various cultures and backgrounds. It's incredible how much we can learn from each other and how much we can grow as individuals and as a society. The world may be vast, but we are all connected by a shared humanity and a desire to create a better life for ourselves and our loved ones.

Caption: A photo I took in 2010 of the Barnes & Noble bookstores at Harbor Inn in Philadelphia, Pennsylvania. Once bustling with people, this splendid building with its elegant interior eventually closed its doors.

OUR DIVERSE BELIEFS and values notwithstanding, we are united by our collective existence on Earth. We can find everywhere beauty, from the vibrant fall foliage of the American East to the bustling landscapes of Washington, DC. It is a moment that gives hope for a future where we can all unite to build a better world for ourselves and future generations. Simultaneously, I find inspiration in the relentless efforts of individuals and organizations striving to transform the world. From entrepreneurs developing innovative technologies to activists fighting for social justice, countless examples exist of people working to improve the world.

Caption: The Center for Aquatic Sciences at Adventure Aquarium at Harbor Inn in Philadelphia, PA.

IN 'THE AGE of Diminished Expectations,' Paul Krugman emphasizes evaluating the actual global nature of markets are truly global (Krugman, 1991). Due to language barriers, Korean entrepreneurs face many challenges to succeed in the worldwide market. However, innovative ideas and determination can help overcome these obstacles. And while there may be setbacks and challenges along the way, I am convinced we can overcome any obstacle and achieve our goals together. Each step we take brings us one step closer to a brighter and more hopeful future for all.

Caption: A restaurant at the State Farmer's Market in Raleigh, North Carolina, serving Southern-style cuisine.

IT'S DESIRABLE FOR Korean entrepreneurs. However, doing business in the U.S. gives them an edge in operating as a global company, given that consumers and partners worldwide communicate in English. Companies like Google, Amazon, Facebook, and eBay dominate the global market. Google represents a new fourth-generation future company that creatively finds and presents the most valuable things to humankind beyond any country. Although Korean laws and institutions emphasize maintaining the status quo, we must boldly pursue the risk of creating a future. Now, Korea is attempting to transform into a top-three company. With rest and a new perspective, it can build a solid foundation for future generations.

Caption: In the distance of the photo, one can see the White House, a symbol of the U.S. federal government.

IN HIS BOOK, THE Essential Drucker, Peter Drucker emphasizes that companies that don't dare to envision the future will face more significant risks from disasters that have already happened (Drucker, 2001). Yet, despite the challenges we face as a global community, we have the power to make positive changes. Whether through small acts of kindness or large-scale initiatives, we can influence the lives of others and the health of our planet. It won't be easy, but building a brighter future for us and future generations is worth the effort.

Caption: My son and his friends are in action on the soccer team run by the town.

AMY CHUA (2007) argued in her book Day of Empire that "opportunity, dynamism, and moral force" are essential qualities for becoming a superpower. However, they are also necessary for becoming better people and better societies. We must embrace these values and work together to create a world where everyone has a chance to thrive and succeed. So, rather than putting up a great slogan and failing to act, we can't help but think about the small steps we can take to impact the world positively. Everything matters, whether volunteering at your local community center, donating to a charity, or being kind to others. If we work hard and believe in ourselves, we can improve the world for ourselves and our generations. With that faith in my heart, I knew I could achieve anything I set my mind.

Caption: Ridgewood High School band performance in Ridgewood, NJ.

AS I CONTINUE my journey, the road ahead may be bumpy; however, I believe we have the strength and resilience to overcome any obstacle. We can create a brighter and more prosperous future for all with hope and willingness to learn from each other. Upon returning home, I felt a new sense of purpose and determination. I knew challenges would be ahead, but I also knew that hard work and perseverance would make anything possible. Looking back on my journey, I knew I would always carry the lessons and memories. From the vibrant colors of the foliage to the stunning architecture of the National Aquarium, it has repeatedly reminded me of the beauty surrounding us. All these experiences reinforced the significance of maintaining optimism amidst life's adversities.

Caption: At the Lincoln Memorial, Martin Luther King Jr. stood in its footsteps in 1963 to deliver his renowned "I Have a Dream" speech, etching yet another historic event at this location.

WHEN I ARRIVED at my destination, the warmth and hospitality of the locals moved me. They welcomed me with open arms and showed me the true meaning of kindness and generosity. Such moments reinforce our belief in humanity's inherent goodness and capacity to shape a better world. We may have moments of sadness, but we must keep moving forward with courage and optimism, taking small steps to build bridges that will lead to a better future. Just as the rolling hills and expansive greenery filled me with awe and wonder, I couldn't help but be grateful for the opportunity to witness these natural wonders. I hope more people can respect and share those values by practicing the small good we can while reminding ourselves of nature's greatness and the Earth's potential.

Caption: While Thanksgiving is an annual fun day for the kids, a couple hosts a party for the adults every year, making the night enjoyable for them.

"Get up, keep moving, eventually build a perfect bridge to keep going."
— Great Summer

FINDING HARMONY

Penned December 3, 2012

Are you familiar with the English adage, 'Every bird loves its own nest best'? Despite its flaws, people often crave the comfort of home after just a few days away. This feeling is even more intense when they stay in an uncomfortable and restrictive place. Of course, people take trips to escape their routine, but finding a place more comfortable than their house can be challenging. Yet, occasionally, people stumble upon such an idyllic spot that leaving feels unthinkable. They might even miss it after they return home. This special place is what we call the "homesick place."

Last summer, I stayed at a hotel for one night and found it more comfortable than my home. However, I enjoyed it so much that I wanted to keep up the same day. Sometimes, even a bird may find a place better than its nest!

In one of my blog posts titled "The High Line and the Forbidden City," I discussed travel and architecture. Whenever we travel, we come across inspiring architecture that makes us think. My daughter is interested in eco-architecture, which is becoming increasingly important. Our ancestors were wise enough to incorporate eco-friendly concepts into their living architecture.

However, we have prioritized functionality and trends instead of listening to their valuable voices. As a result, we have lost many precious things without realizing them. We regret it too late after so many unique traditions and cultures from our ancestors have disappeared.

Traveling isn't just about discovering new places; it's also about absorbing lessons from them. We can appreciate the beauty of architecture and learn from our ancestors to create a better future. So, let us cherish our homesick places and preserve our traditions and cultures for future generations.

SSEATTLE, A DREAMY DESTINATION

Traveling can evoke a mix of emotions, such as nostalgia, excitement, dissatisfaction, and empathy. Have you watched the romantic movie 'Sleepless in Seattle' starring Meg Ryan? If so, what do you feel when you read about Seattle in my writing? I enjoy Jeremy Rifkin's insightful books that deeply understand our era and offer a glimpse into the future. "End of the Working Society" and "The Third Industrial Revolution" are some of my favorites. In addition, Rifkin's book "The Empathic Civilization" suggests that being empathic with others is a beautiful expression of compassion. I hope my writing helps us connect and understand each other better.

Image credit: vecteezy.com/members/316936903976641.

Seattle, a city with a population of 650,000, is in the northernmost part of the western United States. You can drive from Vancouver, Canada, to Seattle in about two and a half hours. The city has a coastal climate, so the weather remains constant throughout the year. Winters are cool and chilly but not freezing, while summers are mild, with temperatures not exceeding 75 Fahrenheit. However, climate patterns are changing, and global warming is causing noticeable changes.

It is not a short trip if you fly to Seattle from JFK International Airport in New York. The fastest direct flight takes around 6 hours and 35 minutes. Still, most people prefer layover flights, which can last up to 8 hours and 45 minutes if everything goes smoothly. Unfortunately, the flight can last up to 12 hours and 20 minutes.

I recently flew from JFK to Seattle-Tacoma International Airport (Sea-Tac). Our flight departed at 7:40 AM and landed in Seattle around 11 AM. Upon arrival, the 3-hour time difference between the East and West Coast was a relief. However, once we disembarked, we waited for a shuttle bus to take us to our hotel, which my wife had reserved. Thankfully, the hotel was only 10 minutes from the airport and was the first stop on the shuttle route.

As soon as we entered the hotel, its eco-friendliness impressed me. This beginning set the tone for our enchanting stay in Seattle, where urban comforts seamlessly intertwine with nature's allure.

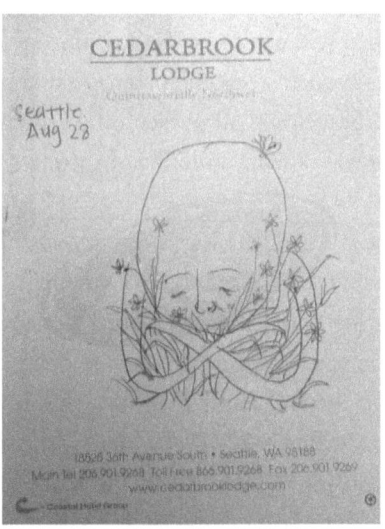

Caption: After MJ drew her image of the hotel on the note, her mother discovered it in our hotel room and returned it home.

GOING TO THAT HOTEL

Cedarbrook Lodge is a hotel on the outskirts of Seattle, Washington. It has gained an elevated level of trust and a well-deserved reputation from the millions of travelers who evaluate the services of the companies they use from sites such as TripAdvisor.com and Expedia.com. Cedarbrook Lodge in Seattle is among the highest-rated hotels on both websites. TripAdvisor always reminds me of the people I know. Every Thanksgiving Day, my family and I have dinner with my German friend Manfred. Ingrid (Senior Director of Merck & Co.), Sebastian (Post-Doc at Virginia Tech), and one of his friends, a young man who works as a developer at TripAdvisor's office in Boston, are part of his beloved family.

He says the company has over 1,400 employees worldwide in the US, Europe, and Asia. In 2011, TripAdvisor officially separated from Expedia, the world's largest online travel portal. According to the engineer, the company has invested and researched heavily to guarantee maximum fairness and accuracy of customer reviews. Nevertheless, I only recently discovered that this hotel received such excellent reviews from these authoritative sites. As I researched this article, my impression of this hotel was purely uninfluenced. Had I known that this hotel is top-rated in the United States, I would not have mentioned it. That was not a pure feeling of mine." Cedarbrook Lodge is an excellent choice if you are looking for a top-rated hotel on the outskirts of Seattle. This hotel has earned an outstanding reputation, receiving high ratings and positive reviews from millions of travelers on TripAdvisor.com and Expedia.com.

TripAdvisor reminds me of Thanksgiving Day when my family and I had dinner with my German friend Manfred. His wife Ingrid, the Senior Director of Merck & Co., and their son Sebastian, a Post-Doc at Virginia Tech, and one of Sebastian's friends, a young man who works as a developer at TripAdvisor's office in Boston, are all part of Manfred's beloved family. TripAdvisor has over 1,400 employees worldwide in the US, Europe, and Asia. The company has invested heavily in ensuring the fairness and accuracy of customer reviews.

While researching this writing, it pleasantly surprised me to discover that Cedarbrook Lodge is among the highest-rated hotels on TripAdvisor (Pucci, 2011). However, my impression of this hotel was that it was independent of its high ratings. Had I known that Cedarbrook Lodge was a top-rated hotel in the United States, I would not have mentioned it. Instead, I wanted to provide an honest and unbiased opinion based on my experience.

Cedarbrook Lodge is on eighteen acres of lush Pacific Northwest landscapes, only minutes from Seattle-Tacoma International Airport. The lodge offers excellent amenities, including a spa, a fitness center, and dining options. The rooms are spacious and comfortable, with all the necessary facilities to make your stay enjoyable.

So, if you are planning a trip to Seattle and looking for a top-rated hotel, consider Cedarbrook Lodge. It is an excellent choice for anyone looking for a comfortable and relaxing stay in a beautiful natural setting.

TripAdvisor.com ranked Cedarbrook Lodge #1 in the US and #17 worldwide in 2011. TripAdvisor is a highly regarded platform used by millions of travelers, making this a prestigious honor. They recognized this achievement and chose the Cedarbrook Lodge as the top hotel in Expedia.com's Insiders' Select list, the world's leading travel booking portal. The hotel is flawless in every aspect, providing top-notch service, excellent facilities, and outstanding amenities.

EXPLORING CEDARBROOK LODGE'S ARCHITECTURE AND DESIGN

Cedarbrook Lodge is a unique and inviting destination that sets itself apart from other hotels with its commitment to service and eco-friendliness. As someone who has traveled extensively, I can attest that the architecture and design of this hotel are awe-inspiring and make it stand out from the crowd.

One of the most remarkable things about Cedarbrook Lodge is its operating philosophy. Unlike other hotels that may seem impersonal, Cedarbrook Lodge calls itself a more friendly and welcoming lodge. The hotel's construction company managed everything from its architecture design to its interior design and landscaping, which they completed relatively quickly. Located just five to ten minutes from the international airport, it caters to guests, including wedding and leisure guests, business customers, and tourists looking for a quiet, eco-friendly hotel.

The hotel comprises three large buildings surrounded by beautiful gardens. The main building is the entrance, and the lodging building on the left has 104 rooms. The lobby is on the second floor, which is accessible by an impressive staircase that leads to a high-quality roof and interior design. The eco-friendly hotel offers a stunning view of the beautiful restaurant and bar.

Image credit: Ahmet Demiroğlu on Unsplash.

The hotel's commitment to eco-friendliness is evident in its design, ensuring guests can move around seamlessly without needing elevators or stairs between the first and second floors. In addition, guests can enjoy a lovely pond and garden when passing through the two guest buildings on the left of the hotel, which leads to the restaurant or bar on the first floor.

One of the most impressive features of the hotel is the annexes and vast spaces of the main building on the opposite side of the lobby, filled with high-quality and genuine artwork. This feature creates a peaceful and familiar environment throughout the hotel, making it feel like Manhattan's Museum of Modern Art (MoMA). As a result, the hotel is an ideal destination for any occasion, from wedding facilities to perfect meeting places.

My family and I stayed on the first floor facing the vast lawn and immediately loved our room. The hotel's design and diligence are remarkable, providing guests with a seamless and natural experience.

The photos of the hotel depict a harmonious blend of architecture and nature, creating a warm and welcoming atmosphere for visitors. The hotel's design is not imposing but blends seamlessly with its natural surroundings. Even when guests appreciate the spaciousness of their rooms and feel free to relax, they book all the rooms in the hotel due to the comfortable and inviting atmosphere that makes them want to extend their stay.

So, Cedarbrook Lodge is a must-visit destination for travelers seeking a natural and wholesome experience. GGLO Architectural Firm created the hotel's interior design and landscaping. Visitors will appreciate the harmonious blend of architecture and nature, much like the works of Antoni Gaudí, a brilliant Spanish architect. The photos of the hotel on Google Maps highlight its vast green spaces and refreshing views, making it an ideal destination for travelers seeking a peaceful and natural environment.

A NATURAL HAVEN IN THE BEDROOM

As I opened the expansive windows, lush greens outside welcomed me. Despite Seattle's humid and dry weather, the landscape outside seamlessly blended with our room. In addition, it was refreshing to have a work desk against the wall; every detail in the interior design displayed the hotel's management philosophy of care and attention. For example, the intricate and beautiful soaps and other items in the bathroom were almost like art pieces. I was so impressed that I asked the concierge if I could buy them separately. However, unfortunately, they were not available for sale.

The value of this hotel became evident after a good night's sleep. Unlike other hotels where I would usually feel dryness and discomfort, the precise calculations in design and construction here meant there was no such discomfort. The bed, sheets, and pillows were perfect, and the humidity in the room was just proper. My family and I even tried to book an extra day, but it fully booked the hotel with other guests. I then realized that this place was even better than home.

This hotel offers eco-friendly rooms throughout the building, with end-less complimentary gourmet snacks that exclude meat. The snacks were so luxurious and promising that my wife and I thought, "Do we need to go to a paid restaurant for a meal when there's enough to eat here?" They offered the snacks for free, without limit, and there was no need to worry about the eyes of others as people were hardly visible. So, we enjoyed our meal while reading magazines, newspapers, and books on the shelves or watching TV in peace. I could not help but wonder if this operation could generate a profit.

However, I also wondered if I paid too much for my stay. As a business, providing services at a loss is only possible for public institutions like gov-ernment agencies. The hotel's secret to delivering such high-quality service is that the room rates are expensive. I brought such delicious food to the room without worrying about people seeing it, which was a nice touch. Some guests even brought luxurious bread, croissants, fruits, milk, and more to their rooms.

MEETING AND PARTING WITH NATURE'S PRINCIPLES

Excitement filled us as we arrived at the hotel. We explored the premises eagerly, yet disappointment crept in upon realizing our time in this delightful haven was limited to just one day. Wanting to make the most of our time, we requested the hotel shuttle service and headed to the nearby Westfield Garden State Plaza, a mall that mirrored the one back home. Competitive large-chain stores are typical in the US, offering a similar shopping experience in different areas. While this has its benefits, it also has drawbacks. We waste precious time and energy in a place we already know.

Returning to the hotel, we discovered it had its farm, providing most of the ingredients for the restaurant inside. The restaurant was renowned for its farm-to-table concept, but the menu was quite pricey. So, opting for a more affordable dinner, we enjoyed what we bought from the mall. As night fell, my wife and I sat in the bar next to the restaurant, sipping a glass of wine. As Koreans, we found the American drinking culture quite bland. However, we enjoyed each other's company in such a pleasant setting.

The complimentary breakfast the following day made up for the expensive dinner. While it was not free, they included it in our accommodation fee of 150 dollars for a room with two beds for our family of four. After inquiring about an additional night's stay, we learned that the standard rate exceeded three hundred dollas. However, my wife managed to secure a reservation at a much lower cost by timing it right and using the right strategy.

In the end, meeting and parting with nature's principles left the biggest impression on us. Every detail of the hotel echoed its commitment to sustainability and the farm-to-table concept, from the lush green outside our window to the ingredients on our plate. And while we were sad to leave such a welcoming environment, we knew that nature's cycles dictated that all good things must end.

Caption: Bill & Melinda Gates Foundation: A Hub of Philanthropy in Seattle.

Seattle and its metropolitan area boast significant companies listed in the Fortune 500, including Costco Wholesale (#18), Microsoft (#31), Amazon (#29), Starbucks (#187), Paccar (#158), Nordstrom (#224), Weyerhaeuser (#355), and Expeditors International of Washington (#418) (CNN, 2012). During our visit to Seattle, we took our son, YW, to the Bill & Melinda Gates Foundation, which exuded a sense of grandeur and dignity. A list of the foundation's most significant donations was visible upon entry. We gained insights into the donors' profiles and the astute management of their generous contributions. We also learned that Warren Buffett donated 85% of his holdings to the foundation in 2006, as the New York Times reported. Mr. Buffett has outstanding generosity; more significantly, it contrasts starkly with Steve Jobs, who does not receive notable recognition for his philanthropic endeavors.

EXPLORING THE HEART OF SEATTLE

We checked out of the wonderful hotel we had stayed in and headed to our next destination — a hotel in downtown Seattle. Before we married, my wife bought a picture of Pike Place Market, which she used to hang on the wall of our home in Korea. I had always wanted to visit this place; as luck would have it, we were finally going there.

Caption: Bustling Farmers Market: Seattle's Energetic Melting Pot of locals and tourists.

As we arrived, the place was bustling with tourists. This market, buzzing with energy, is a must-visit destination for anyone exploring Seattle. I am an avid coffee lover, so we decided to stop by the Starbucks flagship store. While the flagship store was impressive, I found myself drawn more to the city's quieter backstreets and hidden alleys.

That day was my daughter's birthday, and we were looking for a restaurant for dinner. We fortuitously discovered a hidden culinary treasure unmarked by any signboard. After walking down a long staircase, we were in a cozy restaurant where my wife vaguely recalled eating with her friend Liz a long time ago. I ordered the rabbit dish I had not tasted since childhood when I used to hunt in the mountains. My family, discomfited by the idea of eating rabbits, regarded me warily as I savored the meal.

Although we were staying in the city's heart, there was little to do around the hotel. So, I took my son YW to the market we had seen in the pictures a few times. We played games in the arcade for over an hour and had much fun. Our triumphs in the games earned us numerous coupons, elevating me in my son YW's eyes as a proud and accomplished companion. Exchanging the vouchers for prizes meant enduring the store staff's frosty glares. Despite this, the experience was fantastic, and I would not have missed it for anything.

Caption: Seattle is a city that embraces diverse cultures and promotes environmental awareness.

Brimming with organic produce, the city's supermarkets ignite a craving for wholesome, healthy food choices. The city regularly hosts events and concerts centered around environmental advocacy. One of the most memorable events was the exhibition of the movie "Avatar" at Seattle's Science Fiction Museum, which left an impression on visitors.

A VISIT TO VASHON ISLAND

My daughter MJ had been eager to visit Seattle, but once we arrived, she cooped up studying in our hotel room. With exams and summer assignments looming, she had brought a stack of schoolbooks with her, effectively turning our trip into an extension of her desk at home. As the days wore on, my family grew increasingly bored with the hotel and yearned for something more exciting to do.

Caption: Vashon Family: Isaac, Ellie, Liz, and Tom.

At this point, our dear friends Liz and Tom came to our rescue. The couple had known us for two decades. It was renowned in the international film festival circuit, with Liz visiting Korea at our request twice. They had settled on Vashon Island, a large and fascinating island located southwest of Seattle. With just over 10,000 people, Vashon Island is 1.6 times bigger than Manhattan, New York.

Caption: Liz in Seoul, 1997.

Liz's beauty was timeless, reminding me of Audrey Hepburn. After finishing her jury duty at an international film festival in Rio de Janeiro, Brazil, she immediately came to our hotel to pick us up. With his software engineer background, Tom mirrored Liz's friendliness and warm welcome. Upon arriving at their charming home on Vashon Island, we received a warm welcome from Isaac and Ellie, their delightful fraternal twins, whose bright smiles illuminated the room.

As we explored the island, we discovered its charming shops, scenic views, and lush greenery. My family was delighted to be out of the hotel room and to be exploring a new place. We visited a farm where we petted baby animals, picked fresh berries, and even stopped by a pottery studio where we made our pieces. It was a refreshing change of pace from the dullness of Seattle, and my family and I were grateful for the opportunity to explore this hidden gem.

Our visit to Vashon Island was a highlight of our trip to Seattle. We were grateful for the kindness of our dear friends and the chance to escape the monotony of our hotel room.

Caption: The charm of coastal towns during twilight is undeniable.

Even with a less sophisticated smartphone camera, I could effectively capture the moment's essence. The village itself was a poem come to life, its alluring charm rendering it an idyllic haven for romantic escapades.

Vashon Island — A Timeless Escape

As soon as I stepped onto the ferry, I felt a sense of calm washing over me. The boat's gentle sway amidst the stunning natural scenery imbued a sense of being in a grand yet profoundly peaceful and serene amphitheater. As Vashon Island came into view, its unspoiled natural beauty and simplicity immediately captivated me.

Caption: Enchanted Pine Forest: Where family bonds and childhood magic come alive.

This quaint island serves as a tranquil refuge from the frenetic pace of urban living. The streets exude a refreshing simplicity, blissfully devoid of urban chaos's typical hustle and bustle. As my family and I walked around, we felt the gentle caress of Mother Nature at every turn. The forest enveloped us like a warm hug from an old friend. Our exploration led us to a charming cottage in an extensive orchard where a celebration would be held in a few days.

But it was the pine forest that truly captured my heart. The local children often play "The Hunger Games" here, and I could not help but feel transported to another world. As we walked deeper into the woods, I felt like I had entered a different dimension where magic and wonder still existed. I felt surrounded by ancient whispers as if the forest itself was alive with age-old tales.

Vashon Island is a place where time stands still. It is a place where the world's worries disappear, and the soul can find peace. The island's harmonious blend of humanity and nature is like a symphony playing a timeless melody. As I gazed upon the picturesque scenery, I could not help but feel that the sea and the city were like lovers entwined in an eternal embrace, their love ever-growing with each passing moment.

During our stay with the Vashon family, the soothing rhythm of the sea and the gentle touch of the island breeze created a serene atmosphere for us. The island's serene embrace rejuvenated us, giving us the comforting sensation of discovering a second home. Vashon Island truly is a timeless escape, a place where the heart can find joy and the soul can find solace.

Image credit: Vashon-maury.com.

LIZ'S HAVEN — WHERE NATURE AND SIMPLICITY MEET

As we arrived at Liz's house, it felt like we had stepped into a painting with brighter colors and sweeter air. The tall, lush trees surrounding us amazed me as if they were reaching for the heavens, like a crowd cheering on the sun. And the absence of distinct seasons was a gift to the plants that grew and flourished, like dancers in a never-ending ballet.

Caption: Liz's sanctuary: A harmonious haven of simple living and unspoiled nature.

Liz and Tom's lifestyle resonated with the tranquility of a refreshing breeze, embodying the essence of fulfilling simplicity. They dug up fresh vegetables from the garden and baked their bread, living a cost-effective and meaningful life. Their lives harmonized like a natural symphony, free from the clutter of machines and excess, and danced to a rhythm of ease and grace.

The absence of annoying insects and mosquitoes was like a dream come true. In this world, one can enjoy the outdoors without any distractions. The mild temperature that averaged 52 to 75 Fahrenheit from June to August was a haven for those who longed for a respite from the heat of the East Coast, like a cool stream flowing through a parched land. Liz's haven was like a sanctuary where nature and humans coexist harmoniously. That haven hid all the world's obstacles out of sight. Staying with Liz's family on the island was like a blessing, as we got to experience a unique way of life and enjoy the beauty of nature with none of the usual chaos.

Vashon Island was like a black hole, whisking us away from the hectic pace of Seattle and into a peaceful realm. Even the wild ducks coexisted harmoniously with people, undisturbed by our presence. It was like a world where time slowed down, and the beauty of nature was the only thing that mattered.

Caption: KN's Vashon beach house: A masterpiece of artistic and natural beauty.

We dined at a newly opened Japanese restaurant on the island, where the staff appeared Korean like a melting pot of cultures coming together. During a leisurely walk through downtown Vashon, we met a welcoming family who kindly invited us to their home. MK, their fifteen-year-old son, displayed a maturity beyond his years, reminiscent of an old soul housed in youthful exuberance. Meanwhile, KN's house on a hill in Seattle had a breathtaking garden path stretching forever, like a journey through a mystical forest. Her beach house in Vashon was like a work of art, decorated with the eyes of an artist and enthusiast.

Caption: Joyful moments: Boating at KN's beach house, Where generosity meets nature.

KN, an asset investment and management professional, was one of the initial significant investors when Bill Gates started Microsoft. Her generosity extended to Liz's organization like a beacon of hope shining in the darkness. Although my daughter couldn't accompany us, she found peace at Liz's house, reminiscent of a butterfly serenely resting among flowers. And we enjoyed a boat ride on the sea with Ellie, Isaac, and Tom, like a dance of joy and laughter.

Liz's haven was like a place where nature and simplicity met, dreams came true, and the world was slightly brighter.

A SUMMER NIGHT SOIREE IN THE ORCHARD

Chad, the owner of an enchanting orchard estate, hosted a delightful summer party that left an impression on us. As we made our way to the party location in the morning, we stopped by the Farmer's Market to buy two bottles of wine, joining Chad's family, Liz's family, and mine for the celebration.

Chad, a gifted engineer, introduced us to his ex-wife at the market. How natural and cordial it struck their interaction with me. It was a blatant reminder of how American and Korean cultures view divorced couples differently. In Korea, divorced couples usually maintain minimal contact. It is rare to see them attending their children's school events or living in the same neighborhood. However, it is more common in the US, and it was heartening to see Chad and his ex-wife enjoying each other's company.

Caption: Chad and Tom.

As Chad and Tom whipped up various dishes in the kitchen, including juicy hamburgers, we explored the orchard. It was a joy to watch Tom and Chad cooking. Chad's seasonal house in the orchard gave people a sense of ease. We picked apples while taking a stroll through the peaceful bamboo forest. The evening was idyllic, with cool temperatures perfect for the kids to roast marshmallows around the campfire while MK played his guitar and sang.

Caption: Heartwarming gathering: Kids revel in Vashon's tranquil harmony while adults share stories.

We adults had a fun time discussing assorted topics, and I learned more about KN, who had traveled the world for six months with her father when she was a teenager. Her experiences traveling through Europe and Asia profoundly impacted her life. She even had a close relationship with Korean culture, thanks to her grandmother's friend. It was heartwarming to hear about her fondness for Korean food and culture.

As we chatted and laughed, KN shared a hilarious story of how she once got a speeding ticket while trying to arrive on time for a party. It was amusing to learn that the island only had two police officers for its 10,000 inhabitants. However, I soon realized that the low crime rate made it unnecessary to have more. I know Vashon Island for its peaceful and secure environment, and the locals have prominent levels of trust, allowing them to live in harmony.

Overall, the party was an unforgettable experience, and I felt grateful to have been part of it. It was heartwarming to see people from distinct cultures coming together to enjoy each other's company and celebrate life.

VASHON FARMER'S MARKET

My Vashon Farmer's Market visit was a kaleidoscope of colors, sounds, and experiences woven to make a community tapestry. It was a market and a symphony of communication and connection among neighbors.

Caption: Liz's Family: The heart and soul of a welcoming market community.

As soon as we arrived, the market embraced us like an old friend. Familiar faces greeted Liz's family, and locals gathered to meet friends and catch up on the latest news. The pace of the market was like a gentle breeze, inviting us to slow down and savor the moment.

Caption: Vashon Farmer's Market: A symphony of community, fresh produce, and simple joys.

The market featured local farmers selling their homegrown produce, a vibrant display of nature's bounty that celebrated the community's hard work and achievements. The fresh herbs and spices scents filled the air like a potpourri of joy. Fun services like massages and fake tattoos added a playful touch to the atmosphere, like a colorful mosaic that sparkled in the sunlight.

The band played on one side of the courtyard, and the sound of people chatting and laughing mixed with the music, creating a beautiful symphony of community. The market felt like a patchwork quilt of life; each thread represented a unique story entangled to make something beautiful. Compared to Seattle's bustling Pike Place Market, the Vashon Farmer's Market was like a quiet garden oasis. It was an opportunity to slow down, enjoy the present moment, share stories, and build connections.

Caption: Canvas of life: YW and KN collect sand dollars in Vashon's serenity.

The market was not the only masterpiece on my trip. The breathtaking view of the Vashon Sea from KN's stunning summer house was like a canvas of blue and green that stretched as far as the eye could see. Likewise, the artwork adorning the walls was like a collection of stories, each piece telling a unique tale that added vibrant color to the already stunning surroundings.

Watching YW and KN strolling along the beach, carefully picking sand dollars, was like a scene from a painting. Likewise, the lush greenery surrounding Chad's summer house was like a natural tapestry, creating a peaceful retreat from everyday life.

A moment in the dense bamboo forest was like a dream, where one could lose track of time and feel at one with nature. In the lively Farmer's Market, Liz found a pocket of tranquility, relishing the soothing touch of her friend's skilled massage. At the same time, MJ added a touch of rebellion to her look with a fake tattoo on her hand, like a secret symbol of her free spirit.

The Vashon Farmer's Market was like a patchwork quilt. This beautiful tapestry celebrated community and communication, reminding us of the value of slowing down, enjoying life, and building connections with those around us.

WHY VASHON ISLAND TRUMPS SEATTLE: PERSONAL REFLECTION

During a recent trip to Seattle with my family and Liz's family, we discovered that Vashon Island is a better place to live than the bustling city. Despite working in Seattle, Liz frequently drives across the sea to her home on Vashon Island, where ferries run hourly and only charge a fee when going to the island. Moreover, Vashon Island's ports are conveniently located in the North, South, and East, making it easy to access Seattle and nearby cities.

As someone who grew up on land, the idea of living on an island initially made me feel confined. However, after exploring the area, it was clear that Vashon Island offered more than Seattle, which had little to offer those accustomed to the New York metropolitan area. Similarly, YJ was initially intrigued by Seattle when she visited the city. However, upon revisiting the city after living in the US for some time, the excitement had waned. It is a reminder that people's perception of the world changes with their experiences and exposure.

Caption: Captured memories: YW meets Starbucks founder amidst Vashon's rich culture.

I documented my trip to Vashon Island through various photos, highlighting the unique aspects of the island's culture and lifestyle. The first photo features YW with the founder of Starbucks Coffee, which originated on Vashon Island. In another picture, Liz's family prepares a meal. At the same time, we took the rest of the photos at the Farmers' Market, a lively and vibrant place where locals gather to buy and sell homegrown produce.

Caption: Liz and Ellie.

Through my stay with a family on Vashon Island, I noticed significant lifestyle differences between the Northeast and Midwest of the US. While European culture has a powerful presence in the architecture of the Northeast, there is a slower rate of change in the outskirts of cities where larger houses significantly impact architecture. However, the architecture in the Northwest is more efficient, with moderately sized, lavish residential buildings. While wealthier neighborhoods have more extensive and luxurious homes, people in this area tend to build larger houses than necessary. It is a cultural tradition that originated with those who migrated westward in search of gold, where practicality trumped the European-style grandeur of the Old Continent.

Caption: Tom was playing the guitar at his home.

The cars on the streets of Vashon Island primarily consist of public vehicles that people can ride comfortably without a daily burden. Luxury brands are rare, with KN's car being an ordinary Japanese brand. It contrasts with the Northeast, where luxury cars are everywhere, regardless of where you go. In the South, including West Virginia, the brands of cars running on the roads are an indication of the difference between the wealthy and the poor states.

Income levels among states impact living standards, with a more detailed analysis at the county level. For example, King County, including Vashon Island, has a lower per capita income of $29,521 compared to Virginia's Loudoun County, with $119,134, and New Jersey's Warren County, with $66,594. Despite this, Vashon Island's income level is comparatively higher.

In terms of minimizing income inequality, the popular American drama 'The West Wing' often highlights this as a central theme for the liberal US Democratic Party." It is an assignment for the readers to consider ways to address this issue. Notably, Vashon Island is the number one city in the US with the highest percentage of Democratic supporters, with a whopping 99%.

Caption: Island life in frames: From playful kids to Vashon's original Starbucks.

The photographs vividly capturee the island's dynamic atmosphere, show-casing bustling market scenes with lively trading, socializing, and basking in the sunshine. Children run around, play, and get temporary tattoos on their hands. Other pictures feature an abundance of berries, a building slowly fading into darkness, a coffeehouse that was the original Starbucks, and an art exhibition.

THE BEST THINGS IN LIFE ARE WORTH EFFORT

My Seattle trip reinforced the idea that life's finest achievements require con-certed effort and unwavering dedication. In this quaint community, children commence their journey with crew sports amidst the ocean's embrace, laying a foundation of discipline and skills, often proving advantageous for future academic pursuits at elite private universities. Liz's twin children, for example, practice crew into the sea a few times a week after school while also partici-pating in extracurricular activities such as drama and musical performances.

Caption: Heartwarming unwind: Community adults savoring art and culture after work.

After a tiring day at work, the adults unwind by immersing themselves in the rich cultural tapestry of the community. They enjoy art exhibitions and outdoor concerts for relaxation. They attend art exhibitions or outdoor performances held in the area to relax and unwind. Witnessing the community's unique and joyous celebration of life was profoundly heartwarming.

There is a saying that "the best things are hard to come by," and I utterly understand its meaning. It takes effort and dedication to accomplish something truly worthwhile. I also remembered the proverb "no root, no fruit," meaning you must establish a connection to achieve something.

Caption: Contemplating existence and ancient wisdom in Seattle's natural harmony.

Envisioning a future in sync with nature, where our existence melds seamlessly with the natural world, remains a distant yet attainable dream. Thich Nhat Hanh, the revered Vietnamese poet, monk, and meditation master, spoke of ancient wisdom inherent in each grain of corn, from germination to how it bears fruit. We have passed this knowledge down from our parents and distant ancestors and must carry it forward.

This expedition unraveled like a journey across the corridors of time, evoking profound contemplation about the essence of our being and a renewed appreciation for life's beauty. My revelations affirmed that life's most exceptional accomplishments are attainable through persistent effort, unwavering dedication, and enduring patience.

UNEXPECTED BEAUTY

Penned April 8, 2017

BUILDING BRIDGES WITH READERS

Nobel Prize-winning author Ernest Hemingway is often quoted as saying, "There is nothing to writing. All you do is sit down at a typewriter and bleed," (LP, 2016). However, I respectfully disagree with his statement. Of course, his words symbolically express how difficult a writing task can be. However, I find more truth in the words of the great American poet Robert Frost. "No tears in the writer, no tears in the reader. No surprise in the writer, no surprise in the reader," he said (Goodreads, n.d.). (Author's note: As I checked while editing this article, it turned out that Hemingway's words above were not he, but one of several people or an unknown person. Therefore, I leave a note here (QI, n.d.).

When I write, I try to be faithful to my own emotions as a basis. While I may not yet possess the seasoned gaze of a writer, I aim to adopt this perspective momentarily. When I do, I can get closer to the inner depths of some objects I have not seen before. Yet, it's all too easy to overlook the truth or, worse, to distort or exaggerate it. According to Frost, readers cannot sympathize with their writing if they attempt to write about a subject they know nothing about or lack an emotional connection. On the contrary, readers may feel deceived or misled by the writer.

While in Spain, I published several pieces on my blog. However, how many readers have genuinely connected with my work? Of course, my blog does not allow search engine access. Additionally, I frequently set most of my writings to private after a certain period. Therefore, I have limited those who can read my work to a few people I stay connected with. Depending on the type and difficulty of the piece, I sometimes share it with my contacts linked to my chat. Often, I find myself waiting for their responses. In such cases, my works are likely not to resonate with them. Occasionally, I get feedback from them. However, my writing remains the same according to their response. I want my writing to be relatively honest and reflect what I feel and think so that my authorial color is present in the paper. But if I write my pieces with only my contacts and their reactions in mind, my work will likely be fake or deceptive.

Ernest Hemingway believed that good writing resembles architecture more than interior decoration (Poore, 1954). It means that skilled writing is like constructing a solid building, not just stringing together pretty words. David Brin, an American scientist and renowned science fiction author of The Postman, emphasized, "If you have other things in your life — family, friends, good productive day work — these can interact with your writing, and the sum will be all the richer," (Brin, n.d.). Writing ought not to emerge solely from imagination. However, it should be crafted and structured around personal experiences, similar to building an architectural structure where we can apply colors in our own way. Only through this method can a genuine connection with the reader be established.

GOING TO THE GÁLDAR REGION

Yesterday evening, I went to a village in the Gáldar region with my family. The people in that place build their houses inside the steep rocky ravines of the large rocks. It is not a well-known tourist spot, and it was purely by mistake that I went there with my family. Last March, during my daughter's visit from New York, we embarked on a brief 1-day-2-night trip to Lanzarote. The day before leaving, I booked a house on Airbnb. Still, I mistakenly booked a place in a ravine in the Gáldar region of Las Palmas instead of Lanzarote. I set the destination to Lanzarote before searching for the reservation. Still, I later discovered a technical problem with Airbnb; we did not filter the region range correctly.

The Canary Islands comprise seven large and small islands. To go to other islands, you must take a plane or a boat because they are far apart. However, Airbnb ignored this characteristic and made the entire Canary Islands a single region range, which caused the problem. As a result, Lanzarote and the whole of the Canary Islands appeared as bookable information. As a consumer, I did not expect that, so I made a mistake. I tried to cancel the reservation immediately, but according to the policy of the house's owner, I could not get a refund for the rest of the cost except for the cleaning fee. So, I had to change the schedule so my wife could come with me a month later.

My wife YJ recently joined me in Las Palmas. While I'm returning to the US soon, she plans to stay with our son for three months. Therefore, this Gáldar trip was an entirely unplanned venture. Yesterday, my family nearly reached our destination in the deep mountains of Gáldar at 9 p.m.

Caption: My son is in the ninth grade at Atlantic School in Santa Brígida. The school is one of the primary private schools on the island, and many students attend university in the UK.

Caption: The village is high and has many high-end buildings and beautiful scenery.

At 2:30 p.m., my wife and I met with Fernando, our son's Spanish teacher, and the high school principal at his school. This introduction held a bittersweet significance, marking a poignant farewell as I prepared for my impending departure to the US. We arrived at the school in time for the meeting. An Irish lady English teacher, who is in charge of English education at this school, attended the conference for translation. After a lively discussion lasting over an hour, we drove around Santa Brígida until our son's classes were over.

Caption: Hyder Trophy 2017 by NY Squash.

I brought my son to the University of Las Palmas for an hour of squash training with Elena Sánchez Rodríguez. I also took a squash lesson from her for an hour from 11:30 a.m. every few days. Following Monday will be my last squash training with Elena. I have improved my squash skills with her, and I will participate in the squash tournament in Manhattan from May

5 to 7 (NYS, n.d.). I have already applied and am looking forward to an excellent result.

Caption: Tejada Village and a shop selling local products.

MY FAMILY SET off toward our destination around 6:15 p.m.; however, daylight savings had begun by then, and the sun was relatively high in the sky. So, we first stopped at the Village of Tejada, at the highest point of Las Palmas Island. YW wanted to show his mother the town. Clouds swept swiftly over the towering mountains, creating a mesmerizing vista akin to a river meandering gracefully through a lush meadow. This spectacular nature stayed with us until we reached Tejada. This village captivated me. However, YJ was less interested than expected when we arrived at the town. Instead, she showed an interest in a shop that sold almonds and made snacks and bread. So, we bought some bread, snacks, and dinner. She remembered the store because she had recently seen a four-episode documentary about the Canary Islands produced and aired by EBS-TV in Korea.

The breathtaking beauty of the natural surroundings, seeming straight out of a fairy tale, struck me the moment I set foot in the village. The lush greenery, the towering trees, and the serene atmosphere all came together to create a mesmerizing charm that left me completely spellbound. It was like stumbling upon a rare gem in the heart of nature, and I couldn't help but be entirely captivated by it. Moreover, the documentary had a unique perspective on the village. Therefore, I would like to watch the documentary.

People can still have different perspectives by visiting the same places and observing the same objects. It is standard in the world, and any society that tries to impose one angle of view on the world suffocates people. Unfortunately, there are still many such societies in the world. Assessing the world through one's own perspective and values is crucial in the first stage. However, claiming that one's perspective is the only correct one is hazardous. In Korean society, there is an increasing tendency not to accept this. However, the reality is that people have a variety of opinions. It is natural for there to be differences between one's thoughts and those of others. We don't need to compare our values with those of others. We can exist with those with different views, which is natural.

Thus, boasting about thinking differently or feeling discouraged by differing opinions is unnecessary. "I" are all individuals who form "us." If "us" were just a single atom with an identical molecular structure, then "I" would not be necessary. At this point, a replicated human being would be "I." Thus, we are all duplicated humans. But we have not copied humans; we are all unique and independent.

Caption: It is my fourth time visiting this place, but I still fondly love Tejada.

After two months apart, YW expressed his heart-warming emotion to his mom. When the doors of Tejada closed, YW hugged his mother in front of the museum. At 7:40 p.m., we headed toward our destination. Gáldar and I informed Frank, the host, via WhatsApp. Incidentally, people here use this app like Koreans use KakaoTalk. By February 2016, WhatsApp had become the world's largest personal messaging app, boasting over one billion users. Frank said he would wait for us at the café Mima. Although it was only 16.5 kilometers away from Tejada, according to Google Maps, the journey was difficult as most roads were steep and narrow, unlike in the US, where Google Maps rarely directs users to unexpected roads; this sometimes happens in the Canary Islands. Even worse, it can be pretty problematic and time-consuming when this occurs on a mountain road. On that day, it happened twice.

Caption: Our destination was far above 1,000 meters in elevation.

Our meeting with Frank occurred later than anticipated. Our family parked near the café Mima and followed Frank up the hill to the cave house. You can find everything you need in the equipped kitchen. There were many dishes and utensils, beers, and wines in the fridge, and we could even make a meal in minutes using some ingredients. Espresso and fresh beans were also available. Next, they constructed four bedrooms with deep stones to fit beds. Then, of course, someone built the entire house into a cave. Finally, someone designed the bathroom with a large stone tub.

Caption: The area around the cave house was scenic and well-equipped with kitchen utensils for guests.

Frank said the temperature outside at night drops to 6 Celsius. Still, he has maintained the indoor temperature between 17 and 19 Celsius. My wife had prepared a packed lunch in advance, so after having a late dinner, we all went to bed. Even though there were four separate caves and beds in each room, YW slept with his mother. The only regret was the lack of Internet. It was a remote place, and the mountainous terrain intermittently connected and disconnected the Internet. Despite Airbnb's assurance of internet availability, it's hard to imagine someone choosing a location without internet access in today's connected world. Despite the poor mobile signal, it was still enough to access the information.

Caption: In front of the cave house, the expansive garden brings peace to the heart.

THE BUTTERFLY'S TALE: A VOYAGE INTO HIDDEN BEAUTY

I got up early the following day and stepped outside to look around. The sounds of birds chirping echoed throughout the valley. Finally, when YJ and YW woke up, we went to the café Mima to buy bread and snacks for our cave breakfast. We then set off on a walk around the neighborhood.

Caption: The view of Gáldar village is peaceful, with an inexplicable sense of melancholy.

The flowers were blooming everywhere we went, and the bees were buzzing. A tiny symbol and a wooden cross mark its location by the small church in the middle of the village. From the outside, it could see the cave. It was hard to tell if it was a church or an ordinary cave house. Last night, Frank said on WhatsApp that I should find the church if I couldn't find café Mima. The elusive café Mima lacked any signage, and the church's minuscule sign evaded our notice in the cloak of night. In YJ's words, the inside of the church was "primal," with only the furniture that should have been there.

Caption: Amidst rocky terrains and steep slopes, the distant village thrives; residents communicate in bold shouts, children navigate the inclines with ease, and terraced fields line the valley.

I felt warmth among the forty-nine residents of this distant village. Instead of getting close to having conversations with their far-off neighbors, they shout back and forth at each other. It's almost like the birds chirping at one another from a distance. The scene at the bottom of the photo shows an older adult conversing with someone on the road above. To talk in a small voice to the other person, one has to climb or descend a steep slope. Because their houses, built on rocky terrain, spread far apart, they are used to communicating with loud voices. The children are familiar with walking the steep roads. Their health comes in harmony with nature. The steep slopes are no obstacle to the people who raise sheep and goats and open up steep places to farm and live. They use artificial caves on the rocky slopes as permanent houses. Even in narrow spaces, they can cultivate. Across the distant valley, I could see terraced fields carved out to grow crops.

Caption: In Gáldar's Summit, nature and tradition merge with cave-type houses nestled amidst historic canyons.

For these people, nature was the object of harmony. I found many aspects in which nature naturally intertwined with their lives. Fortunately, despite being over a thousand meters above sea level, no chilly winter exists. Although the weather drops to 5~6 degrees during the night, it is still enough for the plants and animals to endure. The Spanish government designated the Summit of Gáldar, formed by a canyon called Barranco Hondo de Abajo, as a Cultural and Historic Site on September 24, 1993. The ancient caves, their derived cultural sites, and their natural environment have sufficient value to be protected. This village clusters traditional buildings: the most outstanding feature is cave-type houses. They formed the artificial caves along the canyon and formed small groups with different names in each area.

Caption: In Gáldar, each cave, from El Callejón to La Poza, carries its unique label, yet to outsiders, they resemble mere house addresses.

EACH CAVE, UNIQUE in shape, bears its own name. Our abode, El Callejón, signified a distinct class of cave-dwelling. The bottom photo shows La Poza, an artificial cave house. In this way, in this village, there are labels in front of each artificial cave designated as a cultural site, so you can tell at a glance what kind of cave it is. However, to me, a stranger to this field, it felt like just an address of a house. There were various labels with names in front of each home, just like an address.

Caption: An unmarked cafe buzzes with community spirit; a local generously shares his meal, epitomizing the village's warmth.

In this neighborhood, the unmarked cafe is essential. While there's a sizable village hall, this eatery is the go-to for those who love music and dance. The man seated next to me, now posing for a photo, generously shared his bread and cheese upon seeing me. Gratefully, I took a bite. After sharing delightful moments with the locals, I departed the village around 12:30 p.m.

Caption: Driving home through captivating landscapes, the narrow mountain path's beauty from the previous night remained unmatched — etched in memory, not on camera.

IT TOOK ABOUT an hour and six minutes to get home to our house in Las Palmas via Google Navigation. The beautiful scenery spread out everywhere made me happy on the way there. However, the most unforgettable scene from this journey was the mountain path I took to access this village last night. It was a narrow road where only one car could barely pass, and the beautiful scenes on both sides made me gasp in admiration. I focused on driving so that I couldn't capture those beautiful scenes on the camera, but I did my best to keep them in my eyes and heart. It was indeed a beautiful flower path that stretched endlessly. It was a natural celebration in itself.

Caption: Reflecting on serendipitous mountain encounters and La Mariposa.

Upon arriving home late for lunch and taking a quick nap, YJ and I walked on the beach near our house. The receding ocean waters were creating a different scenery than usual. Walking along the long beach, I thought of the good people I had met in the mountains and the beautiful villages. Thanks to Airbnb, I made a mistake in my booking and ended up at La Mariposa, meaning "butterfly." Thanks to the artificial cave of La Mariposa, I had a wonderful experience. Now it's Tuesday, and I'm leaving this place, leaving YJ and YW behind, and going to the USA, where my daughter MJ lives. I spent a hectic month here in January, bringing YW to the island on the third. Now, it's time to go back. I'll look back on the time I spent here that I failed to record. With these reflections, I say goodbye to my time in Spain. This marks the end of a chapter, and I wanted to share this final post.

THE BEAUTY OF

IMPERFECTION

Penned June 25, 2017

Joyce encourages us in an interview by saying, "Nobody wants perfection," (Joseph 2017). But, like "gift," she says in an interview with Salon that the word "perfect" is very tricky. Joyce Carol Oates is a Princeton University professor born June 16, 1938, in Lockport, New York. In response to Alli Joseph's question about what she sees as the most crucial advice for literature students, she responded with the following:

I never tell them to try to perfect something because "perfect," like the word "gift," is very tricky, and we don't really know what those words mean. Shakespeare is not perfect, and James Joyce is not ideal. So, the idea is to have energy and momentum and originality, and a verve and a voice that's original that people are interested in. So, it doesn't have to be perfect. Nobody wants perfection. I think it was Sylvia Plath [who said] embodiment has no children.

Perfect writing could have been better for writers like Shakespeare or James Joyce. She advises breaking out of that psychological stress. The ideal essay is impossible. The presentation of a report can vary depending on the intended audience. It's true! We can utilize different approaches to ensure the intended audience quickly understands the report. Joyce says the most crucial thing in writing is "energy and momentum and originality, and a verve and a voice that's original that people are interested in." Perhaps one object we are most interested in is children. By the way, "Perfection has no children," Joyce quotes Sylvia Plath and conveys it to us.

The above quotes do not refer to children. However, no one is living with a surprising momentum with their whimsical voices as utterly interesting, enthusiastic, original, and energetic as children. Children are always a bunch of thoughts, the most unpredictable and the most imperfect beings. Have you ever noticed that perfect beings are always curious and excited? It's incredible how they approach every new experience with enthusiasm and wonder.

In retrospect, every day in my teens was full of things. It must have been such a period that a few words, such as fear, curiosity, sympathy, impulse, passion, and anger, cannot be defined. As Joyce expressed, it seemed "full of mystery" when everything rushed to the head and heart. I can't remember how old my puberty was or whether my entire teens were adolescents when I think about it now. But, of course, I will be able to find out if I calmly recall myself. However, my teens themselves were a period of imagination for me.

Joyce believes puberty, especially the second half, is a fertile time to show your imagination. If you are a parent with a teenager going through puberty, note this. Rather than reprimanding a child for mistakes, a careful and empathetic approach to understanding their thoughts is more effective.

On a Sunday morning, Joyce's words, "Nobody wants perfection," resonate. While hearing 'Perfect!' elicits joy, the real gem is the individual offering praise, seeking to uplift you. True power lies in commendation. Perfection isn't the aim; it's about embracing our flaws and forgoing the illusion of flawlessness. Our passion and uniqueness, not literature or any process, dictate life. It's akin to the shiver that courses through us when a loved one's hand intertwines with ours or the tender union of a heartfelt kiss. If our lives lack that tremor, it's crucial to find someone who looks at us and says, 'Perfect!'

IN PURSUIT OF

EAGERNESS

Penned January 26, 2017

If we are proud of ourselves, we are at the top of life. Let's not hesitate and praise ourselves. If we can't compliment ourselves now, it's time for something. I want to call it 'eagerness.' Finding and achieving this will make me proud. How many people have achieved earnestness in their lives? Most people die without even realizing it. To accomplish this, we must be able to stimulate ourselves continually. Although we live at one hundred, when we look back, our lives are in the blink of an eye. Therefore, we are living a life of a limited time. How precious are the brief moments of one or two seconds in a time-limited life?

In my twenties, I firmly believed that each year should bring intellectual maturity. So, I always tried to maintain my intellectual curiosity. Whenever I explained any complicated issue clearly, I could feel the look of respect that the other party sent me. Whenever that happened, I encouraged myself more. But one day, years later, I suddenly realized that my "confident explanation" was wrong — every time I discovered that, I felt my face flush and embarrassed myself. However, I used to recognize that "then me" and "now me" had taken a step forward. So, I had to grow up intellectually every year to be reassured. That was the case in my twenties.

Even a fleeting time was precious to me. However, I loved it when I married in my early thirties and created my own family. Resolving my family's livelihood was more important than my personal development. So, I had to focus on making money rather than individual development. Still, while living in Korea, I was actively socializing and maintaining tension. Yet, after immigrating to the United States, I felt rapidly regressing. Every day was so hectic that I couldn't even think about it. I had to be faithful to the role of parent. So, my young children could grow up well with no anxiety in this unfamiliar country despite the extreme work-related stress of setting up a safe economy.

I lived without realizing it and without thinking of my eagerness. And I did not give myself a stimulus to shake myself asleep. I may know, but I don't know if I purposely avoided such stimulation. So, for 13 years after marriage, I have been regressing. It's also sped up. I felt like I was gliding endlessly on a well-oiled slide with oil all over my body. So why have I been regressing and have not stopped it? Because there was no deep desire. Because I didn't have it for life, I couldn't express my abilities to the maximum.

IN 2008, WHEN I was 45 years old, I started studying at a university and could barely stop my regression. Delving deeper into new knowledge and reflections invigorated me with each passing moment. Living in the U.S., I only scratched its surface without truly grasping its essence. Delving into American Studies reshaped my understanding of its society and helped me introspect. My grades reflected the need for more alignment between my initial pursuit of business in college and my passion. However, shifting to American Studies reignited my enthusiasm. In my final semester, I excelled in all eight courses, earning straight A+s, and proudly graduated as valedictorian. Those years have marked my commitment to personal growth.

And years have passed. I mulled over my way in my daily routine, read various books, and tried to have multiple pleasurable experiences. However, I had no desire for my own life. I was regressing again. So, in 2015, I enrolled in another university near my home and started studying. Little by little, I gradually recovered my intellectual awareness through the process. At fifty or older, the process could be more comfortable. I was going to a designated place at a set time, attending classes with young people, doing projects or homework, and preparing for exams. Most people choose comfortable and burden-free ones rather than new challenges. I feel connected to them because they are around my age and have a similar economic status.

In my case, I run a small but not deficit company in Korea, the United States, and here in Spain. Therefore, I can spend any time comfortably. I can watch my favorite movies or dramas to my heart's content, meet good people, and have fun together. But I don't want to do that. As an entrepreneur, I admire Professor Peter Drucker the most. In 1997, McKinsey Quarterly said: "In management gurus, there is no debate. Peter Drucker is the one guru to whom other gurus kowtow" (Hindle, 2008). As early as five years, he emphasized, you cannot become an intellectual unless you do a new study every five years. Drucker said you could not be a leader who will lead the times. As he stated, the present era is not for five years, but if we do not always gain new knowledge, we have no choice but to retreat to the era's back door. Our competitors encompass industries beyond ours. It is expanding to visible neighbors or countries and places around the world that are not visible.

Moreover, the opponents of the competition are not only happening between people. Still, they are infinitely expanding beyond that of artificial intelligence or virtual reality. Leading the world requires more than just past knowledge and experience. So, if something we're thinking about connects with our desperation, we must jump in boldly to maximize our potential.

HUMANS CAN ONLY maximize their abilities when they are eager. Without eagerness, creating a good reason to revise or give up on our original goals is easy. 'Eagerness' means 'coming from the heart, and desire is powerful.' Only those who are keen can push their limits. Hence,' eagerness' must be achieved like a burning thirst. It is an eagerness to feel like a person wandering intently, looking for a sip of water to quench thirst. The thought of "It's good if you have it, but it doesn't matter if you don't." is not eagerness. If something burns like a flame in the mind and body, and if something we want to have but never comes easily, that is our 'desire.'

So, we are feeling keen now. In that case, it is a very arduous journey that excites the body and mind simultaneously. If the 'eagerness' holds us, we must prepare to throw all of us to achieve it. When completed, it resembles finding an oasis that quenches thirst in the scorching desert and creates an environment for life. The oasis hopes to be lifelike in a desert with dry sandstorms. When you achieve earnestness, you turn hope into reality.

We must have had many eager feelings in our lives so far. You may have had the experience of wanting to make a person deeply entrenched in your heart, your lover. He may have struggled with eagerness for money. How enthusiastic were we also to get to where we wanted to belong (such as school, work, or a group of friends)? However, the "eagerness" we have created found out how many times we have achieved it. We should praise ourselves if we have had at least one such experience. That's because most people compromise moderately and never reach it. Few people have achieved their limits by pushing them to the limit. What I'm talking about here doesn't mean 'small eagerness.' It means something severe and meaningful enough to bet on all of one's own. Thus, the result is the same as the turning point in our lives. For instance, young students spend all their abilities trying to get into the aiming college a long time. Even with the same learning ability, the results will differ if the quality and energy spent differ.

Sports are the area that best represents this urgency. Park In-bee is an excellent case. She overcame a finger injury, a deep slump, and a severe psychological burden to win the gold medal at the Rio 88 Olympics in Brazil last year. Sports players who have succeeded in extreme competition have proved their eagerness. We applaud them with emotion because their years of learning and practicing skills are like the results. This case is equally apparent in art, such as musicians, artists, and dancers. We can understand the many challenges they have overcome by spending a lot of time achieving their eagerness. That's what hunger is. We must throw ourselves without hesitation if we are enthusiastic about betting on ourselves.

YES. IF WE have found an 'eagerness' to throw out our bodies, we should encourage ourselves to toast. Most people end their lives without seeing enough eagerness to bet their entire lives. Even if we find it by chance, we cling to the matter of living. As the proverb says, we must accept it "as a living." We will probably encounter such eagerness in our late teens, early teens, or early thirties. It is time to always think about your future. If you are young, I would ask you first to find out the most significant 'eagerness.'

Discovering a passion that transforms your life is paramount. Such revelations don't come quickly. A nebulous future hope or goal lacks the clarity and intensity of authentic eagerness. We must strive to achieve it and secure the highest goal at any cost. If our desire makes our hearts beat, we must dive right into it. To accomplish that, we must be confident and brave enough to overcome the countless hardships experienced by successful people in sports and art. If you jump in with that determination, you are more likely to succeed than fail. It is not a good or wrong decision, but the second best. Nothing in the world is easy. If you have already achieved 'eagerness,' I recommend looking for 'small eagerness' again.

Slight eagerness doesn't have to risk my life, nor do I need to deviate significantly from the situation. We can achieve it quickly, so there is less burden. It is appropriate as a "new vitality" to prevent one's regression and escape from identity. Twenty-four hours a day are the same for everyone. Still, depending on how you spend it, 24 hours can vary significantly in quality from person to person. Slight eagerness is the same as what we commonly call a bucket list. But if you think you can live at least 30 more years, I recommend you look for 'real eagerness' right now, and if you haven't tasted it once. No. If you can live another 30 years, that's enough time to challenge yourself, even if you've already experienced eagerness.

The 30 years are enough to create genuine enthusiasm and new willingness. Rather than the immediate comfort, let's find the earnestness that motivates me, makes my heartbeat, and makes my head dizzy. Let's bring up the eagerness within me again. Even if it takes a year or ten years, let's find "my eagerness." It will surely be the pinnacle of your life. Let us hold steadfast to our journey, never relinquishing our drive.

MANY STORIES IN ONE SHOT

Penned January 21, 2018

I am looking at a picture that reminds me of the old days. It was one day in August 1998. Behind Yonsei University is a neighborhood called Yeon-hui-dong. The photograph's background is the house of Mrs. Choi, whom I met while working as a guest researcher at Yonsei University Media Art Research Institute. I hosted an animation workshop with the institute at Yonsei University. Then, she enrolled his fifth-grade son in my workshop. After that, I often talked to her, who graduated from Yonsei. Finally, after being so close to each other, she invited my family to her home. It was a house next to Yonsei University's back wall, with a large and beautiful garden. When I swing my five-year-old daughter MJ, I see her sitting with the dog in a peaceful picture. It was such a fantastic experience that I could not realize there was such an extensive garden in downtown Seoul. I still remember her elegant and intelligent appearance, face, and voice. She's probably in her mid-sixties by now, but she's someone I'd like to see someday.

YEONHUI-DONG AND MEMORIES OF SHORT MOMENTS

I did a boarding home in this neighborhood in the summer of 1989. There was a company in Yeonhui-dong where I got a job after completing a six-month graduate from the Publishing College. The company copyrights foreign specialized books under the United Publishing Promotion Co., Ltd. (UPPC). The company in Yeonhui-dong was a joint investment company established by nine large companies among foreign book importers, including Kyobo Bookstore, Jongro Books, and Kumi Trading. Foreign book importers were over 150 in Korea at that time. The latest newspapers, magazines, and books published in the U.S., Japan, and Europe formed the basis for innovative technology and learning. Universities and national and private research institutions mainly relied on these foreign book importers to purchase books or magazines abroad.

Experts such as professors, researchers, and doctors relied mainly on foreign professional books, including undergraduate, master's, and doctorate courses. Professors often designated foreign books, especially in science and medicine, rarely translated into Korean, as subject books. So, it forced students who took the class to purchase books if it designated them as textbooks. However, the price of one major book ranged from at least $100 to hundreds of dollars, making it very burdensome for college students to buy at the economic level in Korea in the 1980s. Therefore, poor students often use unauthorized copies through copy shops instead of expensive foreign books designated as textbooks. In central university districts, college students frequently copied foreign professional books selected as textbooks without permission and sold them cheaply.

Moreover, a series of copyright infringements have led to problems in which foreign publishers must send importers' demands as samples. Therefore, it was an environment in which both foreign and Korean book importers suffered damage. Many copyright negotiations can be reprinted and sold cheaply in Korea for books designated as textbooks to prevent such issues. Before establishing the UPPC, book importers solved the problem separately. However, they needed more professional human resources and a bigger budget. Therefore, several companies jointly invested and launched the UPPC to solve copyright problems.

When interviewing for a job with the boss there, I asked for a manager's position, and he accepted it. I was full of arrogant self-confidence and had enough social experience or ability to do so. I was twenty-six years old. Korean men had to complete military service for about two and four months as general enlisted soldiers. Then, after taking a leave of absence, they either finished military service or enlisted in military service after graduation.

On top of that, many young people waste years because of the strange college entrance system. Prospective high school graduates who wanted to enter college at that time had to take the college entrance exam only once a year. And the test results were almost absolute, reflecting over 50 percent of the college admissions. Each university selected its first-year students by adding the results that reflected high school grades. We chose most four-year regular first-year university students at once. They allowed them to submit applications to only one university. The primary department selected them.

Moreover, only 10 percent of the applicants (out of about 800,000) wanted to enter the four-year regular university, which was a major social problem. Finally, those who failed the entrance exam were socially wasteful because they continued challenging themselves twice or thrice. Therefore, it was common for men to be 27 or 28 years old when they got their first job after completing their mandatory military service in Korea.

Therefore, it was a very exceptional case for a new employee to assume a managerial position from the beginning of my age. Nevertheless, my extensive social experience made me well-prepared and competent. I've done my business several times, participated as a member of the Hankyoreh newspaper, and had several years of journalistic experience in magazines and newspapers. I had enough experience. But fundamentally, I hated working for someone less capable than me. Korean society has long been given positions based on employment rank and age, regardless of individual abilities. In some cases, they were under the direction of incompetent bosses. I was the type who felt comfortable when I was the leader wherever I went.

I got the job and found a boarding home near my new company. There were only a few things in the trunk, but I put my luggage in a taxi and headed for the boarding home late at night. But the taxi driver wandered from alley to alley to get to the address of the destination I had given to him. At that time, most of the old residential areas in Seoul had narrow and curved streets. If luck was off your side, finding a destination with a home address was challenging. There was no technology such as navigation or the Internet, so everyone went to their destination by address. In a residential area where housing development has occurred several times, finding a specific goal in such a place took time and effort. They mixed the house addresses up in a complicated way. The taxi driver who got lost made a mistake, and the taxi fell on the sidewalk next to the main road from a hill about two meters high, and I had an enormous shock on my back. I experienced mild pain but didn't consider it significant at the time. After I sent the driver without reporting it to the police, I remembered to take my luggage and go to the boarding home.

AFTER WORKING FOR a few months at the company I started working for, it scouted me a company. The new company was Kumi Trading Co., Ltd. (KTC), near Bangbae Subway Station in Seocho-gu, Seoul, founded in 1968. As I found out later, my boss introduced me to the company's president to use my skills further. Then, one day, while I was working in the office, a man in his early fifties with a sparkly head opened the door and stared at me momentarily. The man called me a few days later and asked to meet.

Therefore, he stopped by our office to get information about me from my boss and see who I was. In Korea, the first impressions of people are crucial. When hiring employees, there is a countenance that the owner prefers, so the smaller the company, the higher the appearance. There were rumors that the founder of Samsung Group included a physiognomy expert in the judging panel when interviewing employees and reflected it in the hiring process. Because such a culture remains, the president of KTC looked at me before scouting me. Here's what I heard later. The president of KTC, who needs the head of the company's computer room, announced it one day at a meeting of shareholders of the UPPC. Then, my boss recommended that I be the right person for the position.

I have covered that story in detail in my other article, "A Film Festival Director." All human relationships are closely intertwined. If I hadn't joined this Yeonhui-dong company, I wouldn't have done anything related to the film. And I would have done something completely different. Since I described the relationship realistically in my previous article, anyone who reads my article will understand. A single book or leaflet on a street pole changed us in that direction. And I could meet the book or flyer like that because I worked for KTC. After a while, I visited KTC for my job interview with the CEO. He offered me an Assistant Manager. However, I said they had already given me an excellent position at another larger company and weren't interested in the job change. So, he suggested working for his company, saying that his company has a better outlook and can also treat me better. I told him I would give myself a managerial position. So, I decided to work for the company as a manager.

All the staff gathered when I first came to the company for work. But there was no boss at the time. Rather than feeling embarrassed, the Managing Director introduced me as an Assistant Manager to the team, which deviated from the initial promise. However, the company needed to be more extensive than the size of the previous company in Yeonhui-dong. And all the employees of my age working for the company were plain employees. Employees acting as assistant managers could not get the position after five years at the company but were mostly in their mid-thirties. In short, it was very unconventional for the company to give me the place. Perhaps the president was all against it when he told the company's senior executives after accepting my request. But as a result, they cheated on me. Had I chosen to quit the company immediately, it would have markedly altered the trajectory of my life.

Again, I want to talk about Yeonhui-dong's company for a while. I joined the company as a manager. But there was a male assistant manager in his early thirties, a male manager in his late thirties, a male executive director in his fifties, and two female employees in their early twenties. The boss there was in his late sixties. In particular, the male employees were much older and more experienced in the field than me. Hence, they treated me awkwardly at first. I was concerned about that, but I changed the office's structure. I switched the office layout when I entered a new company. That's because I can take over that space.

After joining the company, the boss took charge of all copyright matters. Although I had previously studied copyright law under Attorney Han Seung-heon — the inaugural director of the Korea Copyright Law Research Institute in 1976, founder of the Hankyoreh Newspaper in 1988, and Chair of the Board of Audit and Inspection of Korea from 1998 to 1999 — at the Publishing College. I gained valuable insights into the practical aspects of the matter. Our two male colleagues were in sales. They spent their days delivering books and generating sales, a process I sought to understand better. Even though our primary focus was copyrights, the company directly imported and supplied books to various universities and research institutions.

HURT MY BACK AND LEARN DATABASE

Near the company, a warehouse kept and managed imported books. Although I seriously injured my back in a taxi accident the day I went to the boarding home, I did not receive any treatment. However, merely two days into my employment at the company, a sizable truck loaded with imported books made its way to the warehouse. I injured my back while blasting those heavy book boxes into the warehouse all day. Because of that, I suffered from back pain for decades after that.

Several female employees managed the book database, a system developed by a researcher from the Yonsei University Observatory. It efficiently managed books, various invoices, and sales by design. Among them was a woman who, due to her actions, had unfortunately made herself a target of dislike among her peers. My tenure at the company was brief, so my memories are hazy, and I don't remember all the specifics. I took the initiative to guide her in building better relationships with her colleagues. Initially, she resisted my efforts. But over time, she came around, expressing her gratitude through tears for my persistent support. There was an incident where she nearly jeopardized her position due to a mistake, possibly involving the database's accidental deletion. I intervened and assisted her through the crisis, and that experience catalyzed my interest in mastering databases.

It has only been an abbreviated time since I joined the company. The program the young women used at work could have been more convenient. I had to deal with the database myself, and I could lose data when the program broke down. Fortunately, the researcher who had programmed the database came and recovered it. So, I overcame the crisis, which made me think I should learn computers properly. So, I enrolled in a computer academy near my company and learned database programs such as dBase and FoxPro. By using that technology, I made it easier for young girls to manage their daily work.

In 1989, only some tiny businesses used personal computers for actual work. It was time for a company run by a reasonably intelligent president to bring one in. Computers operating on MS-DOS, equipped with a 20-megabyte hard disk, relieve 5.25-inch floppy disks for data storage. These floppy disks were prone to damage with frequent use. Therefore, it was necessary to have a copy. It was such a time, but the opportunities were endless for those who learned about computers early. While in such a rush, people around me thought I was a computer hand.

While I was so confused, people around me considered me an excellent, computer-savvy person. Moreover, being in the office daily made me want to run a business. So, the first book I bought was about reunifying the Korean Peninsula. If the professor selected the book, our company could sell quite a few books to the university. I remember taking the book and visiting Professor Lee In-Ho of the Department of Foreign Relations at Seoul National University. Later, she served as ambassador to Finland and Russia and is now the Chairperson of the Korean Broadcasting System.

After considering various options, I realized there were better-fit options than an office job or a sales job. One day, my boss asked me what I wanted to do at work. I told him I would try to make sales because I thought the company needed money, but my boss smiled quietly. Then, he advised me to take time and make it slowly. It had been less than a month since I had been in, and I needed directions. I couldn't understand why my boss picked me. There must have been some reason or purpose for recruiting people, but he gave me different tasks. I can understand the situation now. I would have been an excellent talent to be recruited by such a small company. The boss was in his late sixties, and it was time for him to succeed. Perhaps he chose me in that respect and tried to monitor me.

ASPIRING TO BE A PROFESSIONAL PUBLISHER

I was more interested in running a publishing business than learning about copyright. However, I couldn't just sit and tap on the computer keyboard. I took pride in being a first-term student at the prestigious Publishing College, one of Korea's top educational institutions. I learned the overall process of planning, producing, and distributing books from the best primaries in the field. However, the company wasn't the right place to apply these skills. Before that, the Korean Publishing Culture Association taught the editorial process over a three-month course. However, the association set up a more professional institution. The college was on the second floor of the association building next to Gyeongbok Palace. At that time, no specialized courses taught publication editing and design in four-year universities. Instead, several private editorial design academies in Seoul lasted about three months. Therefore, the news media covered the association's recruitment of first-year students at a new professional educational institution as a big issue.

I submitted my application and took the written test at the test center on the set date. The test center was a huge auditorium at the Kyobo Life Insurance headquarters (the building where the Kyobo Bookstore is) in Gwanghwamun, the heart of Seoul. And they filled the floor with about 1,000 people. Most of them either worked after college or still needed a suitable job. Then, people interested in the publishing field took the exam. They finally selected those who passed the first written test through an interview. They set up about 120 people, dividing the class into day and evening classes. There were mainly office workers in the evening class, most of whom went to publishing companies. However, even if they worked in the publishing field, practically no people have trained adequately in publishing editing.

Many individuals had diverse backgrounds and stories in the daytime class I attended. One of them was Lee Jong-guk, the Chief-of-Editor of Hankook Ilbo in Washington, D.C. I often see him in the U.S. He was also my daytime classmate. The course also included two women in their 50s and 60s and a woman in her mid-forties. Among them, I formed a close relationship with Mrs. Kim Sang-bun. Her husband was a professor at Korea University's Department of German Language and Literature.

One day, Sang-bun invited me to their home, where we bonded over German food. Mrs. Kim supported me, especially when I was making a short 6mm film titled "The Piano." She even offered her house as a filming location, which was immensely helpful. Sang-bun had enrolled in the class to learn about the publishing business, as her late father-in-law ran it. Another woman in the class lived in the most luxurious residential area, Apgujeong-dong. She was there to set up a publishing company.

I was twenty-six years old and the youngest male student in our class. Most of my male classmates were between twenty-eight and thirty years old, a typical age for Korean men to have completed military service and university education. However, the women in my afternoon class were relatively younger, mostly in their mid-twenties, with a few even younger than me. Despite these age differences, we were all navigating through a vibrant period of our lives.

Lunchtime and after-class gatherings became bonding moments for us, where classmates became close friends. During our first week, Mrs. Kim Se-yeon, the school administrator, divided us into three groups to sit together, encouraging us to get to know each other better. The classroom was arranged with ten desks, forming three rows, accommodating twenty students per row. My group consisted of nineteen students, while the other groups had twenty each, making fifty-nine students in our classroom.

My group often spent enjoyable times at Gyeongbokgung Palace right after class, and sometimes we had picnics at Seolleung. I sat at the front of my group next to Mr. Kim Yeong-ro, with whom I became good friends. He was in his mid-forties, with extensive knowledge of challenging Hanja phrases. Although Yeong-ro was well-versed in traditional Korean medicine, he was unlicensed. He operated in a separate space within the Yeollim Pharmacy, run by his wife, a Seoul National University Pharmacy graduate, providing acupuncture and prescribing medicine to patients nationwide who sought him out.

A week later, Mr. Kim Se-yeon held elections to choose one president and two vice presidents. My peers in our group nominated me as a candidate, recognizing my ability to lead with joy and efficiency. The other groups also nominated a candidate, resulting in all-male nominees, including me. Mr. Kim then spontaneously suggested we appoint a female candidate, deciding that one of the vice-president positions would be reserved for a woman. Several women in my group nominated a woman in her forties from our group. This led to a split in votes within our group.

In the election results, candidates from the other groups secured the first and second positions, leaving me in third and the woman from my group in fourth. As a result, I missed out on the vice presidency. A genuinely fair election would have awarded the vice-presidential role to the female candidate and subjected the top three male candidates, including myself, to a runoff. If the female candidate had received the most votes overall, she could have become president, with the next two males serving as vice presidents. However, her fourth-place finish, mainly as she was from my group, meant our group members split our votes, which could have been more challenging for me.

The election was a contest between groups, with our group at a disadvantage for having two candidates. For fairness, each group should have nominated a female candidate as well.

Had there been a runoff or if each group had nominated an equal number of male and female candidates, the outcome might have been significantly different. Despite not winning, I remained active in various fields, continuously learning and building friendships with my peers.

TWO MEMORIES REGARDING RUNNING FOR CANDIDACY

Although it may be a little uncomfortable to call it an elected office since it's not a public position and simply selecting someone from a small group, a few moments stand out in my memory. One such moment was when I became the student council president. Previously, the school had appointed its president rather than holding elections. However, that year's election was free for some reason, where fourth to sixth-grade students directly voted for their president and vice president. Students recommended three people for the position, including myself.

In our world, the election was the talk of many small towns. The atmosphere was electric, with children abuzz with excitement and anticipation. I, too, was caught up in the excitement, and I did everything I could to win the favor of the students. I canvassed the neighborhood during my free time, campaigning vigorously to persuade everyone to vote for me. My younger sister Min-jeong, a third grader, was my most enthusiastic supporter at that time. In her unique way, she championed my candidacy, enthusiastically spreading the word among her peers.

However, another person particularly caught my attention. The fourth-grade girl had excellent academic and leadership skills. I developed a slight crush on her and enlisted her friends to promote my candidacy. She agreed, and it was the most crucial factor in my victory. She came from a village with the most sizable number of students, the same village as my friend Kim Chang-sik, my strongest competitor. It was essentially a strategic splitting of votes, similar to a process called 'mitosis.'

The election was a three-way battle, with Kim Chang-sik, who always studied first and had a good heart, from the largest village, and the now-deceased Ham Joo-ho from a town with more students than mine. It was intense competition, with Chang-sik appearing to have the most significant advantage. He had always been the class president and the school's favorite student.

But to my surprise, the children in the villages of Heatya 1 and 2-ri supported me. It was unexpected, and it divided only 35% of the students in Heatya-ri into two or three units. Nonetheless, I emerged victorious, and Joo-ho came in second.

The result shocked the entire school, including the principal and teachers. They had always favored the best students who excelled in school. However, the students voted for two guys as president and vice president instead.

After the election, I went out as a student representative and held the ceremony at the stadium's morning meeting. However, it was evident that the principal disliked me, as I overheard his comments about me to the vice-principal. Since then, the student council has disappeared, and I have never gone out in front of the students again.

I graduated doing nothing, just by name. They did not fire me along the way because the school had no justification for dismissing the elected president. Yet, I felt like a mere figurehead, puzzled by the principal and vice-principal's decision.

After I graduated, I heard from my sister Min-jeong that the school changed back to appointing the president and vice president. Through a robust academic foundation, the school aimed to nurture its students into outstanding and upstanding individuals. However, it must have been because the results differed from their expectations.

Dohak Elementary School, where I graduated, was a small school in the deep mountains of Gangwon-do. My victory sparked a conversation that lingered for a long time. I may always wonder why the principal and vice-principal made that choice. However, I will always cherish the memories of that fierce election battle.

MY SECOND MEMORY of being elected was going out to society. With my heart racing, I stepped onto the vibrant KAIST campus, filled with eagerness to establish myself in the world of venture business. The venture boom was at its peak, and KAIST had established an innovative program to foster scientific and technical management talent in partnership with venture entrepreneurs from the school. Cyber KAIST, an online graduate school, was the talk of the town, backed by successful venture companies such as the Madison Group, chaired by the legendary Lee Min-hwa. With billions of won invested, they had built a campus in the heart of Gangnam, the symbolic street for ventures in Korea.

The campus was a hive of activity, with the best and brightest minds from all over the country vying for a spot in the program. The competition was fierce, with only 190 sites available for the first year. Most of the applicants were seasoned professionals with impressive resumes.

But I was determined to make my mark. I had seen some press articles about the program and knew I had to apply. I had poured my heart and soul into building my venture company and was ready to take my skills to the next level. The KAIST brand was strong, and most of the professors at the school gave direct lectures. I knew I would learn best from the business if I could get into the program.

As I made my way through the campus, I felt a sense of excitement and anticipation building within me. Finally, it was my chance to prove myself, to show that I had what it took to succeed in the world of venture business. I was ready to take on whatever challenges I lay ahead, work hard, and learn all I could.

And so, with my head held high and my heart full of determination, I stepped into the world of Cyber KAIST, ready to make my dreams a reality. When running a business, it is essential to find new learning opportunities constantly. One of those opportunities was taking a course called the e-CEO Academy. I did a similar study the previous year, but the content needed to be improved. However, the e-CEO academy was different. It was a weekly breakfast lecture series at a luxury hotel in Gangnam, focusing on building a network of people in agreement rather than simply learning something new.

Among them, KAIST lectures were incomparably beneficial. We provided online courses and graduate programs covering broadcast production, planning, management, and promotion. I took the time to attend the lecture despite my busy schedule.

They provided a virtual message board for students to post inquiries and receive answers regarding the course content. But there was one more student-only bulletin board where we could talk to each other freely. Being well-versed in cyber activities, I stood out on this board and built a network of people who trusted me.

When the lecture lasted about a month, the school organized a meeting with venture capitalists at the Ramada Renaissance Hotel in Yeoksam-dong. They conducted an event following the meeting to elect the student council president. I was nominated for the first time as a candidate for Chairperson by someone's recommendation. Despite the university's efforts to recommend additional candidates, I was the only candidate. This embarrassed university officials because it is customary to nominate a few people out of courtesy.

The college encouraged additional nominations for approximately 10 minutes, but no other candidates came forward. People couldn't think of anyone else to replace me because they knew my online presence and how I had mediated and overseen various critical issues. I was also quite embarrassed by the situation, and especially the dozens of venture capitalists there were very curious about who I was. Since there were no other candidates, they elected me without a vote. It was an honor because it meant my colleagues would send me infinite trust. I tried to maximize the capabilities of my fellow students by building and operating an independent website where we could share our mutual development and impressions.

At the graduation ceremony, I received a merit award from the university and became an icon of the program. The university continued using me in many ways as an ambassador to recruit subsequent courses.

WRONG DIRECTION

In 1988, I registered a publishing house in a distant province from Seoul to publish a book titled "Deulpul." At that time, I was part of Hankyoreh's founding team. I was actively involved in the region, a newly established newspaper distributed nationwide. Not long after I arrived in the area, I organized a group named "Deulpul" with the local residents, focusing on cultural, literary, and civil rights activities, which led to the book's publication. I realized the need for professional knowledge to create a book, which prompted me to apply to the first class of the newly launched Publishing College a year later. At Publishing College, I systematically studied publishing, editing, and marketing. I attended classes daily, from Monday to Friday, 9 a.m. to 3 p.m. Over six months, I thoroughly learned various subjects, including editing, planning, design, production, spelling, copyright law, writing, computer editing, and proofreading. The faculty comprised the most reputable experts from the Korean publishing industry and other fields. For instance, I learned writing from Kim Byung-ik, one of the best literary critics of the time, and book design from Jung Byung-kyu, who first introduced the concept of book design to the Korean publishing industry. What I cherish most is the enjoyable times spent with my classmates.

After completing the course, I joined United Publishing Promotion Co., Ltd. (UPPC), but it turned out not to be the right place to utilize my knowledge. The company primarily negotiated with foreign copyright companies to allow expensive books adopted as textbooks by Korean university students to be reprinted affordably in Korea. The constraints at UPPC limited the application of the knowledge I gained at Publishing College. I don't remember exactly how many months I worked there, but my boss at the time was aware of the issue. Consequently, he introduced me to the representative of another company where I could more effectively apply my skills. People remember my boss as an academic intellectual who upheld high moral standards. Whenever I think of Yeonheedong, located behind Yonsei University, it remains a precious space in my memory despite being a place where I briefly struggled to adapt.

PHOTOGRAPHS, MOMENTS OF RECORD

Caption: My daughter on the swing.

Looking at the picture of my daughter sitting on the swing, I strangely thought about various things related to Yeonhui-dong. A photograph is surprisingly expansive in this way. There is a saying that "all that remains is a photograph." Memories fade with each passing day, but photos record those days. There are many cases where a single image changed history. Robert Capa's "The Falling Soldier, 1936," widely publicized the futility of the Spanish Civil War, is one such example.

It later debated the photo over its authenticity. There was a debate about whether it was staged or natural and increased the possibility of being produced. However, people at the time thought a lot about war because of this picture.

Photo Credit: The Metropolitan Museum of Art (TMMA, n.d.).

In 1936, a female photographer, Dorothea Lange published a photo titled "Migrant Mother, 1936," showing the wretched lives of the American West, which caused a sensation at the time of publication. Though later exposed as a staged photograph, this image is a testament to the power a single picture can hold.

Recently, a photo of the death of a young child found on the Mediterranean coast among Syrian refugees shocked the world. Yet, with this one picture, countries worldwide are accepting Syrian refugees. Getting people's attention with a photo like this is unnecessary, but Koreans often say, "What's left is a photo." So, let's record our precious moments frequently. Our descendants will remember us in the distant future through the images we leave behind. I recommend increasing the image size and quality to the maximum for taking pictures.

Photo Credit: Library of Congress (LOC, n.d.).

In my case, in the early 2000s, I took images with low-quality digital cameras. To be displayed on today's high-definition monitors, it must render the grades at a lower resolution or smaller size to conserve memory. When we direct the screens we use these days towards 4K or 8K, they cannot use those images from the past. So, we will have to create a photograph with the highest quality to see it to prepare for such an era where the device's image quality will be higher resolution.

Also, one image is good, but I recommend often leaving it as a video. Many places lend storage space for free these days, so if we put original photos and videos there, we can take them out and view them anytime. And while it is good to leave pictures of family and friends, I recommend we take pictures of ourselves whenever possible. As time passes, we notice that our appearance has aged, and we look older than before. If we leave it a year earlier, looking at the image in the distant future, we can reminisce about that time and change our mood.

EVENT FOR MY WIFE

I was hesitant to share this post but ultimately decided to. Yesterday, I set up a beam projector in the basement. I looked through photos to comfort my wife, YJ, who had a particularly tough day. She's been battling a severe illness, and just a few days ago, her father passed away. We couldn't attend the funeral in Korea because we were informed by my sister-in-law only after it had occurred. Her father passed last Sunday evening, and even if we had been notified sooner, traveling there in time would have been impossible. My sister-in-law knew about our situation in America. We were in the middle of our U.S. citizenship examination, which restricted our ability to travel abroad. Though it was technically possible to go to Korea with U.S. immigration authority permission, it wasn't simple. My family had important commitments here. My son YW had been working on a research thesis for a year and was in the midst of his final exams, requiring him to submit it to MIT. My daughter MJ and I were planning to move her belongings to a new rental apartment this week, as her second semester is starting soon. Despite our complicated situation, I know YJ would have gone to Korea for her father's funeral under any circumstances.

YJ was devastated upon learning about her father's death after his funeral had passed. His prolonged illness had somewhat prepared us for this loss, yet it only intensified her sorrow. Being her father's eldest daughter and myself as the eldest son-in-law, I felt a profound sense of duty and regret for not being able to lead the funeral rites. During this time, YJ became seriously ill, suffering from intense body aches. On the Friday evening after YW finished his final exams and thesis submission, I shared the sad news with our children. To my surprise, they were less affected than expected. Since moving to America nearly 13 years ago at a young age, their memories of their grandfather were faint.

Their bond with their grandmother was more robust, as she had visited the U.S. several times, and they had spent considerable time together during visits to Korea. I knew they would be deeply impacted by her eventual passing as well.

Nevertheless, I scanned the photos I had of tribute to their grandfather. I also scanned images of her when she was young for my wife's mood swings. I took the pictures in an album, checked them individually, and watched them together with a beam project in the basement yesterday afternoon.

Caption: This is a picture of my parents-in-law's second wedding anniversary and YJ's childhood.

Caption: To be closer, my father-in-law moved from Seoul to our Jugong apartment complex in Geumchon, Paju. He often spent time playing with MJ before YW was born.

FIRST, I SHOWED my father-in-law's handwritten message to his grand-children. Then, we discussed our memories with him by projecting pictures of him from his youth to recent years on the screen. Among them was a scene where my kids played with their grandfather as babies. Few people remember the situation in a photograph taken when they were young, even if it is a photograph of themselves. Therefore, explaining the relationship between people with these photos is only possible. However, my children said they remembered the images I took when they were a little older. That is the power of a single shot.

Caption: This is a picture of YJ working as an in-flight interpreter for Northwest Airlines.

After that, I showed YJ's pre-wedding pictures. Seeing her mother at the same age as she amazed MJ, who is now 21 years old. "I wish I could go back in time and be friends with my mom," she said. Since my wife's college days, YJ has worked as an interpreter and volunteered at several prominent international events, including the 1988 Seoul Olympics. Since her early twenties, she has made a fortune traveling to many countries. After graduating from university in Korea, she had two German women who became her close friends while studying at Keio Graduate School in Japan. Her album contains many pictures of her friends. There were photos of her friend who visited YJ's Korean home and YJ visiting a German friend's hometown. An exciting thing happened last year. My wife took YW to Germany from Spain, where she reunited with her old friends. Each time such a picture appeared on the screen, YJ's voice became brighter as she explained it to her children. It was time to talk about the old days of their mothers. My children didn't even know about it. Although MJ is now her mom's age, she realizes her mom was once as young as her. We pass on memories, but they will never disappear if forgotten.

Caption: Those photos amazed my kids at their mom's professional landscape photos. Her 35mm camera images were well-composed and impactful, unlike her usual smartphone shots.

SEE THE DESOLATENESS OF RURAL AMERICA

Consequently, we discussed how beneficial it would be for YJ to carry a film camera regularly. As a result, the event I had been planning for several days was a great success. Not only was it possible to share YJ's father's memories with her children, but it also changed my wife's mood. I am now lying in bed at a small Inn near Cornell University. Next to me is my daughter MJ, who is tired and asleep. When we arrived at MJ's apartment, something completely unexpected happened.

The story goes like this: After the last week of commotion with my family subsided, on Sunday, I loaded MJ's belongings into the car and headed to Ithaca, NY. Looking at my daughter's luggage, I realized how much a female college student had for just one semester compared to male college students. If I had been a male college student, I would have packed everything in two large suitcases and gone to school, but we packed my daughter's luggage in my big SUV.

MJ spent last fall semester at the hotel where I am writing this. As she returned to school after studying at SVA in New York, she missed the right time to sign a rental contract, forcing her to live in this hotel, which rents a room for long-term stays at cheap rates. But my daughter signed up for a three-bedroom apartment this spring semester so she can live with the other two. They don't know each other because they signed a contract online.

We arrived at our destination in the middle of the day. However, MJ encountered an awkward situation when she spoke with the apartment's manager. First, she had to take her key from the janitor to open her room, but the man was not on duty because it was a Sunday. Furthermore, since he was the sole employee, MJ sought help from her colleagues. Thankfully, she was able to get in touch with one of her roommates. Unfortunately, the girl said she could only arrive at the place after 5 p.m. Left with no other option, we decided to have lunch at a Thai restaurant in downtown Ithaca and waited for her call at a nearby coffee shop. However, even after 6 p.m., there was no contact with the girl. We eventually gave up the connection with her and spent one night in this hotel MJ once used as her lodging. Recognizing my daughter from her months-long stay, the hotel staff happily offered us a room at half the regular price.

Caption: MJ's apartment is spacious and has large buildings behind it, including the one in the photo and a parking structure. Surprisingly, just one person manages the entire complex.

I was tired of driving all day and waiting. So, as soon as I lay on the bed, I fell asleep. Thinking of going to bed early, I turned off the lights and lay down, then got up to write and sleep. Unfortunately, I planned to drop off MJ's luggage and go straight home, so I only had my cell phone. So, I've been writing this post for hours on my cell phone. In the meantime, I was far away from sleep.

After driving for about two hours from home, I took a break at a shelter. From there, MJ said she would move. Thanks to her offer, I could get to my destination comfortably while sitting in the passenger seat, dozing off, and looking outside. I make it a point to document my travels wherever I go. The passing scenery out the window frequently drew me to abandoned houses as I gazed. I gave that road back and forth several times, but I didn't know it was such scenery back then. But when I sat in the passenger seat and looked out carefully, I could see the lives of the people living in the mountainous villages to some extent. I wanted to know what work people do to make a living in these places. Occasionally, we saw a lumber mill placing various agricultural implements in the farmhouse's yard. Sometimes, we demolished abandoned houses.

Caption: The central town building, still displaying a 2016 Christmas party sign, looks dormant. Nearby, similarly suitable but empty houses echo its vacancy.

Even in still-inhabited areas, the view from the window imbues a sense of loneliness. Living in this world with the old way of life is becoming increasingly difficult. For instance, I recently met with the accountant handling my company's taxes since 2004. His company is in New York, and I talked to him about various things. When I first met him, he was in his late forties, but now he is in his sixties. He has now turned over the management of his company to his junior accountant, who says he wants to try something else.

NO RETIREMENT

My accountant, Mr. Kang, had some experience with computer programming during college and expressed a desire to revisit it. He has had considerable financial success, having built his building in New York a few years ago, with another one nearby. Mr. Kang plans to buy a farmhouse that covers one acre of land in the north of New York for $150,000. Currently, he is diligently researching to find a suitable farmhouse. He is particularly interested in one with low taxes as his hobby involves renovating homes. An affordable farmhouse in an appropriate location would hold significant meaning for him. The house he is considering is likely in a better area than the abandoned farmhouses I encountered on my way to Ithaca today.

Nevertheless, the farmhouse he intends to purchase will likely have a similar atmosphere. Locals are looking to leave their homes, while retirees aim to acquire a place that feels like a vacation home. Hearing about his plans has brought to light the potential crisis the accounting industry may face soon.

Retirement is no longer what it used to be due to advances in healthcare and longer life expectancies. Additionally, technology is eliminating the need for physical labor, with cheap and convenient services available to move heavy furniture, for example. With primary economic power, we can delegate physical tasks and engage in more stimulating activities even in old age. Thus, as long as our brain's health is good, we can enjoy life to the fullest until we die. It would be a denial of life to wait for our brain to deteriorate instead of using it to its fullest potential. We're fortunate to live in a time when we can lead rich and fulfilling lives well into our later years. Now I must sleep for tomorrow.

COMMENTS

As the morning sun rose, I remembered my conversation with MJ the night before. She had woken up quickly just as I finished a post on my blog. We talked about assorted topics, but one that stood out was the photo of "My Daughter on the Swing," which inspired my article. MJ reminisced about seeing those pictures often when she was a little girl. Even though she didn't remember being there, she yearned for the carefree childhood days depicted in the photographs.

We shared a common trait of being able to reminisce about familiar places. For instance, if we had lived in the same house for over 20 years, we could recall every nook and cranny of the site with our eyes closed. We could even visualize the tiniest details in our mind's eye, even after several years had passed. However, moving frequently or entirely changing our home could blur those memories. Taking just one picture could be a powerful aide-mémoire, jogging our memories when needed.

It may seem insignificant then, but let us take pictures occasionally. In the future, that one snapshot may hold significant meaning for our children and us, reminding us of the moments and memories that make up our lives.

PART THREE

A STORY OF

PERSEVERANCE

Penned February 11, 2017

I suggested to my son YW that we take a trip to Tejeda to distract ourselves from the anxiety of waiting for his private school admission decision that night. It would be a better way to spend our time than just waiting anxiously for the results all day. Additionally, I planned to celebrate his admission pre-emptively, confident that he would be accepted. The admission announcement was at 4 p.m. Eastern Time, which is 9 p.m. here (UTC). Our spirits lifted under the bright moon above the towering mountain range on our return from Tejeda. I encouraged YW, saying, 'Strive to be like that moon, illuminating the darkness.' He replied, "I'm feeling the stress from your words." He was cheerful about the beautiful scenery but soon tensed up again because of the upcoming announcement. I also felt a little anxious. Feeling anxious, we conversed to distract ourselves, arriving home just after 9 p.m.

As soon as we got home, YW immediately logged onto his laptop. I climbed up to the second floor and knocked on the screen of my room's laptop. When he had checked it first, he went to the second floor and said, "I don't like feeling," then went into the bathroom. I sighed and took a seat. Hoping he might be joking, I checked the school's website and only found that YW was 'Waitlisted' instead of accepted.

Nevertheless, given his position on the waitlist, I was optimistic about his chances. Manhattan's elite private schools typically announce their accepted students in March or April. Therefore, some students who applied to the Dwight-Englewood School (DE) may give up on their final enrollment. That is because DE is a safety net for those students. However, YW had to experience the sting of failure once more. He was going through a series of trials.

I embraced my son as he exited the restroom and immediately noticed how much taller and bulkier he had grown since we settled down here. His physical growth marked the beginning of his journey into adulthood. He was more mature and experienced than his peers. Despite the intense competition for the limited spots in the 10th grade, which the school allocates while maintaining a gender balance, YW managed to secure a place. In this situation, it is essential to keep a hopeful outlook.

The school considered the racial ratio and awarded a white student one of the two spots. Consequently, non-white male students, including Black, Hispanic, and Asian, faced intense competition for the remaining spot. Among the Asians, the competition was primarily between Chinese, Indian, and Korean descent. Therefore, if a Korean student were selected, they would have had to compete again among themselves for the spot.

My son asked about other options if he didn't receive the final DE acceptance. I informed him of different options, such as United High School in Manhattan and some good public high schools. Moving to a town with these options would provide an alternative. However, I assured him YW would likely receive additional acceptance from the Dwight-Englewood School. He could register in order after paying the initial tuition fee, increasing the likelihood of approval. My son asked whether attending a public school in California or pursuing his dream of movies or television would be better. I advised him to take his time since California was not the foundation of our family's life and to wait until the announcement of additional acceptance. Although I comforted him, it saddened me that YW had to experience the same disappointment of failing to secure admission to private boarding schools as in middle school. Nevertheless, I encouraged him to persevere, as only a few succeed through trials, and such processes make him stronger.

YW HAS LIVED in Ridgewood, a town, for over 12 years since my family moved to the US. He asked if we would have to shift to DE's town if he attended DE. I considered his request, recognizing the challenges of a three-year commute, as it takes over 30 minutes by car and more than an hour by school bus. However, since we rent a house, my family can move to a more convenient location anytime. Therefore, if we proceed to the town where DE is located, it will benefit everyone. Despite his anxieties, YW had been well-prepared psychologically to discuss his alternatives and plans. Eventually, he will understand that persistent hard work leads to the most remarkable achievements through further preparation and effort, as nothing in the world is free.

Yesterday, YW had to call his mother via video, so I went downstairs to check in. My wife informed us that she planned to leave a hotel in Busan for Seoul early in the morning. I could sense a deep sadness in her eyes on the smartphone screen. Her eyes seemed to be on the verge of tears at any moment, yet she continued to smile for YW.

Later, YW went to bed at 1 a.m. and asked me to wake him up at 10:30 a.m. He then retreated to his room. I, too, had been up late, finishing my account of our recent trip together before finally succumbing to exhaustion and drifting off to sleep. YW had mentioned that his entire body was aching from using many machines at the fitness center with his trainer. My own body, including my head, was also throbbing with pain.

As I reflected on the emotional video call with my wife, I couldn't help but feel a pang of sadness. The distance between us seemed impossible at times. Nevertheless, seeing YW's determined spirit and resilience in the face of such challenges gave me hope for the future.

As I glance out the window at the rain pouring down, I know it will be impossible for my son and me to engage in our usual outdoor activities. On weekends, we usually drive around the seaside towns together. However, today, we must settle for indoor activities such as going to the gym, shopping and buying a new swimsuit. Although my shoulder is throbbing with pain, I am determined to approach the day with enthusiasm. YW remarked yesterday that no one understands and spends time with their father as he does with me.

Since we arrived here, there has been no conflict between my son and me. We sometimes have disagreements in the US, but I laugh it off even when YW annoys me. As he realized it wasn't my true nature, he no longer reacted sensitively, regardless of how I responded. YW has always been able to read our mental state accurately through our tone of voice, facial expressions, and gestures and respond sensitively. As a result, we can now spend time together without getting annoyed with one another.

It has been almost a month since YW began attending his new school. Recently, he has expressed a desire to be invited to a friend's house. As a result, starting next week, I plan to give YW as much time as possible to integrate into his classmates' daily routines. Rather than spending weekends with just the two of us, it would be better for him to spend more time with the locals and learn Spanish quickly. In these circumstances, striving to do our best is the ideal strategy.

I WAS IN THE middle of a squash lesson when my phone rang. My wife, YJ, has just returned from her trip to Korea. Despite the early hour, it filled her voice with excitement as she told me the news: they had accepted YW to the Dwight-Englewood School (DE).

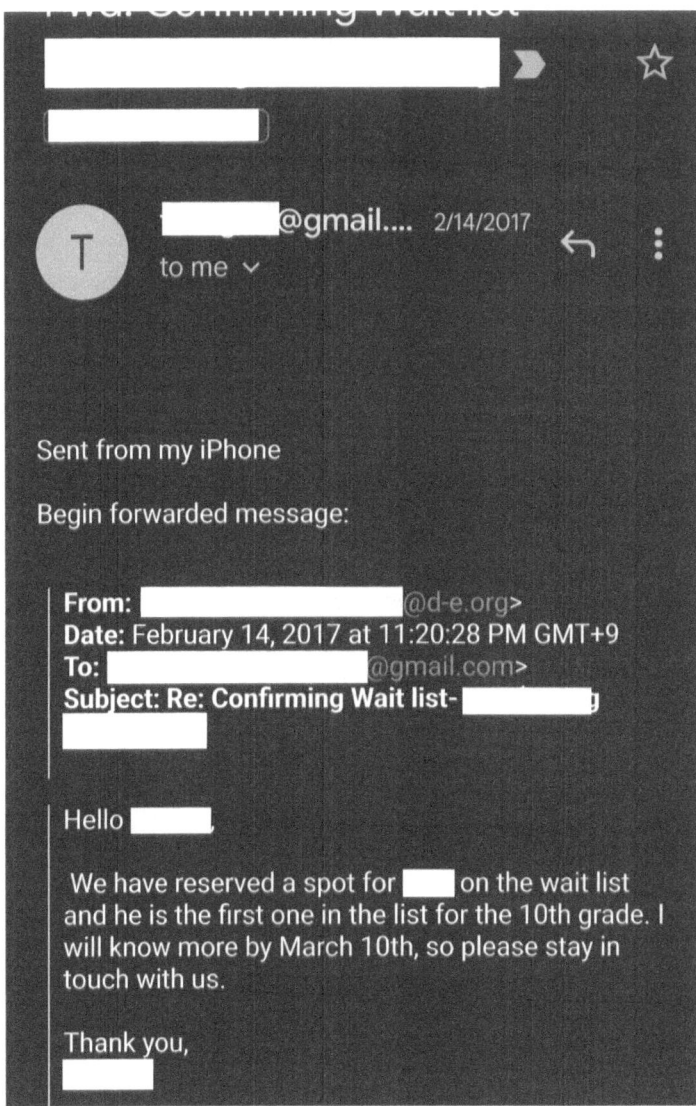

Sent from my iPhone

Begin forwarded message:

From: [redacted]@d-e.org>
Date: February 14, 2017 at 11:20:28 PM GMT+9
To: [redacted]@gmail.com>
Subject: Re: Confirming Wait list- [redacted]

Hello [redacted],

We have reserved a spot for [redacted] on the wait list and he is the first one in the list for the 10th grade. I will know more by March 10th, so please stay in touch with us.

Thank you,

[redacted]

After a long and anxious wait, YW had finally achieved its goal. YJ emailed the DE's admission office director in February to inquire about the decision. Ms. Kavita Bafana replied that the school had reserved YW as their first choice and that they would notify them after March 10. As we anxiously waited, days filled with hope and prayers for YW's acceptance ticked by. Finally, our hopes received an answer, and I couldn't wait to share the good news with YW.

As I hung up the phone, I felt a sense of relief washing over me. YW had applied to only one school, DE, due to his schedule in Spain, so we had been counting on his acceptance. Thankfully, his hard work and dedication had paid off.

As I finished my squash lesson, I couldn't help but think about all the other students who had applied to DE. It is a prestigious school, and many students aim to attend it, even if they can commute. For example, in the 1980s, Ms. Brooke Shields was a star among the high-teen demographic and an alum of this esteemed school. As a student, she relocated from Manhattan to Haworth, New Jersey, where she resided until eventually enrolling at Princeton University. However, YW had put all his eggs in one basket, and I was proud of him for taking that risk.

I couldn't wait to see YW's reaction as we drove home. He had worked so hard for this, and I knew his joy would be uncontainable. It was another reminder that when we face adversity, we can become more assertive if we overcome it wisely.

FROM STRESS TO SUCCESS

Penned February 12, 2017

I had an appointment with YW's school on February 10, 2017, at 2:15 p.m. Upon racing the front doorbell, someone inside saw me through the camera and opened the door. I parked my car on the side of the road as the school blocked the road to it with concrete blocks for unexpected vehicle terrorism prevention. Samuel was going to help me with the meeting. WS, a lawyer in the area, has been a longtime acquaintance. He has helped my son with his studies at the school since January 2017. After a while, he arrived by car, and we entered the campus together at the Atlantic School.

Caption: Atlantic School, Las Palmas, Spain.

We saw YW chatting with his friends on one side of the campus. YW also looked a little embarrassed when he saw us. His friends looked over at us curiously. We moved to the conference room on the second floor, and after waiting for a while, the meeting started. It had been almost a month since YW came to this school.

Six people attended the meeting, including Mr. Don Fernando, who teaches Spanish to my son's homeroom teacher, the high school assistant principal, and an English teacher, Mr. Don Javier, who manages the school's middle and high schools. I have primarily communicated with Mr. Pedro Pablo Gutierrez, Head of the School, since the beginning, while Don Javier, the principal, was in charge of the meeting.

Our conversation was about how YW could more effectively receive the services of the school. Among the subjects he is currently taking, some issues exceed his Spanish level, and there is a plan to replace them with self-study Spanish. Ultimately, the day's main focus was discussing how YW can learn Spanish more effectively.

ATLANTIC
SCHOOL

The Atlantic School's Headmistress

CERTIFIES

That   _   _ **has most successfully completed the**

first semester of 3 ESO in our Centre during 2017.

Santa Brígida, 20 June 2017

Juani Guerra Arencibia
The Headmistress

Fernando Montesdeoca
The Teacher

Antonio Jesús Monzón
The Secretary

Gustavo J. Navarro Nieto, 23 · 35310 Santa Brigida · Las Palmas · Tel 928 356000 · secretaria@atlanticschools.net · www.atlanticschools.net

Image Caption: This is the certificate that YW completed
in the second semester of the ninth grade at Atlantic School.

My son received permission from the school to attend only the second
semester of the ninth grade at Atlantic School, a private school. Therefore, he
is not a formal student recognized by the Spanish government. Consequently, he won't get credits but a certificate of completion. So, my son is not a
traditional Atlantic school student but an experiential learner. So, YW only
had to attend some of the regular classes. While the school offers courses in

English, most subjects are taught in Spanish, posing a challenge for him in some advanced subjects.

However, recently, YW brought up a concern that he needed help understanding some of his classes at his current Spanish level. He questioned why he needed to continue attending those courses and sought my advice. While his Spanish skills may be at a different level than required to fully comprehend the classes, continuing to follow them until the end of the semester would benefit his language improvement. However, I also recognized that YW felt stressed due to the sudden changes he faced when he arrived in Spain without proper preparation. As his father, it was vital for me to consider his circumstances.

After explaining YW's situation to my friend WS, I asked him to meet with Pablo Gutierrez and sort out the issue. Samuel had many connections in the area as a local, and I trusted him to oversee the matter. In addition, I had previously sought WS's advice when I was looking for a private school in Spain, and he had introduced me to the president of Atlantic School. So, it made sense for him to speak to Gutierrez rather than for me to approach him directly. Thanks to Gutierrez's prompt and decisive actions, we could quickly schedule the meeting with six people despite everyone's busy schedules. I am genuinely grateful for his leadership and swift response.

During the meeting, I learned that YW's homeroom teacher, Don Fernando, had already had several conversations with my son before the meeting. As a result, he had a good understanding of YW's situation and needs. His initiative-taking approach impressed me. After the meeting, it assigned YW to an excellent teacher well suited to his needs. I expressed my gratitude to the school for being so considerate and accommodating. YW had only studied Spanish for a year or two in the US, so keeping up with ninth-grade classes in Spain was challenging.

Nevertheless, Don Fernando designated it as 'YW's Week' last week and organized a particular project for YW. His friends individually created a project to help YW learn unfamiliar words and expressions. When YW first started attending this school, Don Fernando had seated him next to a fluent English student so that he could receive additional help. However, YW only spoke in English with that student. Therefore, Don Fernando recently switched his seat to sit next to a student who needed to improve their English skills to provide YW with more opportunities to practice speaking Spanish. This meeting showed me that the school considers several factors to support my son's learning.

So, the primary teacher leading the discussion was Don Fernando. He agreed with YW that there were some classes he didn't need to attend. Don Fernando explained that YW had already completed the ninth grade in the United States, so some subjects wouldn't require him to relearn the material. Additionally, some issues might be more relevant for YW as an international student to study for only one semester. Don Fernando suggested that YW does not participate in some classes, including science. He said he would prepare and provide the necessary materials for YW to learn Spanish independently during the newly created time. Furthermore, he offered to motivate YW to read by selecting books that could help him learn Spanish.

Doña Juana Guerra Arencibia, Headmaster of Atlantic School, 35007349 Code Center, located at c / Gustavo J. Navarro Nieto, 23, 35310 Santa Brígida, Las Palmas (Spain),

CERTIFIES:

That student   , Passport No.   .   .. from   , resident in Ridgewood, New Jersey USA, has been admitted to our College during the Semester from January to June 2017 to join 4th year of ESO (Secondary Education) with thirty hours of study per week, attending these subjects:

- Spanish Language
- Mathematics
- Geography and History
- Biology
- Physical and Chemistry
- Catholic Religion

Image Caption: The above letter is a letter of acceptance sent to YW by the Atlantic School and the subjects he will study during the second semester.

DURING THE MEETING at YW's school, the teachers discussed his unique situation as an international student attending for only one semester. Although he cannot receive formally accredited courses, they still want him to have a fulfilling experience learning about Spanish culture and history while improving his language skills. Don Fernando, YW's Spanish teacher, commended his cheerful outlook toward learning and believed he could gradually speed up his progress.

Don Fernando also shared that YW is a bit shy but has been coming out of his shell and playing pranks with his friends. In a light-hearted moment, he suggested that the quickest way for YW to become fluent in Spanish would be to get a girlfriend, which made everyone chuckle. To help YW become more comfortable with the language, he encouraged his students to invite him to social events and parties. Don Fernando even asked YW's father to enable him to accept such invitations. Social activities can help someone learn a language faster.

The teachers also discussed which courses YW should take, considering his background in the United States. Don Fernando recommended that YW skip some unnecessary courses, such as science, and focus more on learning Spanish independently. He even offered to prepare and provide the necessary materials for YW to study independently.

Although YW cannot receive a report card due to Spanish education law, the teachers still want him to have a meaningful experience at the school. They recognize that YW has unique circumstances and are willing to collaborate with him to ensure he has the best learning experience.

We focused on finding ways for YW to learn Spanish effectively while having fun with his friends. Don Fernando, YW's Spanish teacher, asked about YW's favorite sport and suggested encouraging his classmates to play squash with him. He also showed that YW is more confident and louder when giving class presentations.

At the meeting, there was also a discussion about giving YW homework assignments in Spanish, math, history, and art. Even though it may be challenging for YW initially, completing homework assignments will eventually help him learn Spanish. As a result, Don Javier, the school principal, agreed to allow YW to do homework in those subjects.

Caption: Mr. Pablo Gutierrez.

The meeting, despite the challenge of language differences, was engaging and lasted around 40 minutes. After its conclusion, we encountered Mr. Pablo Gutierrez, the Head of the School, outside the meeting room. A brief exchange of pleasantries followed before we went our separate ways, marking the end of a fruitful session. The teachers showed a commendable eagerness to assist YW in his Spanish language learning and to help him become more integrated within the school community.

Post-meeting, Samuel shared his high regard for Don Fernando, a YW school teacher, praising his exceptional dedication. He noted that Don Fernando's commitment to his students' success was rare and not often seen in other schools.

After the meeting, Samuel went to another school where his children attend, and their classes ended earlier than YW's school. As for me, I went to the University of Las Palmas to play some squash and then came back to pick up YW. On the way home, I explained everything discussed in the meeting, and he felt a bit more relaxed. Overall, it was a productive meeting, and we produced some clever ideas on how YW can improve his Spanish skills while having fun with his friends.

TODAY, FEBRUARY 12, 2017, YW and I agreed to have dinner at a restaurant in Tejeda. I stumbled across the town at the highest point in Las Palmas last time and wanted to revisit it. According to TripAdvisor, I was curious as one of the town's restaurants had the best ratings in Spain's Canary Islands. Furthermore, the school will announce the results tonight for the application that my son submitted before coming to Spain. So, it'd be better for YW to forget about it than to wait for the results after school. And I intended to congratulate him on his acceptance over dinner.

After leaving the school gate, YW got into my car, and I headed straight to our destination. YW told me about a meeting with Don Fernando, a Spanish teacher; Don Fernando asked his students to invite YW to future parties and gatherings if possible. Then he found students playing squash and advised them to play with YW. Don Fernando is really nice. He implemented what he had said at the meeting a few days ago. And in math class, his math teacher smiled at YW, saying he was happy to be able to give him homework from now on.

So, I ended up making a big decision for my son. Most of all, I had to get YW to drop out of school before he could take his midterm exams. Then, YW needs a report card for this school, so his records are meaningless. So, in mid-October, he submitted his resignation letter with the consent of his parents. And on November 30, 2016, YW received his acceptance letter from Atlantic School. He was due to attend one semester at this school from January to June 2017. YW's goal was to start in 10th grade at Dwight-Englewood School (DE) in the fall after returning to the United States. To do that, he had to get a good GPA on the Independent School Entrance Exam (ISEE), one of the essential procedures for admission to DE. The only date YW could take the ISEE was December 10, 2016. The DE's application submission deadline was a few days later. This way, YW could come to Spain after submitting his documents and completing the interview safely.

So, at Ridgewood High School (RHS), YW also needed more trust in the teachers due to the terrible relationship between the two teachers. However, I had many thoughts as I received unexpected support and consideration from the Atlantic School community. RHS is a vast public school with over 1,700 students, so it is impossible to consider each student's circumstances. Since YW is a new student who transferred from another private school, the academic schedule had to be different. RHS decided on the educational plan unilaterally, even though they should have considered such aspects when assigning YW classes. As a result, problems arose in several subjects. However, the school did not offer solutions, blaming the cause of YW's issue.

In contrast, Atlantic School offered YW opportunities to immerse himself in Spanish language and culture, demonstrating a caring and supportive educational environment, as evident from our recent meeting. Although education in the United States is highly competitive and the academic standards are high compared to Spain, students in Spain experience little stress in school. One day, YW told me this. "Dad, these kids love getting a 70 because they passed the test criteria." In my son's case, it was stressful not to get a score of 96 or higher, but the Spanish students cheered on the 'pass.' It makes me think a lot."

JUGGLING

RESPONSIBILITIES

Penned May 5, 2018

YW took the Spanish SAT II this morning. He aims to complete four SAT II subject tests before graduation. His original plan was to take only three courses required by Ivy League schools. Recently, he added Georgetown University to his list of safety colleges. The college requires applicants to submit four subjects for SAT II. Therefore, he's contemplating subjects like Math, Spanish, English Literature, and one Science subject. As he enters his junior year, crucial tests await him. First, this summer, he's taking the SAT. Once he gets the score he wants, he can finish it once. He grabbed the PSAT last April and outperformed his sister without any preparation. In 2014, his older sister, MJ, achieved grades in the top 0.6%.

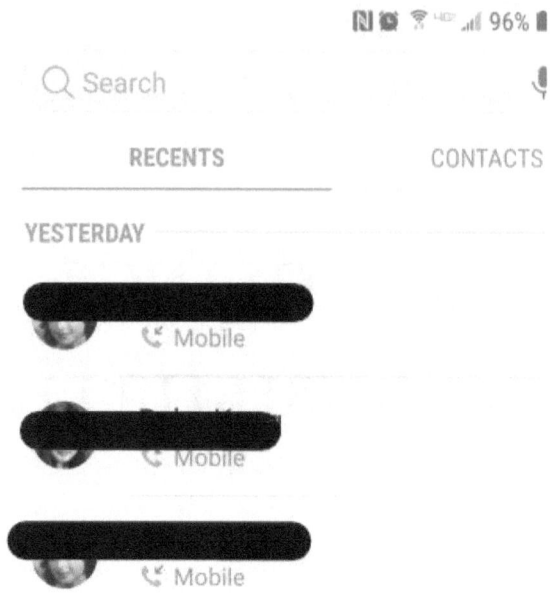

Image Caption: I made thirty-nine calls to my daughter by 7:23 a.m.,
according to my call log on May 4. Shortly after, at 7:48 a.m.,
my wife called me and informed me that it had resolved the issue.

I returned around 7:40 a.m. after dropping my son at Fort Lee High School, which is close to our home. However, I had to head out again almost as soon as I arrived home. Because MJ needed to answer my calls, my daughter called me at 3 a.m. this morning and asked me to wake her up at 3:45 a.m. I didn't sleep and waited and called her several times at 3:45 a.m., but she fell asleep. Finally, she barely answered my call and asked me to wake her at 5:50 a.m. Ultimately, I set my alarm for that time and tried to close my eyes, but I couldn't sleep properly. At 5:50 a.m., I called to wake MJ up. I called more than thirty-nine times from 5:50 a.m. before picking off YW at the test center. Concerned, as soon as I got home, I set out for Ithaca, where my daughter was.

MJ told me on the phone at 3:00 a.m. that she hadn't slept for three days because she had been working in the architecture studio. I am worried because overwork can lead to severe heart problems no matter how young a person is. But again, I couldn't call the university police, so I hurriedly drove with my Z4 quickly. If I move fast, I'll get caught speeding a few times, but I'll be there in about three hours. I would have to keep on the phone if I didn't stay home. While I was going to Ithaca, my wife tried to find a way to contact her daughter.

WORST OF ALL is when something terrible happens to MJ. If I start when I know that fact, it's already too late to respond. So, I function as quickly as possible when faced with a problem like this. In that respect, my wife and I differ in how we solve those problems. Fortunately, if MJ wakes up on my way, it's fortunate, and I must go home. Coincidentally, not long after I set off, I got a call from my wife. Fortunately, we resolved the issue.

And on my way back home, MJ called. She fell into a deep sleep so entirely that she couldn't hear anything. She slept for three days, from 3:50 a.m. to 7:50 a.m. It was indeed fortunate. Her brain might have suffered a severe shock if she hadn't slept so deeply. My daughter does her schoolwork this way for a few days a week without sleep. Being an architecture major, she will spend most of her time in the studio.

Caption: There was an SAT at Fort Lee High School, a public school in Bergen County.

I ate breakfast and took a break to pick YW up at the test center, but I spent an hour and a half waiting in the confined space of my car. I stayed because I was distracted all morning and needed more precise information on when his exam would end. Finally, my son ended by almost 10 a.m., but when I told him I'd waited in the car for so long, he clicked his tongue in disbelief.

AFTER THAT, MY wife and I took YW to Palisades Park, a Korean town, to a restaurant that makes Jajangmyeon. This restaurant is well known for making hand noodles and serving Korean-style Jajangmyeon. Customers can watch the process by beating the dough through the glass window. Then, as you watch the lump of dough gradually split into thin noodles, your order of Jajangmyeon comes out. The menu we eat at this restaurant is always two types, as above. My wife said she was always delicious and that she should come often. I also ate until I was full. I got home and immediately went to bed. Today was an exhausting Saturday from dawn. Fatigue came on suddenly. I closed my eyes despite knowing it's not ideal to fall asleep right after eating. After I shut my eyes for about an hour, my condition improved a little, but instead, my stomach felt bloated.

In the late afternoon, I found a Danish TV drama called "The Rain" on Netflix. It is a story about tragedies created by a series of scientists and the people who risked their survival. Then I had dinner and went to the cinema with YW to see a movie. Avengers: Infinity War is rewriting box office history these days. I have watched most of this series. Of course, I watched this series thanks to my son, but I prefer something else to these kinds of movies. So, I just watched the film when and where he wanted.

My son, YW, said something was at the end even though the movie was over and told me to wait. And most of the audience sat there as if they knew something. I felt bored to the point of feeling like this was the first time I'd experienced a movie with such long credits. I could have been more impressed with this movie. Finally, after all the credits, the director left a brief hint on the screen. These Marvel movies are like over-the-top action movies in the Hong Kong style of the seventies. Most American superhero movies portray success and money as directly correlated to the skill of exaggeration. For me, it's just one of the boring genres.

We walked out of the AMC Theater in Edgewater after the movie. At that time, YW stepped forward to drive. I object that my son, who has a Graduated Driver's License, cannot move past 11 p.m., so he counters that it was still 20 minutes ago. Reluctantly, I handed him the car keys. Although the distance from here to my home is 15 minutes, it is a challenging road for beginners to drive. When I put on a disapproving expression, YW retorted, "Then when will I learn to drive?" He would have missed the red light if I hadn't warned him while driving.

Nevertheless, he is getting used to driving these days. I remember the first time I learned to run when I was my son's age. My older brother drove a truck and sold briquettes, and I always sat next to him on the move to help him. At that time, I used to do simulations by myself. Then, one day, my older brother asked me, sitting in the passenger seat, to get behind the wheel of a moving car. Mainly, when he was smoking, he invited me to do so. One day, when I got used to driving, he allowed me to drive. I was unlicensed then, but since there were very few cars on the road, it was fine unless I got a ticket for an accident or a traffic violation.

THE WORLD HAS completely changed since then. My son must have a licensed driver over twenty-one beside him when driving. Of course, when he moves, I usually accompany him and give him warnings or advice depending on the situation. Now, after this summer break, my son can drive alone. After that, I won't have a chance to interfere with my son's driving habits, so teaching him well before then is essential. Once established, habits tend to last a lifetime.

I talked about my life yesterday and today, but most of my time, including my wife, revolves around our children. As with their parents, we must go where we want and move when we want. Tomorrow morning, I have to go with my son to a place about an hour's drive away. Of course, because my son likes it. He will attend a fundraising event contest for the non-profit organization StreetSquash. He plans to capture the critical moments on camera and video. We intend to stay there for about 4 hours. Sure, I'm excited to go to those squash courts for a long time; even so, that's different from my plan. In a way, our children dictate my wife's and my schedules.

IMMIGRANT PARENT'S SACRIFICES

Penned April 12, 2018

My son YW's door bears a sign reading "The Office," the title of his favorite American sitcom. Created and produced by Michael Schur, the show is his most well-known work alongside Parks and Recreation (Wikipedia contributors, 2018). On his sister's recommendation, YW started watching this nine-season sitcom a few years ago. By now, he has likely watched the entire series at least six times. Therefore, Michael Schur's influence probably inspired his declaration to become a producer someday.

Caption: The sign in front of my son's door.

Caption: YW's desk displays self-made posters of his favorite TV shows. Next to his bed, he displaced Ryan Shazier's uniform and helmet from his favorite Pittsburgh football team.

Caption: YW's wall displays camera equipment and posters of his favorite movies. Today, a new poster joined his expanding collection.

Caption: The wall beside the closet showcases' cameras on the left and front sides.

Caption: A skateboard given to him by MJ, YW's older sister, hangs at the top center of the face.

When I entered his room while he was away at school, I immediately saw how he decorated his room and what was occupying his mind. I feel sorry for my children because, since coming to America, my family has been unable to find a permanent home. Every four years, we've moved, renting in three different places. Then, finally, we moved to this town, and we were here for a year for YW's high school.

We will stay in this house for another three years until YW goes to college in the fall of 2020. As a parent, I regret not allowing them to decorate their rooms. Each move requires us to redecorate their rooms, yet they should be free to design them as they wish. We cannot change the structure of the rental house, and we cannot transform the wall material or color. Even something as simple as putting nails in the walls is prohibited. Changing windows or curtains in a house that isn't ours seems futile. Thus, in every rental home, we only manage temporary decorations for their rooms. My daughter is deeply sorry about this. However, She wants to decorate her room as an artist but needs help, too.

Therefore, I intend to purchase a permanent home after my son starts college. It allows my children to have their own space in their parent's house, creating lasting memories to cherish as they grow older. But now, it might be too late for them to create such memories. They will only have their own room after they have already grown up.

During this spring break, my daughter MJ came home and said, "I'm going to live with mom and dad after graduation," which she had told me a few times before. My children love being at home. My mind drifted to my daughter's dream of becoming an architect after MJ finishes her studies; she is likely to work in New York City, where many attractive architecture firms exist. I knew that meant we could not leave the metropolitan area anytime soon. Still, it also meant we needed to find a permanent home for our family.

Also, YW, who is likely to work in the film or TV industry, will have a high probability of finding a job in Los Angeles. Still, New York City is also the next most likely area. If my children settle in the United States, they will likely stay in close contact with us, their parents. To make it easier for them to remain close to us. Buying a condominium with a few rooms in New York City would be nice if I created much money in a few years.

STANDING IN MY son's room, I could not help but feel a pang of guilt in my chest. My children deserved a stable home where they could make memories and grow without fearing constant displacement. But as an immigrant family, we had to work twice as hard to provide for our children, which sometimes meant sacrificing stability.

As I left my son's room, my thoughts turned to the future. I wanted to give my children a place they could call their own, where they could make memories and grow, and where my children could come back no matter how far they ventured into life.

I own a condominium in New York and aim to buy an adjoining unit if the chance presents itself. Removing the wall between the two units could create ample space for our family's comfort and security.

My children drive my hard work; they are why I rise each day and dedicate long hours. I wanted them to have a home they could be proud of and feel safe and loved.

As I sat at my desk to work, my mind turned to my daughter's visit in the spring. I could not wait to see her, to hear about her plans, and to tell her about my plans for a permanent home.

I smiled, grateful for my family, their love and support, and the hope for a brighter future. No matter where life takes us, we will always have each other and the memories we created together.

A FATHER'S LOVE

Penned May 2, 2018

On May 1, 2018, I called 911 to ask for help yesterday. Unfortunately, my daughter MJ, who studies at Cornell University, was unreachable. Specifically, her phone was either dead or not working, and my wife and I had been waiting to hear from her for hours. Facing a 4-5 hour journey to reach her, I had no option but to call 911 for assistance in ensuring her safety.

The text conversation below shows that on May 1, my wife and I must attend a ceremony. At 12:01 a.m., my daughter messaged me, saying she could not sleep.

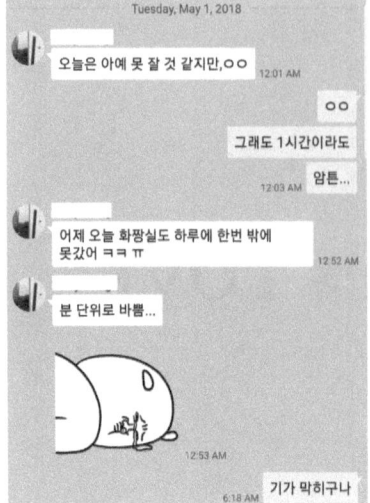
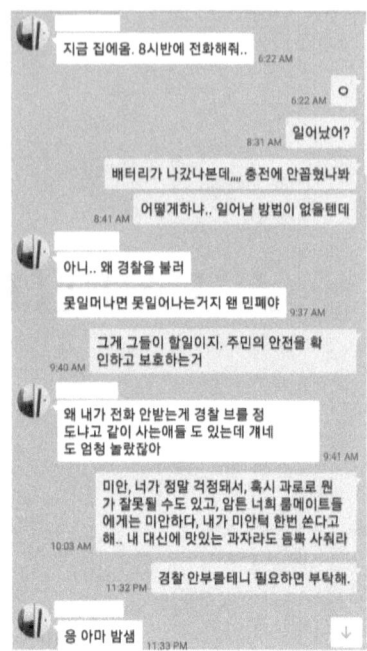

Image Caption: Message conversation between MJ and me

Tuesday, May 1, 2018:

MJ: I don't think I'll be able to sleep at all today, haha

Me: Haha

At least try to get an hour

Anyway...

MJ: I've only been able to go to the bathroom once a day for the past couple of days, haha. So busy, down to the minute...

Me: That's insane

MJ: I just got home. Call me at 8:30

Me: Okay

Did you wake up?

Your battery must have died... I guess it didn't charge

How can you wake up now? There's no way

MJ: No... Why did you call the police?

If I can't wake up, I can't wake up. So, it's not a nuisance

Me: That's their job, though. To check and ensure the safety of residents

MJ: But why would you call them just because I didn't answer the phone? I have roommates, too. They were really shocked

Me: I'm sorry, I was just really worried about you. I thought you might be overworking yourself, and something could go wrong. Anyway, apologies to your roommates for me, and I'll make it up to them. Buy them some delicious snacks on my behalf

Ask the police for help if you need it

MJ: Yeah, I'll probably pull an all-nighter

This situation had been ongoing for a day or two, which wasn't surprising. That is why I messaged her, saying she needed to sleep for at least an hour. However, this didn't guarantee it would happen.

In response to my question, she said she only went to the bathroom once on April 28 and 29 and was busy down to the minute. After going to bed early, I sent her a message at 6:18 a.m., saying, 'Sounds crazy.'

It was an extraordinary situation. Last fall, when my daughter returned to Cornell, she could not take architecture courses because she had already completed them in the fall of 2015. Cornell's architecture program is a five-year professional program with a set curriculum from first to senior year, so since my daughter finished all the architecture courses in the fall of 2015, she could not take any more architecture courses even if she returned in the fall of 2017. Therefore, she took various classes in English, Culture, and other subjects she was interested in. Even then, she occasionally stayed up all night but still slept and did what she had to do.

However, since January of this year, when she started taking architecture courses in the second semester of her first year, she has had numerous nights where MJ could not sleep at all and had strange experiences where she only slept a few hours a week.

ONE MORNING, I woke up at 6:18 and replied, "That's insane," to MJ's message. She then texted me, asking me to wake her up at 8:30, as she had just returned home. This meant she had pulled an all-nighter at a studio or library and stopped by home to shower and change clothes. Until recently, MJ had never asked me to wake her up, so she would often stay up all night and head back to school without sleeping to avoid the risk of oversleeping. However, after I recently offered to help wake her up so she could at least catch some rest, MJ asked for my help occasionally.

So, I called her at 8:29 a.m., but she did not answer, and I had a momentary thought that since MJ had set her alarm for 8:30 a.m., I should let her sleep for one more minute. Therefore, I hung up and redialed at 8:30 a.m.

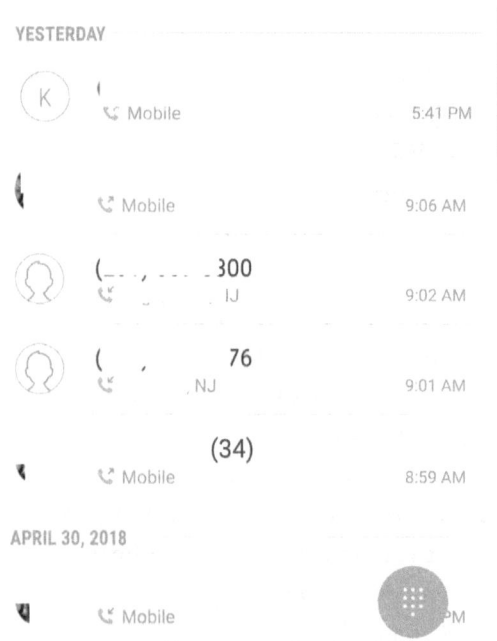

Image Caption: The image above refers to 34 times I called MJ.

Looking at my phone log, I called MJ 34 times until 8:59 a.m., but there was no answer, and she turned off her phone. She lives in an apartment off campus with three other students, each having their room, but they only see each other briefly in the morning and do not know each other well. Regrettably, contacting them was only possible with their emergency contact information.

Of course, I did not think anything unusual happened to my daughter, but the fact that she was busy and could not sleep worried me. If she kept sleeping like that, she would waste all her effort studying. So, I decided to seek help from the police. I called 911 and explained the situation, and after a while, I received a call from our local police station. They told me to contact the Ithaca police station, where the school is located. I asked my wife to explain the situation and get to the police station. She called the campus police station first, but they said they could not help because it was not a dormitory situation. Hence, she called the Ithaca police station. She explained the situation and asked for help. The calls that came in at 9:01 a.m. and 9:02 a.m. were from the police stations in Fort Lee and Englewood, our neighboring towns, respectively. There is no police station in Englewood Cliffs, NJ, where I live, so Englewood police station covers our area. As mentioned, I received a text message from my daughter at 9:37 a.m.

My daughter needs to follow proper grammar when sending text messages. She thinks it is a waste of time, and if the recipient understands the news, it's good enough. She does not bother correcting typos or errors because she is always in a hurry.

My daughter MJ asked me if not answering her phone was an emergency and if I needed to call the police. Her roommates were surprised, which was a big concern. From the text she sent me, she must have been pretty angry. It was one of the few times I have dealt with her while living together. But even though the police officers had worked hard, I would not be sorry if my daughter had gone months without sleeping properly and remained in that state. I would naturally worry as a parent if I could not reach her. Moreover, that day, I had to receive my important a certificate at 1 p.m., but since I could not attend her college, it was the best I could do.

Wednesday, May 2, 2018

8:48 PM 한숨도 못잤니?

○ ○

오늘도 11:07 PM

11:15 PM

Image Caption: Message conversation between MJ and me.

Wednesday, May 2, 2018:

Me: Can't you even get a wink of sleep?
MJ: Yeah
Today as well

NO ONE WILL believe me when I explain this. How can a university student survive without any sleep? Cornell University's architecture program is known for being intense, which makes this especially notable. Last fall, my daughter attended general education classes outside of the architecture program, and other students could not believe she was an architecture student. There is a day once a year when first-year architecture students have Dragon Day, which is open to the public to come and watch, and that is the only day when regular campus students can see the architecture students. The curriculum is so rigorous that she barely has time to prepare for other classes, much less do the homework properly.

MJ says that she and other students in her program are always pulling all-nighters to complete assignments for the core subjects because there needs to be more time to focus on other issues like architectural history. Despite all the professors knowing the situation, they continue to push these intense academic schedules, which my daughter needs to help me understand. It is a clever use for money if students can learn and understand the material properly. She needs to spend more time than other students due to her slower pace. The other students are in similar situations. They cannot shower or change clothes before class to get as much sleep as possible. However, my daughter always makes sure to shower and change clothes even if she has not slept at all. That is why I ask her occasionally if she needs me to wake her up.

Image Caption: Message conversation between MJ and me.

Saturday, March 10, 2018:

MJ: (emoji)
Me: Do you eat seven meals a week?

MJ: Yup

I finally slept after three days yesterday...

Haha

Me: Sleep more... Why did you wake up so early?

MJ: I'm already up (laughs). Eating breakfast

The above conversation was on Saturday morning, March 10. Since it was Saturday, MJ could at least sleep for a few hours. Naturally, they cannot afford to eat properly. So, I asked, "Do you eat seven meals weekly?" My daughter replied that she had slept for the first time in three days.

On March 19, MJ texted me at 2:53 a.m. asking if I was sleeping.

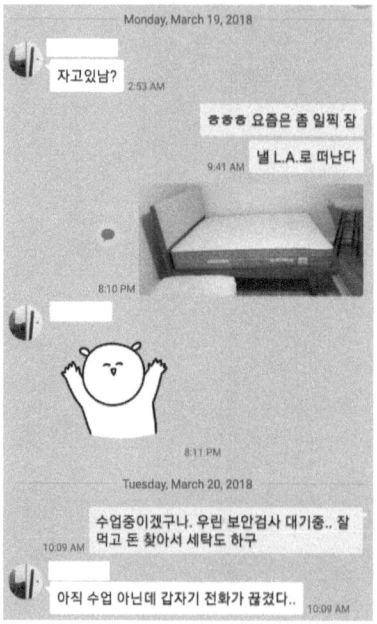

Image Caption: Message conversation between MJ and me.

Monday, March 19, 2018:

MJ: Are you sleeping? 2:53 a.m.

Me: Hahaha, I've been going to bed a bit earlier these days

I'm leaving for L.A. tomorrow

MJ: (Emoji)

Tuesday, March 20, 2018:

Me: You're probably in class. We're waiting for the security check. So, eat well, find some cash, and do the laundry

MJ: I'm not in class yet, but the phone suddenly disconnected

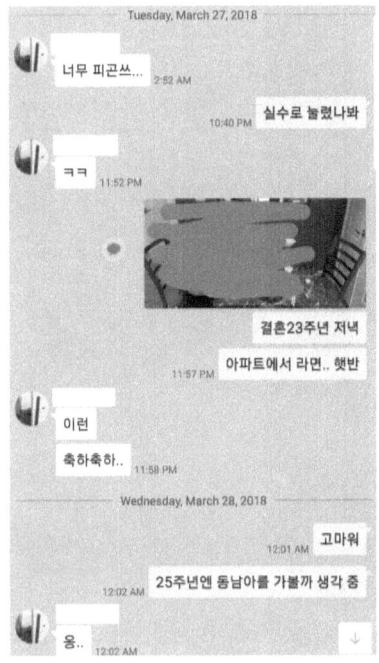

Image Caption: Message conversation between MJ and me.

Tuesday, March 27, 2018:

MJ: I'm too tired...

Me: I must have pressed the button by mistake

MJ: Haha

Me: 23rd wedding anniversary dinner. Instant ramyeon and micro-waveable rice at the apartment

MJ: Oh, no. Congratulations
Wednesday, March 28, 2018:
Me. Thanks
Considering a trip to Southeast Asia for our 25th anniversary
MJ: Okay

On March 27, she left a message at 2:52 a.m. saying, " I'm too tired..." The rest of the family was on a trip to California, so I felt sorry for my daughter.

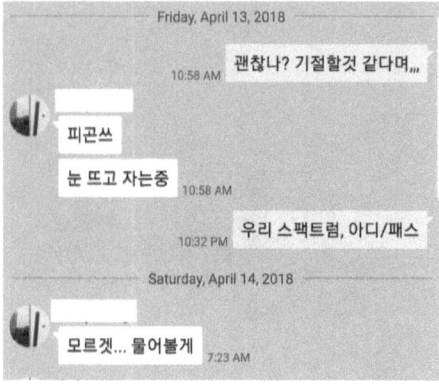

Image Caption: Message conversation between MJ and me.

Friday, April 13, 2018:

    Me: Are you okay? You said you felt like you were going to pass out,,,
    MJ: I'm tired
    Sleeping with my eyes open

My daughter sometimes mentioned feeling like she would pass out. During our conversation on April 13th, I asked about her health since she'd previously expressed this feeling.

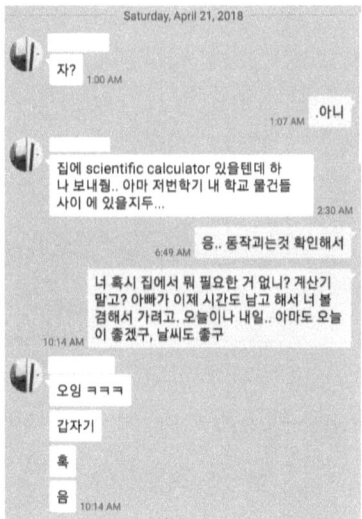

Image Caption: Message conversation between MJ and me.

Friday, April 21, 2018:

MJ: Are you sleeping?

Me: No

MJ: There should be a scientific calculator at home... Can you send one to me? It might be with my school stuff from last semester...

Me: Okay... I'll check if it's working first

Do you need anything else from home besides the calculator? Dad has some free time now and is thinking of visiting you. Maybe today or tomorrow... Today might be better since the weather is nice.

MJ: Oh, haha.

Suddenly?

Hmm

Well...

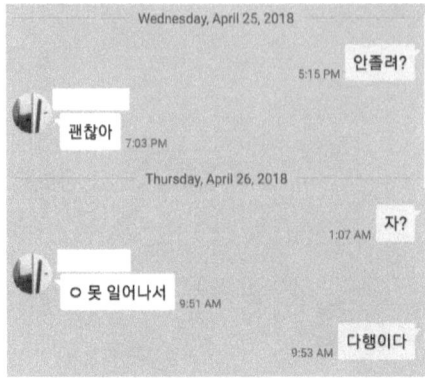

Image Caption: Message conversation between MJ and me.

Wednesday, April 25, 2018:

Me: Aren't you sleepy?

MJ: I'm okay

Thursday, April 26, 2018:

Me: Are you sleeping?

MJ: Can't get up

Me: That's a relief.

The conversation above might not make sense to ordinary people. But, at 1:07 a.m. on April 26, I asked, "Are you asleep?" She did not respond to my question until 9:51 a.m. that morning. It meant she could not wake up. Perhaps she had unknowingly collapsed and slept that early morning. That is why my response was, "I'm glad." As a father, I am relieved that my daughter managed to get some sleep that way.

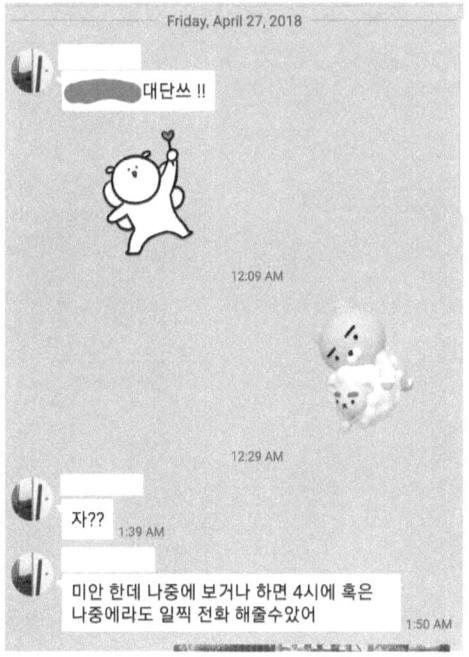

Image Caption: Message conversation between MJ and me.

Friday, April 27, 2018:

> **MJ:** Amazing!!
>
> **Me:** (emoji)
>
> **MJ:** Are you sleeping?
>
> **MJ:** Sorry, but if you see this later, can you call me early, at 4 o'clock or whenever you can?

On April 27th, at 1:50 a.m., MJ texted me, asking me to wake her up at 4 a.m. I did wake her up at that time that day. I often check my phone in the early morning to see if there are texts from my daughter.

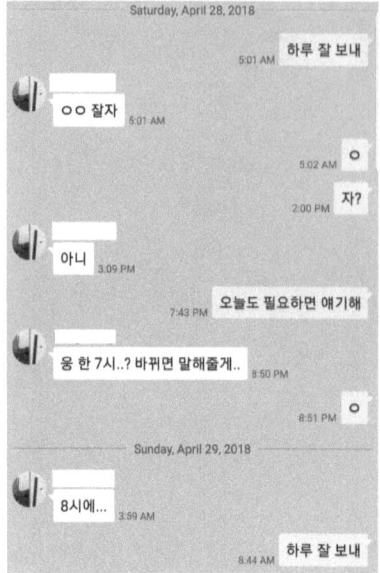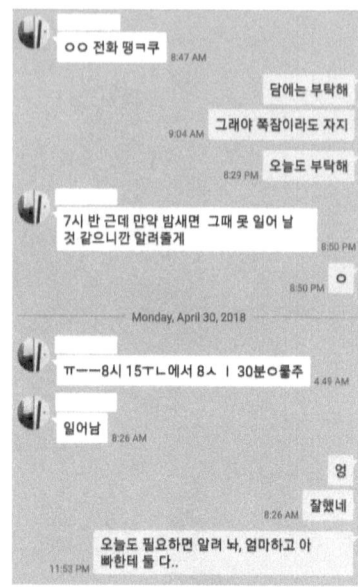

Image Caption: Message conversation between MJ and me.

Saturday, April 28, 2018:

Me: Have a good day

MJ: Yeah. Goodnight

Me: Yeah

Are you asleep?

MJ: No

Me: Let me know if you need anything today

MJ: Yeah, maybe around seven? If it changes, I'll tell you..

Me: Yeah

Sunday, April 29, 2018:

MJ: At 8...

Me: Have a good day

MJ: Yea. Call me at 8

Me: Ask me next time

That way, you can at least nap

Ask me again today

MJ: 7:30. But if I stay up all night, I might not be able to wake up, so I'll let you know

Me: Okay

Monday, April 30, 2018

MJ: 8:15 to 8:30

MJ: Woke up

Me: Oh

Good job

Let me know if you need anything today, both Mom and Dad..

THE CONVERSATIONS LEADING up to the incident are as follows.

On April 28 at 5:01 a.m., I sent my daughter a message saying, "Have a good day." On the 29th, MJ left a message at 3:59 a.m. asking me to wake her up at 8 a.m. Finally, on April 30, she left a message at 4:49 a.m. asking to be woken up, and the writing shows that she was not in her right mind.

She intended to write "8:15 to 8:30" but left a message saying "ㅠㅜ---- 8시 15ㅜㄴ에서 8ㅅ ㅣ 30분ㅇ룡주," indicating that she was on the verge of collapsing.

Still, lately, I have been taking care of her in the early morning so she could nap like this.

However, after yesterday's police station incident, my daughter probably will not ask me for a favor for a while. Given her schedule, she might not even have time to sleep, eliminating the need to ask. With everything, including exams, piling up before the break starting May 20, she'll likely manage only minimal sleep. On top of that, her laptop broke down completely a few days ago, and she requested a recovery from the school's tech team while borrowing a computer from the school. Architectural programs consume many CPUs. The computer motherboard likely died because it could not manage the heat from the continuous operation.

Cornell University has a reputation for its demanding workload. Students are known to commit suicide by jumping off the high bridges over the campus gorge due to stress. A few years ago, they installed nets under the bridges to prevent deaths from falling. However, students continue to die from excessive study pressure. According to my son, MIT has the highest suicide rate among colleges. That is believable.

Today, I met with a real estate agent, Mr. Jung, and discussed this over tea. He said, "After studying so fiercely, there should be nothing difficult in the world." He might be right. Intense college competition fosters individual competitiveness. However, I am not sure about the current situation in Korean universities, but I wonder if they go to the same extent. I question if architecture students in Korea go through the same situation as my daughter.

My daughter often calls when heading to school or working late in the studio. She does this to ward off sleepiness, as talking helps her stay awake. When working on computer modeling, which consumes a lot of her time, she sometimes calls me to discuss diverse topics when she feels sleepy.

My daughter shared a poignant moment when one of her closest friends broke down in tears during dinner, overwhelmed by the intense academic pressure. This friend is navigating her third year in the rigorous 5-year architecture program at Cornell University. MJ is just beginning her first year. In her initial semester in 2015, MJ formed a strong bond with two friends — one hailing from California and the other from an international high school in Seoul.

Originally, MJ planned to resume her studies at Cornell University after a two-year hiatus at the School of Visual Arts (SVA), focusing on graphic design. Yet, motivated by the deep connection she shared with her friend from California, MJ chose to return to Cornell a year earlier than planned. She realized that delaying her return would mean less time spent with her cherished friends, especially since they were not just friends but soulmates to her. The trio had already signed a lease to share a living space for the upcoming fall semester to ensure they could maximize their time together.

Her Californian friend, a multifaceted talent, has captivated a broad audience with her drawing videos on YouTube, showcasing her diverse skills. Life as an architecture student at Cornell is notoriously demanding, with the relentless workload often leading to emotional breakdowns among students. This close-knit group of friends supports each other through the highs and lows of their rigorous academic journey, valuing their friendship and the solace it brings in their high-pressure environment.

My daughter has four more years like this, and I want to know if it is the right thing to do. Primarily, her health concerns me. Therefore, upon her return around May 23, I will ensure she rests and sleeps throughout the summer. MJ wishes she could store sleep like a battery when necessary, and she wishes there were two of her to manage everything.

As she goes through such an intense academic experience, it is hard to know whether this path is right for her. Nonetheless, she must develop resilience and determination to tackle future obstacles. Though Korean universities may present different situations, acknowledging students' global educational struggles remains crucial.

As a parent, worrying about your child's well-being is natural. However, offering support, understanding, and encouragement can significantly aid your daughter through these challenging years.

EPILOGUE

After writing this post, I texted my daughter to ask if she was sleepy. She replied that her body was hurting, and my heart ached for her.

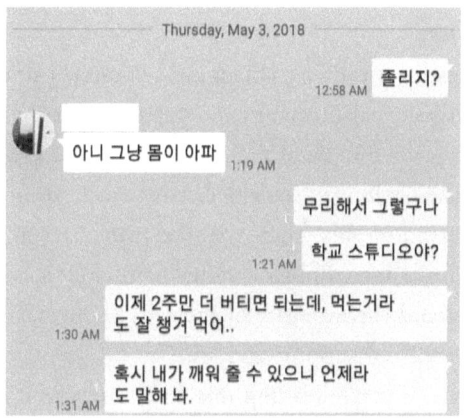

Image Caption: Message conversation between MJ and me.

Thursday, May 3, 2018:

Me: Are you sleepy?

MJ: No, my body just hurts.
Me: You must be pushing yourself too hard.
Are you at the school studio?
Just hang in there for two more weeks, and make sure to eat well.
If you need me to wake you up, let me know anytime.
She still needs to read my message. Instead, she might be lying in bed, feeling unwell.

I've realized something profound about love and responsibility in sharing these intimate moments with my daughter, MJ. To love someone deeply is to revel in joyful times and stand by them during their challenges — no matter how insurmountable they seem. As a father, my heart aches with each text of exhaustion and every call of frustration. Still, it also swells with pride for the resilient and fiercely ambitious young woman she's becoming.

In a world that relentlessly demands more, losing sight of one's limits is easy. It's even easier to overlook the quiet endurance that keeps us going daily. But if there's one thing I wish for MJ, it's that she understands the value of rest as much as the value of work — that she learns how to fuel her aspirations and recharge her soul.

As she prepares for another challenging semester, I find comfort in the little things: a text received, a call answered, a moment shared — even if it's just a fleeting one in the middle of a stressful night. Our lifelines are momentary triumphs in the prolonged struggle between aspirations and well-being.

To any parent reading this, know that the struggles you see today are but the forging fires for the incredible individual your child is becoming. We may not always understand the intensity of their experiences, but we can always offer the constancy of our support and love.

And to you, MJ, if you're reading this, know that your mother and I are immensely proud, even if you're too exhausted to realize it. You're not just storing up knowledge and skills for your future; you're storing up a reservoir of love and support from those who believe in you the most. So, remember you're never alone when the nights are long and the load feels unbearable. Hang in there, sweetheart. Two more weeks, and then you can rest.

A TEENAGER'S QUEST

OR JUSTICE

Penned February 9, 2019

This writing chronicles the transformative journey of my son YW from a curious teenager to a committed advocate for social justice, with a particular focus on his exploration of Latin culture and his efforts to support immigrants awaiting deportation in the United States.

YW started researching Latin culture and history a few years ago; he became interested in various issues he would typically have overlooked. He participated in Latin-related film festivals, and YW became interested in the lives of immigrants and became aware of the human rights and lives of minorities in the United States. Academic research is a process of discovering contemporary issues and ideas that other scholars have yet to be able to deal with before in the subject area one is exploring and theoretically uncovering them, unlike simply authoring articles at the level of the papers. This kind of research is an in-depth field of inquiry required for master's programs and above.

Caption: New York Public Library, Stephen A. Schwarzman Building. Copyright: New York Public Library.

YW delves into high-level research, submitting paper abstracts to various relevant summer vacation enduring a hellish routine. He could not understand why he had to dig through boring specialized academic books that he could not quite understand on a sweltering summer day. I bore the brunt of his complaints. On the one hand, he understood, but on the other hand, he could not understand the situation in which he had to lock himself in a stuffy hole in the New York Public Library Main Branch on 42nd Street in Manhattan. At the same time, his friends went on a cruise.

YW realizes he needs to improve his exceptional artistic talent or other overwhelming skills like his older sister. Therefore, he knew he could enter the university of his choice only when YW focused on the area he was best at and produced outstanding results. But he was too young to go through such hardships for such a thing. He traveled to New York every weekend during the semester. However, this effort didn't yield notable results for the entire year. He spent most of his time reprocessing in the library during vacations and breaks. The person who guided him was a professor teaching student at Princeton University.

Then, while YW spent a semester at a private school in Spain, he came back mentally mature. That year, in 2017, his research skills improved so much that he began digesting and arranging 40-50 pages daily (the time to read books in earnest is about 3 hours a day). Last summer, his advisor reached the point where he commented that YW was the best student he had ever had. Recently, the professor praised YW, suggesting that a career as an academic researcher would suit him well. Only after this development did YW focus on research during summer vacation. He usually finds time to travel to and from New York every Saturday. He spent most of his winter break at the New York Library Stephen A. Schwarzman Building on 42nd Street in Manhattan. Only something comes.

Caption: Bergen County Jail

I AM WRITING THIS right now from the waiting room of the Bergen County Jail. Currently, my son is visiting an inmate imprisoned here. So, of course, they will be conversing in Spanish.

First Friends NJ NY, a non-profit organization, assists undocumented individuals in the United States who are arrested and awaiting deportation. My son wanted to serve there. Participating in a First Friends NJ NY seminar and expressing your intention to join allows you to become a member. My family joined last year. Many individuals awaiting deportation from prison lack connections in the United States. First Friends NJ NY arranges pen pals with them, and if necessary, visits them directly at the prison and visits them to find ways to help.

YW is preparing to set up a First Friends club at his high school to raise funds for those waiting for deportation. A $2,000 bail can release some inmates. Upon release, they may find better ways to defend themselves and contact their families back in their country to ask for help. So, for those who are undocumented and incarcerated, bail is significant. My son is considering a fundraising plan to release ten inmates from his school. He would not have paid attention to these things if he had not researched that field in Manhattan.

During this spring break, he plans to visit an immigrant prison in Spain. He intends to make a documentary about the local situation, including interviews with local Red Cross volunteers. My son is still young, but I no longer treat him as a child. Instead, there are times when I feel that he is thinking more maturely than I do when I talk to him about an issue. As his father, it is a pleasure to see his spiritual growth.

As I watch my son mature into a committed advocate for justice, my feelings alternate between pride and awe. YW has grown not only in academic prowess but also in moral stature. He has come to understand that knowledge bears the responsibility of action. Sometimes, when we discuss various issues, he enlightens me as much as I hope I have inspired him.

CULTIVATING PASSION

Penned February 18, 2023

In 'Juggling Responsibilities,' I explored how my son YW's transformative journey under Professor John Glavin at Georgetown University shaped his vision as an aspiring screenwriter.

My son, YW, is in the final semester of his junior year at Georgetown University. And he has been consistent with his dream of becoming a screenwriter, producer, or director. His stage and screenwriting class from the previous fall semester significantly inspired him. This is because Professor John Glavin, who has been teaching the subject for several decades at this university, is truly a legend of this university. He has been a professor in the Department of English at this university since 1967, guiding stage and screenwriting for talented and enthusiastic students. Ryan Bacic's article about Professor Glavin, published in the Washington Post on December 3, 2017, highlights the following key points (Bacic, 2017). Professor John Glavin at Georgetown University has impacted his students academically and professionally. Known for his rigorous yet inspiring teaching approach, he has mentored many successful writers, including Jonathan Nolan, co-creator of 'Westworld' and co-writer of 'The Dark

Knight.' Nolan attributes his success crafting engaging stories and characters to Glavin's teachings. Professor Glavin challenges his students to elevate their writing skills and offers practical advice for succeeding in the competitive world of screenwriting. He maintains a close relationship with many former students, who often turn to him for guidance or collaboration on new projects. His instruction extends beyond mere technical skills, fostering creativity, confidence, and a disciplined approach to the craft. Thanks to his influence, many of his students have gone on to win awards and build successful careers in various writing fields.

One of my favorite drama series is "Westworld," co-written by Jonathan Nolan and his wife. He is also well known as the younger brother of film director Christopher Nolan. While listening to Professor Glavin's lectures, my son talked about his class to his parents. Despite being over eighty, Professor Glavin maintains perfect posture and consistently dons a business suit, a testament to the class's rigor. He said that every Sunday at 1:00 PM, his students must watch some films designated by the Professor on the screen on campus. However, if someone misses even once, the student can no longer participate in his class. For example, a Korean international student had to complete the course before graduating. He signed up for the class for the final semester but did not participate in watching the screen on the first day, so he could no longer participate in the class. Professor Glavin also said that when students submit their papers, they maintain the strictness of presenting documents in the format and binding. Professor Glavin specified, which makes it exceedingly difficult for students.

But YW told me about an episode while talking on the phone a few days ago. He has already been taking the Professor's class for the second semester. In the last lesson, a female student was 15 minutes late for class and did not bring a printout to turn in during that time. YW thought, "That's a big deal, man." The female student explained, "I couldn't bring the assignment because the printer malfunctioned." Surprisingly, the Professor accepted the excuse, saying, "That kind of thing is a common problem for me too."

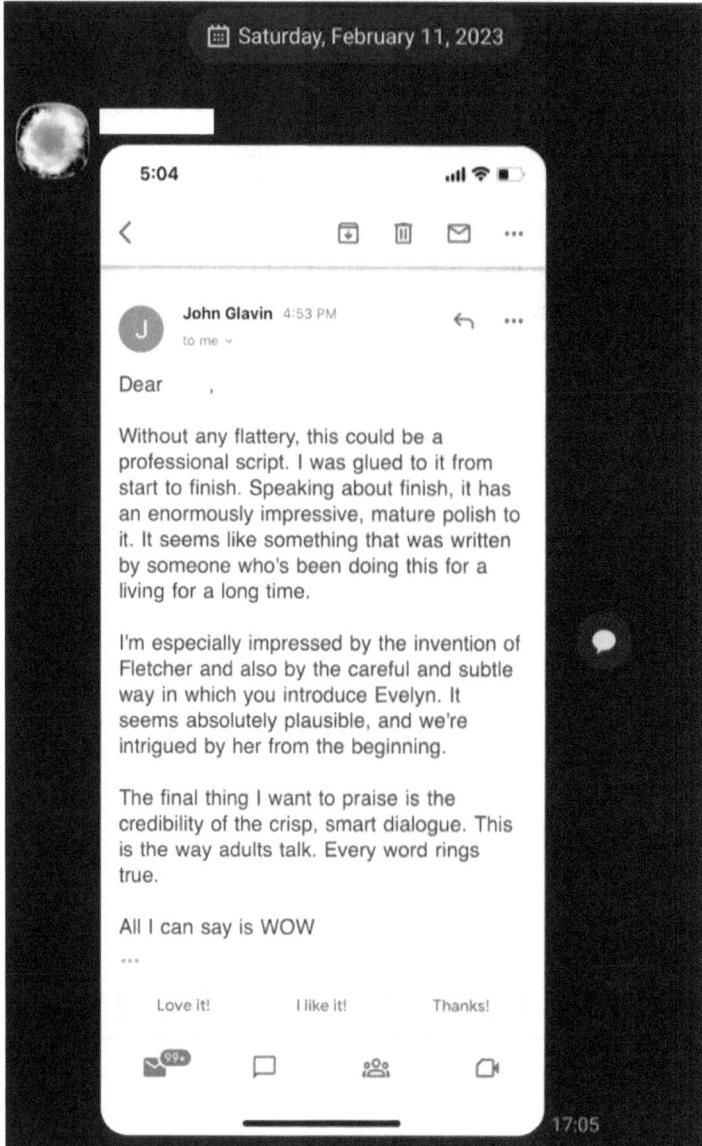

Caption: Professor Glavin's email

What was even more surprising was that when the students in the back row handed over the assignments to be submitted that day to the students in the front row, my son looked through the works and found that most of them were staples, let alone binding — even some assignments with titles written in pencil without covers. My son was still strictly following Professor Glavin's guidelines in the first class of the first semester. Ultimately, he understood that he was the only one adhering to the rules. He then expressed his approval and said he would keep following them because he had grown accustomed to them.

The Professor then singled out a student, inquiring, "You haven't scheduled a 1:1 meeting with me yet; when will you do it?" My son had delayed a one-on-one meeting with the Professor for a few weeks during the fall semester. He explained that he had postponed the meeting to prepare thoroughly for their discussion. As much as that, YW regards the Professor as a tight-fisted person.

YW holds immense respect and a bit of fear for Professor Glavin, driven by his desire for the Professor's acknowledgment. Therefore, whenever the Professor occasionally mentions the examples of his ex-students he produced during class, my son has a strong will to succeed later like them. To do that, he knows very well that it is possible to become the best disciple that Professor Glavin picks.

I read my son's feedback via email from Professor Glavin about his first writing and submission during the fall semester. Glavin seldom mentions the students' assignments but replies that he wants to praise YW's writing. His email encouraged my son immensely.

ADDITIONALLY, LAST SATURDAY, he sent me another screenshot. He read Professor Glavin's email to him and immediately sent it to me. YW must have told me that his Professor, whom he respected and was astute, had praised him. I cannot get more compliments than this.

When YW was in junior high school (11th grade), he could not concentrate and made big mistakes in some subjects. He wanted to go HYPSM (Harvard/Yale/Princeton/Stanford/MIT), which his parents wanted (of course, he desired). YW had an enormous burden on his heart that my son could not get into those universities. At the time, they accepted him into Vanderbilt University, UC Berkeley, UCLA, USC, and New York University; however, he either wait-listed or failed at the universities he wanted. Fortunately, YW is delighted with his college life at Georgetown University. At first, he struggled with his majors, such as Spanish, English, and American Studies. However, he finally finished the third year, listened to Professor Glavin's lectures, and seemed confident in his future career.

By coincidence, he has a scheduled internship at a Korean broadcasting program production company this summer. He will start to have hope for his future self in many ways. Of course, it is never easy because you must prepare for a long, unemployed life as a screenwriter or after graduation. Nevertheless, I'm proud of my son, who firmly committed to his chosen career path from an early age.

The fact that Korean culture is attracting global attention in various fields will also greatly help my son, who is both Korean and American. When YW came to the United States at four, he was familiar with the American education system from kindergarten until now. However, he can speak fluently and understand Korean culture to some extent, which will also significantly boost him. When my son once refused to talk to Koreans, it helped a lot that I took him to Korea for a month and gave him a branch to make him proud of Korea.

Whether you were born in the United States or grew up as an immigrant, if you lose your Korean identity, you forfeit your American identity as well. Because when you were born, you were destined to inherit Korean blood, and you became an American because you grew up in the United States. Among Americans, all races, except Native Americans, have their roots in their country. For instance, Italian Americans, Jewish Americans, British Americans, German Americans, and others draw their heritage from the lands of their ancestors.

Therefore, on American soil, there are only Native Americans in the true sense of the word. So, among Americans, the only difference is whether their ancestors immigrated to this land 30 years ago or two hundred years ago. To lose one's roots in one's homeland is to lose a part of one's identity.

I look forward to seeing my son grow as a writer, embrace his cultural heritage as a Korean-American, and add another layer to his storytelling under Professor Glavin's mentorship. Although his future may be uncertain, the skills and perspective he has gained will provide a solid foundation for his future.

PART FOUR

THE EVOLUTION OF
PHOTOGRAPHY

Penned December 13, 2017

In Professor Noah Epstein's class, 'A History of Photography from Da-guerreotype to Digital,' we explored vital figures who shaped the history of photography, tracing its evolution from daguerreotypes to digital forms. As Edgar Allan Poe's 'The Daguerreotype' illustrates, people initially found early photographic inventions simply marvelous (Giordano, n.d.). However, people with intellectual curiosity have changed their surroundings and the world through their cameras. Specific photographs have garnered significant public attention, achieving more dramatic impact than any other medium. Also, many photographers have devoted their lives to advocating for the recognition of photography as an art form comparable to different artistic disciplines. Some people have played an enormous role in the development of humanity by recording and accusing the world of cameras and devotion to their beliefs. The advancements of these photographs are developing into new art forms after other fields of art combine and fuse with them. Now, it is impossible to predict how the digital age will evolve. In the digital era, capturing, expressing, and sharing photographs with the public has become accessible. The question then arises: how will professional photographers establish their domain and influence the masses in this new era? Yet, the field of photography is continuously developing and evolving.

As I mentioned before, in the early days of the invention of photography, people started expressing strange things with mere designs. However, certain photographers have made significant historical contributions by documenting and altering the world and communicating with the public. Mathew Brady (NA, 2021) and Alexander Gardner (Wikipedia contributors, 2023a) were pioneers in realizing the purpose of documentary and photojournalism.

THIS PHOTOGRAPH EXEMPLIFIES my consistent habit of documenting the life around me. In 1988, I organized an event in an organization where I led the group. After a long time, this single photograph proved to be an essential event in Korea. Gardner (*Historic Photographs by Alexander Gardner - Antietam National Battlefield:* USDI, n.d.) and Brady, who recorded the Civil War, had a noteworthy influence by systematically recording historical events (NA, 2021). I made detailed records of the event at the time. However, although it is not a major historical event, it remains essential in at least one area.

However, I can't discount Alfred Stieglitz as a photographer who created works of art, even though he was also a street photographer who documented people's daily lives (Hostetler, n.d). There was another photographer with the same viewpoint, overlapping with Stieglitz. He is Eugène Atget (ICP, n.d.-a.), who records the neglected streets of Paris and the buildings that will soon disappear.

THIS PHOTO CONTAINS a couple living in an isolated, high-mountain village. The couple, weak enough to rely on canes, sit in front of their house in the afternoon sun. The woman holds a cigarette, and the man opens his mouth, challenging them to breathe with their small dog beside them. A doghouse uses a large yellow barrel. It made the dog a bowl of stone, often found in the area, sitting heavily between the house's walls and the doghouse. Eugène Atget links this photo of me to the ordinary people on the streets of Paris.

I TOOK TIME and tried to get one of these photographs in the best position. I waited for the most suitable time to shoot. And I had only a smartphone, so I plugged it into my mind with little skill. I liked that place. It was the most beautiful and noble place I have ever experienced. This picture reminds me of "The Hand of Man, 1902" by Alfred Stieglitz.

Paul Strand tried to show the city's health and hope for the future, centering on Manhattan (ICP, n.d.-b.). I see some of the Empire State Building on my condo rooftop on Manhattan's 30th Street. Every time, I am proud that I belong to New York City, the center of the world. I photographed the building going on for almost one hundred years. Though not as much as Paul Strand felt one hundred years ago, New York City is still the center of the world.

AN ENVIRONMENTALIST, ANSEl Adams (TAAG, 2023), put his magnificent natural beauty in his camera-like decorative paintings. The entire island of Lanzarote has been the UNESCO Biosphere Reserve since 1993. However, this photograph shows a different region producing vines using volcanic rocks. The uniqueness of nature is genuinely abundant.

EDWARD WESTON (EF, n.d.) was a photographer who stepped up his photographic art by expressing nature and objects beautifully. For example, he took fruits and vegetables as still life, linked to Laura Letinsky's work (Laura Letinsky, n.d.).

TIMOTHY O'SULLIVAN RECORDED the Civil War as a documentary photographer (TJPGMC, n.d.). However, after the war, he moved west and recorded nature. He was the first photographer to understand nature architecturally. So, I had the experience of going up to a mountain and looking analytically at the spectacular view before my eyes. At the end of the screen, the sky and the sea were in contact. And there were multi-storied roads and dots along the massive valley from the coast.

MOREOVER, THEY LAYERED the ridges together and formed a vast valley; a small lake is tinted green at the bottom. On top of the mountain were all kinds of flowers, including cactuses. It was like a giant orchestra of nature. O'Sullivan would have felt the greatness of spirit in the western wilderness. So, it conveys to us the belief that humans and nature can harmonize.

THERE IS A SECTION like "Body Farm during Sally Mann's work (SM, n.d.). I took the photographs to reveal the cause of the body's death. This photo shows an abandoned house that was left unchecked 30 years ago. This family house was a decent mental hospital people had abandoned for decades and was about one hundred feet from the hospital building. I forcibly opened the door and went into the house. In a room that seemed to have been used for storage, the belongings of the forgotten individual remained untouched. Such neglected items appeared to tell the situation of the forgotten person. A single picture can tell numerous stories. Sally Mann's "Body Farm" section describes the dead account.

LAURA LETINSKY (LCA, 2014) elaborately and beautifully works on people's everyday lives. Families enjoy a delightful conversation while watching T.V. or listening to music near the fireplace. However, people need to pay more attention to burning firewood. This photograph shows warm attention to the firewood, showing people do not care about others.

THIS PHOTO SHOWS the spring of my birth home, where I grew up. In the house's backyard, the Koreans call Jangdokdae (Wikipedia contributors, 2022b). Koreans make various spices for healthy and delicious food through this method. For this purpose, there are big pots for storing soy sauce, miso, and Gochujang. Historically, it has played a significant role in Korean food. However, as urbanization has taken place, these kindergartens are almost disappearing. Therefore, it may be a clue to my grandson's understanding of Korean culture long after this photo of me.

Photography transcends the mere act of pressing the shutter. Photographs gain significant value when they share the photographer's vision and feelings with others. Furthermore, if it could connect to future generations, it would become even more meaningful. Edgar Allan Poe (Poemuseum, 2018) recalls what he saw when people first invented photographic techniques. As we study the history of photography through this class, we have learned that photographers have kept their work's meaning distinct from that moment (Laurent, 2017). Instead, they pressed the shutter for their community and loved ones. As global citizens, photographers channel their beliefs and talents through their cameras, expressing love for, protecting, and preserving nature, linking the past, present, and future.

HEALTHY FUTURE

Penned April 12, 2020

THE MOST URGENT ISSUE

Last night, I had a lengthy phone call with my friend SJ, whom I've known since my early twenties in Seoul. She has been running a private after-school academy in Gangbuk almost her entire life. She also majored in education; from then until now, she has only taught children. Therefore, she serves as a teacher, mentor, and entrepreneur in the educational field. We are lifelong friends, but even if we don't talk on the phone or meet each other, we live by guessing roughly how each other lives. After quite some time, our phone conversation began with personal anecdotes. Then, naturally, it moved to concerns about the future of our descendants and us. The discussion focused on how Korean society can remove the darkness of the future and move forward to a community of bright hope.

This article summarizes what I have said while talking with SJ. This article will be the most macroscopic alternative at present. The pressing question is: what is the foremost issue in Korean society, and how can we address it?

In Korea, the presidential election, held every five years, is the most crucial political event. According to the constitution, the most powerful place is the elected president. The President of Korea represents the country externally as the head of government and the head of the country. The president's constitutional authority to appoint critical public officials is also broad and robust. As a result, the nation's destiny hinges on the president's vision and decisions. Voters strive to select candidates who align with their interests. This is especially true for groups rather than individuals. Specific unions, alumni, and hometown associations intertwine their interests in the Korean presidential election scene like a spider's web.

Candidates also identify advantageous points among interest groups and tailor their pledges accordingly. Korean presidential candidates' detailed and elaborate election pledges underline their significance. Embroider colorful words that cover all voters in their favor. For example, the collection of promises of the With Democratic Party of Korea, which is currently in power, can be viewed as an e-book, a whopping 389 pages. They must furnish a comprehensive blueprint to all government departments, incorporating all critical details without superfluous elements. They must then implement a plan accordingly. Even if that were the case, it wouldn't address the fundamental issues of Korean society. For example, if we randomly asked twelve people about their ideal society, their responses might include the following ideas:

- Eradicating Corruption
- Eradicating Corruption
- Securing Fairness
- Creating a Democratic/Civil Rights Society
- Creating Jobs
- Securing Economic Growth Engines
- Local Equalization Policy
- Addressing the Low Birth Rate
- Civil Livelihood/Welfare/Education Solution
- Peaceful Country
- Society Safe
- Gender Inequality Resolution
- Cultural Enrichment

In the spring of 2016, most Korean society supported the critical pledges of Moon Jae-in, the current president, during his presidential campaign. The main goal of these promises was to secure votes from individuals interested in each industry. Similar promises are standard among other political parties and independent candidates. However, this approach will remain the status quo of Korean society, even if repeated ten more times, because it fails to tackle the core issues. The influence of a party's ideology or character pervades from the central government down to regional levels, rendering election promises by politicians, no matter how appealingly presented, ineffective. If voters continue to be swayed by such superficial pledges, addressing Korean society's fundamental challenges will remain daunting.

WHAT ARE THE critical issues in Korean society that demand our immediate focus? The crux of the issue lies in education. Previously, we looked at the significant areas of the twelve pledges made by the current administration, but the problem lies in education. Adopting a macro perspective, rather than focusing narrowly, is essential for securing the future of our society and nation. Until now, solutions to educational problems have been tackled from a microscopic viewpoint. They have improvised most policies to achieve short-term goals within the administration's term or to set up significant barriers to prevent rapid changes by subsequent administrations, even in the event of a transition.

However, meaningful educational results often require a decade or more of patient waiting. Growing a tree takes years or even decades, but how can it not take enough time to develop a person? Thus, any education policy catering to the ideology or preferences of a specific regime is likely to be less effective or even counterproductive.

In this article, I won't dwell on the shortcomings of past education policies, as there is a consensus that improvements are necessary. Thus, our focus shifts to fundamentally resolving this issue. Suppose the reader of this article is a parent with a toddler, a parent with a kindergartener, an elementary school student, a parent with a middle school student, a parent with a high school student, or a parent with a college student. In that case, they need help figuring out what the problem is from their point of view. Will be able to raise

What is the problem and how to solve it? Here are some conversations I had with my friend SJ.

CONVERSATION WITH SJ

Me: Is your son in the army now? When are you discharged?

SJ: The year after next year. He went this summer.

Me: Okay. Your son's going to have a challenging time with his military life.

SJ: His army life is amazingly comfortable these days. He lives with about eight people in an inner class, beds far apart, a large TV, and many washing machines. So, their military life is wonderfully comfortable. It's better than I thought, so I was surprised.

Me: Your son loves music, but I hope he will do what he wants after military service.

SJ: Yeah. But he still doesn't know what to do. When I was young, I used to challenge myself with things I didn't understand much, but he didn't try to do anything. Because my husband and I make him comfortable by giving him everything, he attempts to settle for it. Various club activities are essential when you're in school, but kids need more time for that. It's just passively driven by the tight time limit. They are on their cell phones when they have free time.

Me: That's right. Didn't you have many club activities when you were in school?

SJ: Right.

Me: You're a really great person that I've been watching all this time. But I don't know if we can expect kids to have that personality these days.

SJ: Ha ha ha. Thank you, friend. I read an article that said 70% of college students these days have mental problems. It's shocking. And it should be enough. It would help if you discovered how amazing it is to do prior learning because elementary school students are solving high school math.

Me: No, how is that possible? Of course, among elementary school students, we can gift math to people who can do it well enough, but most are ordinary children.

SJ: Right. However, to some extent, it is possible due to the ongoing coercion of children into studying. Some time ago, a relative who lives in Seocho-dong, Gangnam, called me and complained. Her kid is just in kindergarten, and all the kids around her are studying math. Once, her child took an assessment to enroll in a private math academy but failed because of inferior performance. It means that even kindergarteners are already in an era where they know how to solve mathematics in first to third grade since the reality is that her neglects, like her, cannot afford to study math, even at the private academy in her neighborhood.

Me: Really shocking. Korean students are really good at math, but there are only so many scholars who excel in math compared to others. Of course, there are geniuses in every field. Intellectuals stand out in any circumstance, but the vast majority are ordinary people like us, and that's normal. In Korea, children excel in math, leading to an ironic phenomenon. When they enroll in American universities, they find the math subjects remarkably easy, almost like they are being given away for free. Having experienced this, Korean students tend to underestimate the mathematics level at universities in the United States. However, as they progress into master's programs, they gradually lose their edge and fall behind their peers. Consequently, the number of Korean mathematics majors advancing to doctoral programs has significantly decreased. Therefore, it is common for American students who could have improved in undergraduate mathematics to stand out powerfully. Why?

SJ: Because there is no creativity. They lost interest.

Me: Yes. It is possible to respond efficiently to diverse types of problems by solving a lot of mathematics. However, when it goes beyond that, the level is different. Then, of course, you must go crazy because you really like math to reach a certain level in that discipline, but how many students who have studied in Korea are so good that they go crazy? Very few, or both.

SJ: Right. After the school classes, the kids do forced self-learning and then come home and do private tutoring. And when there are no self-learning classes or holidays at school, they spend all those precious days clinging to private academies, tutoring, or building specs. Among my fellow academy directors is a senior who graduated from Seoul National University's College of Engineering. Many of his peers have so-called envy jobs, such as doctors and lawyers. But when he sees them, his doctor friends must look at the patients constantly grimacing in pain, and his lawyer friends must make up plausible stories for scammers and criminals. It's their job. Of course, lawyers also work for wrongful victims. My point is that the jobs everyone in Korea prefers could be better, and how dangerous and pitiful it is to apply for such a university regardless of one's aptitude.

Me: If people ask what the most important thing is, they will answer that it is a matter of making a good living. That's right. Eating well is the most fundamental issue. However, among the problems of living well, people who have children or those who will have children in the future are most worried about, and the part that costs a lot of money is their children's education. Therefore, even if the actual issue of eating and living is the most important, in the end, the importance of children's education is absolute. Even that kind of thing is a burden, so it happens that you don't get married or don't have children, or even if you give birth, you only have one. The rapid decline of the young population is a real problem that is very dark for Korea's future. No matter how specific fields compete for the lead in the world, society can only survive if the young population is rapidly declining. Therefore, the issue of education is of paramount importance.

SJ: You'll be happy because your kids are all doing well.

Me: That's right. I talked with my wife about it a few days ago about what we would have chosen for our children's education if we had continued to live in Korea. It didn't come to mind at first. At the time, my daughter was attending an alternative elementary school. But as her parents, we were curious if we would have kept her through her alternative high school. We weren't sure how happy she would have grown up if we had put her in the standard public education system. One thing is for sure: We agreed she was still studying art because she is gifted and enthusiastic about it.

SJ: Really, I don't know where to start. My academy also runs a program to develop children's creativity and character. However, neither the parents nor the children are interested. They only care about raising their school grades. However, such a program cannot teach in groups of four or five people, like teaching academic subjects. The one-on-one time required is a significant financial burden, but as an educator, I cannot simply ignore these children. The lives of Korean children appear bleak and pitiful. They constantly consume information on their phones during their free moments. News of an elementary school student making ten million won monthly on YouTube, often through activities like Mukbang, captures their attention. When peers produce such content, it resonates strongly with them, influencing their consumption habits and aspirations.

Me: Children turn into defenseless consumers of advertisements. YouTube and Facebook are incredibly popular in Korea. My kids have Facebook accounts solely for keeping in touch; they don't actively post or engage with the platform. However, in America, many teenagers do use it actively. Thus, it's the older generation that primarily engages with Facebook.

SJ: There are no kids in Korea who don't use Facebook. They always hold it in their hands and review information about friends of friends and friends of friends. They are always at war with their parents because they waste all their precious time on useless things. When students come home from school or the private academy, they don't take their bags off properly, and they don't take their eyes off their phones.

Me: But really, I can't blame the kids. It's fun, but you can't force yourself to stop it. However, society does not offer an alternative. I feel a lot while raising my children here.

SJ: You are amazing. Going to another country, your daughter is studying at the best architecture university in the world, and your son's future is bright.

Me: Yes. It's just that I'm lucky. I've raised my son from the age of four and my daughter from the age of nine here, so I'm experiencing real American education.

EDUCATION IS A BIG PLAN FOR 100 YEARS

My conversation with SJ, a leading figure in Korean education, left a deep impression on me. Korean society is deviating more than I had previously thought. Political parties, driven by their ideologies, often disband and merge, occasionally altering the education system to garner votes. In particular, political parties in Korea are not as stable as in the United States, so they have repeated a strange political phenomenon in which we repeat dissolution and formation every few years for decades. Thus, more than any other factor, Korean political parties pose the greatest threat to Korea's present and future progress.

Consequently, political interference should be absent in establishing and implementing Korea's education policy. However, the reality is that politicians are the key actors in making laws and enforcing them. Moreover, they persistently attempt to influence future voters to seize future power. Therefore, they are constantly intervening in the educational world.

A country's education policy must not be sacrificed to political greed, as it is pivotal in nurturing future generations and directly impacts the nation's rise or decline. Formulating an education policy demands long-term planning spanning 10, 20, and even 30 years. Entrusting such a crucial task to politicians focused on short-term results spanning just four or five years is impractical. The education policy of a country should remain consistent, irrespective of which party holds central or regional power.

Education policy should ensure stable continuity regardless of regime change. Our ancestors wisely stated that education is a 100-year plan. Given that education looks a century ahead, we must devise policies with a future-oriented vision. Therefore, it must be a plan that is effective and vital in the long term. A country's long-term goal of education should not change in a brief time to support the ideology of a specific regime, nor should we neglect it because it cannot be effective within the terms of any extraordinary power.

However, this article does not intend to present any grandiose education plan. In the conversation with SJ, I showed above what you, who live in Korea, would choose as a critical keyword. It may depend on your values and interests; however, the above conversations do not mention the keywords I value most. First, it is the physical strength of students. If Korean society is healthy and Korean culture is to nurture future generations properly, an education policy that values students' physical force is necessary. Of course, Koreans reading this article will not agree, saying that my argument is absurd. I would disagree with that assertion if I lived only in Korea, like you, without practical experience.

PHYSICAL POWER IS A NATIONAL POWER

One of the slogans I often heard when I was young was, "Physical Power Is a National Power." It was the driving force that brought Korea, the poorest country in the world, into an advanced country. Fitness isn't just about increasing physical education time at school. Physical fitness makes all members of society healthy. The adage "A healthy mind resides in a healthy body" is accurate. This slogan of Korea in the 1970s, which I had never thought of while authoring this article, fits very well with the point I am trying to make. Achieving any educational goal by exhausting our children's physical strength is doomed to fail, and we should never glorify it. Nobody wants excessive studying to mar their children's lives. The key is learning to balance academic work with physical development. Sadly, in Korea, people often overlook the negative impacts of education due to their circumstances. Yet, the truth is that the education system can harm children's physical and mental health.

What are your thoughts on the case mentioned in our previous conversation with SJ, where a preschooler was denied a spot in a private cram school math class due to competition from peers who had already completed elementary school grades 1-3?

If you think enrolling in another academy that matches your child's class is okay, you're missing the point. Most people believe that teaching elementary math should begin when your child is in pre-k or kindergarten. However, you know the reality of education in Korea surrounding you is different. So, we all created an environment for our children to focus on their studies so that our children could get into good universities. Some even went to prestigious universities in the United States and would have thought it had rewarded them all these years. But, like the case of doctors and lawyers pointed out by SJ, does the current way make our future generations happy?

A research paper published ten years ago found that 44% of Korean students entering prestigious American universities drop out, which shocked us. On October 3, 2008, reporter Park Si-soo of The Korea Times wrote, "44% of Korean Ivy League Students Quit Course Halfway," Known (Park, 2008). It is what Samuel S. Kim revealed on Friday, October 1 of that year, in his doctoral dissertation at Columbia University, "First- and Second-Generation Conflict in Education of the Asian American Community." From 1985 to 2007, Dr. Kim taught at 14 top universities in the United States (Harvard, Yale, Cornell, Columbia, Stanford, UC Berkeley, UC Davis, Amherst College, Duke, Georgetown, Brown, Dartmouth, and UPenn). After tracking 1,400 Korean international students enrolled at Princeton, 44% claim to have given up their studies. He claims this proportion is significantly higher than 34% of American students, 25% of Chinese students, and 21% of Indian students. Dr. Kim tracked and uncovered 23 years of data to support his doctoral thesis. Although someone published his view ten years ago, many Korean students still enroll in these prestigious universities and give up their studies in the middle.

As of 2007, Korean students enrolled in undergraduate and graduate programs at prestigious universities in the United States accounted for 6,667 out of 62,392 total Korean international students in the U.S., representing 10.7%. This statistic is notable because Korea's ratio of international students is twenty times higher than that of India and China. Reporter Park (2008) highlighted this trend by noting that 37 Korean students were studying at Harvard, representing the third-largest national group after Canada and the

United Kingdom. This reflects Korea's strong emphasis on elite education and its citizens' significant presence in top global academic institutions.

However, Dr. Kim argues that the high dropout rate of international students in Korea results from their children studying under the pressure of their parents rather than participating in extracurricular activities themselves. Self-driven extracurricular activities are essential for international students to assimilate into American society and secure employment. Dr. Kim's thesis reveals that Korean students dedicate 75% of their time to studying and only 25% to community service or extracurricular activities.

In contrast, Dr. Kim argues, American students and students from other countries tend to allocate academics and other activities equally. For example, according to statistics of senior executives of Fortune 500 companies in the United States, there are 10% of Indians and 5% of Chinese. In contrast, Dr. Kim argues that only 0.3% of Koreans have eunuchs. In an interview with reporter Park of the Hankook Ilbo, Dr. Kim expressed his opinion.

I've seen Korean students become isolated from their American communities as they focus on their studies. To succeed in America, you must give up what they used you to in Korea.

Although I did not do research and analysis to draft a research paper on this field like Dr. Kim, I have my own opinion on this issue based on the experience I have gained from bringing my children to the United States and sending them from pre-K to university. Why do so many Korean international students drop out of their studies at prestigious universities with such fierce competition? Why do Korean students graduate with excellent grades but cannot adapt to American society and return home to Korea? I searched variously through the university library to check the entirety of Dr. Kim's thesis, but I could not find it. Therefore, it is impossible to refute or quote the contents of his thesis directly. However, while respecting the results of his research, I disagree with him on why the rate of Korean students dropping out of prestigious American universities is high and what to do to prevent it.

THEN, WHY IS the dropout rate of Korean students at American universities so high? First of all, I want to point out stamina. Of course, my answer will be absurd. But this answer is accurate. Students who completed high school in Korea and then entered prestigious U.S. universities have exerted considerable effort. In other words, they've been engaged in continuous study since childhood. Of course, there will be physical education classes at school. Even if you keep that time, you can never compensate for the physical strength of students who cling to studying from early morning until dawn. However, teenagers possess inherent physical resilience, allowing them to cope for a year or two, even at prestigious universities like Harvard. However, the more they go up to the juniors and seniors, the more they feel the limits of their physical strength.

On the other hand, people who went to school in the United States have different physical strengths. Those who have only experienced this in Korea and have not raised children directly in the United States will not be able to understand my argument. I will now explain why the physical strength of students from Korea differs from that of students from the United States and why physical fitness is vital to successful college completion.

The saying' Physical Power Is a National Power' I mentioned above is true. Weak physical strength inevitably leads to diminished national power. Therefore, physical force should develop naturally from an early age. However, achieving this in the Korean environment proves challenging. Having grown up in Korea and raised children there until their early elementary years. And since 2005, I have raised a 4-year-old and a 9-year-old in the United States. My first child is attending university, and my second one is in his senior year of high school. In the meantime, I enrolled in an online university in 2008, majored in American Studies and International Relations, and received first prize at the graduation ceremony in 2011. This year, I graduated from Fairleigh Dickinson University (FDU) in the U.S. with a business major, receiving the Dean's Award. To that extent, it is a belief I gained while raising my children and experiencing myself in the field of study.

AMERICAN SPORTS EDUCATION EXPERIENCE

When raising my kids in America, my most memorable experience was sports. I have always marveled at and been thankful for the town government's providing opportunities for high-quality sports education to kindergarten children. Thanks to this, my son has experienced almost two distinct types of sports by the time he finishes elementary school. He has played golf, football, soccer, baseball, basketball, swimming, lacrosse, tennis, and squash. Individuals played some sports, while the town-managed teams played others. Unfortunately, my son hasn't demonstrated any unique talent or passion for sports. In my son's case, he was highly interested in soccer, so when he was in elementary school, he participated in the summer soccer camp held at the United States Military Academy, participated in the soccer team run by the town, and played away games. Then, when he failed to place in the best class he wanted in the annual tryout (a test to determine his potential for the game), he lost interest and quietly quit.

On the other hand, children recognized for their potential through such a process can continue to exercise even after entering middle school. Therefore, they can be assigned to school sports classes by level, even after high school. In addition, children who like sports sometimes run as athletes seasonally. In the United States, seasons divide high school sports. For example, fall sports include cross-country, football, golf (women), tennis (women), volleyball (women), and water polo (men and women). Winter sports include basketball (men's and women's), cheerleading, dance, soccer (men's and women's), and wrestling. On the other hand, they classify spring sports as baseball, golf (men), lacrosse (men and women), softball, swimming and diving, tennis (men), track and field, and volleyball (men). Therefore, in the case of students who like sports and are talented in sports, they are also active as players in all seasons.

In the case of my son, he has been a squash player since middle school and started with the purpose of going to the best private high school in the United States, such as Phillips Academy. And in fact, prestigious private high schools select many students with talent in sports. The reason is that the first is to get superior results in the league competitions of prestigious private high schools. It is much easier for excellent athletes to get admission opportunities from the best universities. In other words, it is easy for outstanding athletes to attend excellent universities, so prestigious private high schools prefer such students when they select first-year students.

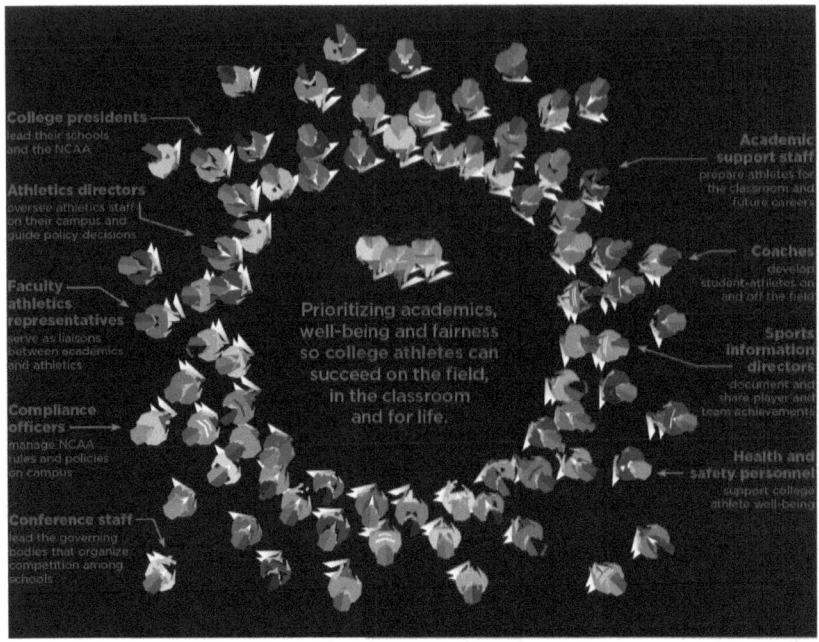

College presidents
lead their schools
and the NCAA

Athletics directors
oversee athletics staff
on their campus and
guide policy decisions

Faculty
athletics
representatives
serve as liaisons
between academics
and athletics

Compliance
officers
manage NCAA
rules and policies
on campus

Conference staff
lead the governing
bodies that organize
competition among
schools

Academic
support staff
prepare athletes for
the classroom and
future careers

Coaches
develop
student-athletes on
and off the field

Sports
information
directors
document and
share player and
team achievements

Health and
safety personnel
support college
athlete well-being

Prioritizing academics,
well-being and fairness
so college athletes can
succeed on the field,
in the classroom
and for life.

Image credit: NCAA.

SPORTS ACTIVITIES ARE BENEFICIAL FOR HIGHER EDUCATION

Then, from now on, I will explain in earnest why there are many advantages for active student-athletes in the United States. The United States has a non-profit organization called The National Collegiate Athletic Association (NCAA). One thousand one hundred seventeen universities in the United States are members. It is a crucial organization for American college athletics that cooperates with one hundred athletic conferences and forty athletic organizations. The organization has nearly 500,000 collegiate athletes on 19,750 teams. They divided into divisions 1 through 3 and held 90 NCAA championships in twenty-four sports. For example, Harvard University has forty-two varsity sports, sixty-six club sports, thirty-two houses, and sixteen freshman leagues. Five hundred twenty-five thousand people visit the school annually for these sports activities. According to Harvard University, up to 80 percent of students participate in some sport, and nearly 100 percent cheer or support their games (SLA, n.d.).

The sports events of Harvard's varsity teams are as follows: baseball, basketball, crew, cross-country, fencing, field hockey, football, golf, ice hockey, lacrosse, rugby, sailing, skiing, soccer, softball, squash, swimming, diving, tennis, track and field, volleyball, water polo, and wrestling (HU, 2023). One thousand two hundred thirty-nine people (726 men and 513 women) are active in thirty-five sports teams. That's 18.5% of Harvard's 6,700 undergraduate students (Wikipedia contributors, 2023c). It is to select about 310 first-year students out of an average of 1,675 students per year for the college sports team. This selection is called recruiting. American universities support early and regular admissions, including students selected through recruiting in early entry. With Harvard, the class of 2022 (students graduating four years after admission in 2022). Therefore, in the 2018 admissions process, Harvard passed 964 students through early admission and 998 through regular admission. Out of 2,056 students, the university has enrolled about 1,665 students, including approximately 310 sports athletes, making up 85% of the total. Depending on your academic ability, you can take the same subjects as regular students. However, many of them must take unique courses designed separately. Universities provide exceptional guidance to these students so they do not perform poorly. It is why only some players are good at sports while having poor academic abilities in Ivy League universities, where they have to do both simultaneously because of such a system.

On the other hand, athletes at large state universities known for their sports programs can balance athletic activities with academics due to the relatively lower academic demands. This article emphasizes that excelling in sports while maintaining good academic standing can simplify admission to top U.S. universities, including Ivy League schools. However, gaining admission to a university like Harvard without athletic involvement generally requires a high school diploma and a perfect SAT score. According to NCES data for 2009-2010, there were 23,176 public and, as analyzed by the Washington Post (Mathews, 2011) from 2007-2008 data, 7,341 private high schools in the U.S., totaling 30,517 high schools. This suggests that at least 30,000 top graduates compete for only 1,600 spots at Harvard yearly, with about 310 reserved for athletes. Seats are also filled by remarkable musicians, artists, actors, writers, and Olympiad medalists in STEM fields, as well as legacy admissions and children of faculty and alumni. The Crimson reports that applicants tied to financial donors receive preferential treatment, with more than 10% of the class of 2019 on the Dean's list, indicating a significantly higher admission rate for these applicants than the general pass rate.

Considering that sports scholarship students account for roughly 18.5% of admissions, donations influence another 10%, and a variety of exceptional admissions criteria fill the next 50%, about 70% of admissions slots are effectively pre-allocated. This situation leaves a highly competitive battle for the remaining 30% of spots, equating to approximately five hundred positions. The lawsuit that the Asian Group filed further delineates the complexity of this competition, revealing intricate admissions classifications based on race, region, individual schools, and countries.

Therefore, even if you graduate from high school with top grades and have perfect grades, including the SAT, you can never guarantee to pass Harvard. In the case of Korean students, it reassigned them within the number assigned to Asian countries. According to Dr. Kim's research, as of 2007, there were 37 Korean students enrolled in Harvard's undergraduate and graduate schools, and there were about twenty-five undergraduates alone. This group is only 0.37% of the total 6,700 undergraduate students. Even if all thirty-seven students are undergraduates, it is only 0.55%. Therefore, about 6 to 9 Korean students enter the school every year. Why is this number so significant? Students aspiring to Harvard in Korea are not in competition with American high school graduates or those applying from Europe, South America, or Africa. It is a competition between applicants from Korea and Korean applicants worldwide, including the United States.

ADMISSION CHANCE FOR KOREAN APPLICANTS WITH NO SPORTS ACTIVITIES

Hence, the admissions committee reserves approximately 18.5% of admissions for sports scholarship students, allocates 10% of admissions based on donations, and fills the remaining 50% through various outstanding entries. Consequently, approximately 70% of applicants receive access in some form.

In comparison, tens of thousands of applicants (some five hundred people) fiercely compete for the remaining 30%. Moreover, the current lawsuit filed by the Asian Group reveals more complex and detailed admissions classifications, including classifications based on race, region, school, and country.

Thus, even if you graduate from high school with top grades and have perfect rates, including the SAT, you can never guarantee to pass Harvard. In the case of Korean students, they reassigned them within the number assigned to Asian countries. According to Dr. Kim's research, as of 2007, there were 37 Korean students enrolled in Harvard's undergraduate and graduate schools, and there were about twenty-five undergraduates alone. This group is only 0.37% of the total 6,700 undergraduate students. Even if all thirty-seven students are undergraduates, it is only 0.55%. Therefore, about 6 to 9 Korean students enter the school every year. Why is this number so significant? Students aspiring to Harvard in Korea are not in competition with American high school graduates or those applying from Europe, South America, or Africa. It is a competition between applicants from Korea and Korean applicants worldwide, including the United States.

However, if Korean applicants fit under 70% of the above, their competition is even fiercer. Therefore, if you win the Korean competition, you have to compete with students from Asian countries. If you go one step further, you will compete again with all the applicants for international students. However, it no longer competes with non-Korean applicants who have completed middle and high school in the United States. This is because universities mostly pre-determinate the ratio of international students. They decide within the limits of that ratio for each continent, then for each country, and again for each high school. Therefore, the fiercest competitor is closest if there are multiple applicants to Harvard from the same school. That's why selecting many people from one school is impossible since only a few can choose.

These selection criteria also apply to US high school applicants. Each of the fifty states sets a certain number of candidates. And they subdivide each state into regions. For example, New Jersey divides New Jersey into northern, central, and southern parts, assigning each area a selection person. Each high school sets a limit on the number of applicants. In addition, they make the selection by applying a range of factors, such as race and background, school grades, SAT or ACT scores, extracurricular activities, letters of recommendation, and interviews. Therefore, the closest competitor is, of course, the one most similar to oneself. It is an actual competition regarding school, race, region, etc.

Hence, you will benefit greatly if you can get admission to sports in the United States. Even if you are an international student, you receive a full scholarship and unique benefits from the school. But why do we treat athletes so favorably? The actual goal is to unite the current students and, at the same time, continue to receive donations from alumni. In addition, Ivy League universities compete with each other by holding many competitions and risking their pride. Therefore, it is significant for one's home school to win against a rival school. Therefore, running a sports team may be a more critical strategy than anything else for a university.

HARVARD WELCOMED A KOREAN SWIMMER, LEO

A few years ago, I planned and published an autobiography of Leo, who was active as an athlete on the Harvard swimming team and graduated. When I first met that student in June 2012, he was just out of high school so that he would be a first-year student at Harvard in two months. It liquefied him as a swimmer. Of course, he goes through all his admission procedures despite being recruited. Although he finished high school in the fifth grade at an elementary school in the United States, he was still a Korean student by visa status. However, he received support from the school for all tuition, textbooks, and dormitory fees. He continued to write from when he met me to write his autobiography through his sophomore year at Harvard, publishing a book while still in school. Therefore, I know more vividly than anyone else the many stories I experienced while living as a Harvard student.

Image credit: The Crimson.

Harvard's Crimson selected Leo as one of the 15 most promising students annually among first-year students (THC, n.d.). He mentions in his book that he was an ambitious student who aimed to befriend all of Harvard's students and that the school recognized him for his excellence. While many Korean graduates have made headlines for achieving outstanding grades, Harvard's alum community has yet to realize them fully. It is because contributing to the community is essential for recognition. We know many of these students for their dedication to their studies, often spending long hours in the library. However, this singular focus on academics may prevent them from being recognized as notable Harvard alumni, even if they graduate with excellent grades.

In contrast, Leo represented the school as a swimmer. Throughout his school years, he actively participated in community service. He even established two official school clubs, a feat that is almost impossible to achieve. After publishing his essay, I needed more information about Leo's activities. However, when he entered a famous investment company in Manhattan, New York, after majoring in economics and statistics at school, I referred to his request.

WHY AMERICAN UNIVERSITIES ARE SO INTERESTED IN SPORTS ACTIVITIES

There are many reasons why American universities prefer students who have played sports. As mentioned above, it is not only directly helping the school with honor and finances but also recognizing the process if it is talented enough to represent the school through sports. In other words, it is to acknowledge the arduous process of achieving excellent grades or achievements in a field through sports. It recognizes many things, such as a long-term struggle with oneself, cooperation with team members, responsibility, leadership, the spirit of sacrifice, and service. Even if their academic level is lower than general students, recognizing their achievements enough to offset it is reliable accumulated data based on hundreds of years of experience in school society. It is because university authorities are well aware of the virtuous cycle structure in which, even after graduating from school, they succeed based on their careers and contribute to the school community.

On the other hand, I expect little from international students, especially those from Korea who live school life only for themselves. This is because American society's success rate after graduation is relatively low. As a result, it also showed that Korean graduates who contribute to the school community are rare in the data. Hence, no matter how good the applicant's specifications are, we try not to widen the entrance door to them if possible. Again, this is because they have a high dropout rate and do not significantly contribute to social activities or school development during or after graduation.

The phenomenon among Korean students arises because, growing up, I didn't learn those things. The reliance on school grades and academic ability tests for college admissions leads education policy authorities, school operators, parents, and society to overlook other development aspects. This approach is why we end up nurturing deformed students. Developing physical strength from an early age requires dedicating significant time to physical activities, from which we can expect the benefits of sports activities. Should South Korea's admissions system begin to value sports activities as done in the United States, it could lead to dramatic changes in Korean society.

From elementary school to high school to university, it comprises students who currently play sports or only do professional training. These are the so-called elite sports students. They focus on sports rather than school classes. They go on to the next level of higher school with those grades to become elite athletes because Korea uses a select sports policy. In the United States, even athletes representing their schools take the same classes as regular students and participate in all assignments and tests. In particular, athletes do not receive exceptional benefits. Therefore, your studies have little disruption even if you stop sports in the middle for assorted reasons.

Therefore, prestigious universities prefer applicants with excellent academic records who excel in sports. But, of course, if you want to be a professional sports player after graduating from college, it is expected to go to a state university with more strengths in sports than to a prestigious private university. It is ultimately a matter for students to decide when choosing their career path. So, with so many options, high school students are okay with participating in competitions while traveling by bus for regular training and hours each week. Instead, suppose the university admissions authority recruits you while doing such player activities. In that case, the probability of passing is higher than that of general applicants.

Therefore, parents and students prefer engaging in competitive sports early on. And almost without exception, children enjoy various sporting activities from an early age. My daughter has been devoting much time to her art activities, so she is relatively inactive in sports. However, in the last year of elementary school (fifth grade) and first year of middle school (sixth grade), he was a softball player and won a regional championship. In high school, he competed in a judo championship and won a gold medal. Physical training like this plays a massive role in maintaining concentration and stamina when they study at university. American students obsessed with sports activities like that stay in even though they look at the university library until 2 or 3 a.m. while doing school sports activities after class.

Furthermore, extreme competition pushes out Korean students who must train their stamina in their junior and senior college years. It amazed them at their extraordinary energy, saying, "American guys study until dawn, but they're fine the next day." It is possible because of the stamina accumulated through regular sports. Therefore, understanding the essence of education is crucial, and any changes in education policy in Korea ultimately stem from this need. Fundamentally, as long as they prioritize the study, it cannot be groundbreaking, no matter how many policy changes.

THERE IS NO SUBSTITUTE FOR THE VALUES OF A HEALTHY SOCIETY

Physical power is a national power. If all students have muscular physical strength, they can develop a healthy mind. For adolescents with a lot of stress, a healthy way to relieve it is to do sports activities. When you sweat, it will reduce your pressure before you know it. We cannot improve it by establishing a policy to keep children locked up while ignoring the obvious. No matter what regime changes, the education problem will still be unsolvable. The school paradigm needs to change. School playgrounds need to be designed better and offer more space than they currently do. It is necessary to nurture experts who can teach various sports subjects. Experts should be people with an understanding of the education and health of students rather than those who have experienced elite sports as they are now.

And the community must provide students with sports services that local schools cannot offer. For example, when my son was in the 3rd or 4th grade of elementary school, in that city with a population of about 25,000, he brought in coaches from England's professional youth teams as soccer class leaders. And people made up of various volunteers participated in coaching and supporting the program. It can operate such a phenomenon according to the characteristics of diverse local communities. Likewise, cities can provide sports activity services to children as part of their service to citizens. Therefore, schools and districts must support various stimulating activities so children can enjoy sports early.

During our conversation, SJ asked me whether working as a lawyer or a doctor brings me happiness. Geniuses with the best brains in Korea mainly choose a medical school, regardless of their inclinations or intentions. It is a tremendous loss, both nationally and personally. Suppose we expose children to an environment from an early age where they can participate in various sports activities, and the community encourages them. In that case, they will grow up loving sports that benefit their physical and mental health. Some may have succeeded as world-class athletes because they showed a natural aptitude for a particular sport. We have produced the second and third Kim Yuna players countless times in various sports fields. Every year, we significantly reduce youth problems such as suicide, school violence, mental and physical weakness, and social inadequacy. Of course, this is a claim that I do not provide a separate basis for this prospect, but it is generally correct.

Therefore, it is essential to recognize the importance of physical education, which is wholly excluded or formal in Korea's education field. And it is crucial to closely analyze the educational effect that will ripple through it and reflect it in education policy. Therefore, it is essential to recognize the importance of physical education, which is wholly excluded or formalized in the education field in Korea. We must closely analyze the educational effects that will ripple through and reflect them in education policies. Korean education must integrate sports into the student curriculum to achieve these goals. It is possible only with the efforts of the education authorities. The local community, including schools, must work together to reach a healthy society. The culture becomes incredibly beneficial when the whole organization agrees, and our children get accustomed to sports activities from kindergarten through high school to college. A healthy society has irreplaceable values. It is only possible through the efforts of the educational authorities. The community, including the school, must work together to achieve a healthy society. This way, when the entire organization agrees, and our children become accustomed to sports activities from kindergarten to high school or college, culture becomes hugely healthy. A healthy society has values that we cannot exchange for anything else.

POEMS OF LIFE AND RENEWAL

Penned January 13, 2020

Today, two volumes of a pale-blue poetry collection arrived at my door, packaged in a brown envelope from my younger sister, Young-ju, in South Korea. The postcard, dated December 20 of last year, finally arrived today.

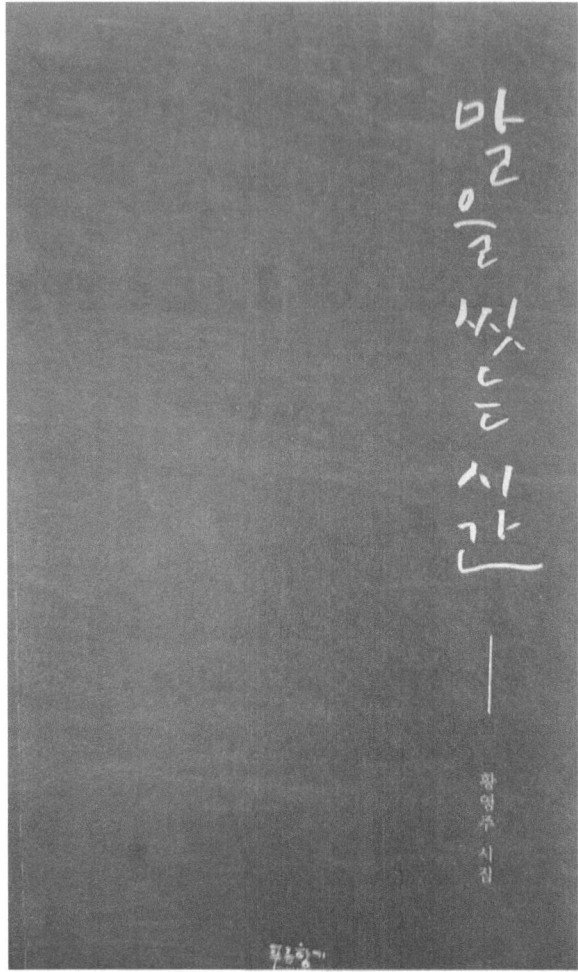

Caption: Hwang Young-ju's first poetry collection, " The Time of Verbal Rebirth," published in Prunbook, settled into my hands and my heart as if it had crossed the Pacific Ocean just for me.

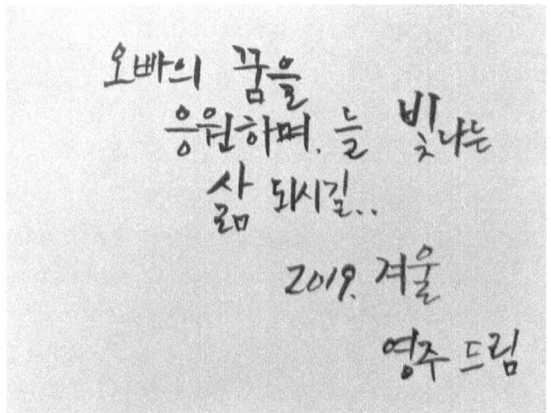

Caption: Young-ju learned calligraphy, writing her collection's title in her own hand. Though she could not include it in her collection, she left me a sweet message on one of the pages.

Young-ju and I are the sixth cousins on my mother's side. Her late father, who often appears in her poems, and my late mother were fourth cousins. I first saw Young-ju in the early 2000s. During that time of my desolate twenties, with no accomplishments and no hopes, her family was living in the back alley of Jongam Police Station in Seongbuk-gu, Seoul. She was then a high school student with three younger sisters, and her father always wore neat glasses. Her father was tall and may have been around my age or younger. Her mother is a typical housekeeper who always smiles brightly. I often visited her home and was happy to see four lovely younger sisters. Then, suddenly, her father passed away, bringing trials to Young-ju as the eldest.

Hwang (2019) writes, " Before the splendid days arrive, / Hastening to fold its life, / Taking all away, / You, / Live well, / Do just that, / Father, embracing winter's slumber" in "When the Camellia Falls" (p. 48).

Despite her sadness, she persevered with determination, saying, " When the camellia falls, / A radiant spring shall come." When she was over fifty, she published her first poetry book. When I held her book in my hand, it moved me. But my emotions did not end there.

I read her book in one sitting. Reading a poem in one breath without savoring it insults a poet. The poet carefully crafted each poem and invested significant effort and time in selecting, washing, seasoning, and arranging each line. We cannot just use our eyes to read a poem. At least with a poem, one should read it aloud to get the proper flow. Therefore, poems have rhythms like music.

For some reason, the mail of the day arrives at my house every evening around 6 p.m. The correspondence she sent took so long from Korea to the eastern United States, but at least it arrived at my home in the evening when the day ended. Is it because of the long wait? I first put her books on my bookshelf when I opened the envelope. The purple book of poetry harmonizes well with foreign language books. It looks best when placed on a bookshelf. Unlike novels, it is good to put poetry books on the bookshelf behind a chair and occasionally pull them out and open them to read a few pages.

There were many books when I shipped my luggage from Korea to the United States. Among them were collections of poems such as Poet Go Eun's "Maninbo (萬人譜)." However, after I bought his poetry collection in the late 1980s, I only flipped through a few pages and did not read anymore. To me, his poetry was already dead then. Despite that, I felt guilty about throwing them away and kept them whenever I moved. I discovered the poet was an inferior person who was a sexual abuser, so I finally threw his books in the trash. Ms. Choi Young-mi, a brave poet, revealed to the world that he was an ugly monster (Ryu, 2018). I wondered why people read Young-ju's poems at once rather than pedantic poems written by people who pretended to be noble, like Go Eun.

When I was with Young-ju, I always felt at ease. So, I lay in bed and read Young-ju's poems. It divided the anthology of poems into four sections: "Drawing People," "Touching the Landscape," "Asking Life," and "Embodying Life." Ultimately, the poet is telling life stories. She witnesses, yearns for, touches, and questions these people, eventually stitching their stories into her own life. It is, of course, the poet's own story. Therefore, her poems do not need to be complicated or philosophical. This is because her lyrics are precisely like the poet herself, composed of words woven together with care. The collection's title, 'The Time of Verbal Rebirth,' is likely taken from her poem of the same name. Reading this poem reveals how the poet approaches poetry.

Hwang (2019) writes, "Can one touch others with hands alone? / The heart speaks through words, / To cleanse them / Is to reshape oneself anew" (p. 89).

For her, poetry expresses her heart, which is her words. It is a pure object she rinses clean, puts in the sun, and shares it with herself.

Hwang (2019) writes, "Gently washed and rinsed, / Filled to the brim with sunlight, / Tomorrow, one may freely share their heart" (p. 89).

How eloquent is this expression?

One can only write poetry if one possesses skill in art. We must register it with excellent character. Even if one has talent in art, their poetry will be bland without sympathetic character. They focus on deceiving the world to hide their insipidity. The poet Go Eun proudly proclaimed that his work, Maninbo, comprised records of the people he had encountered, amounting to ten thousand. His poems written through his meandering life only reached me a few pages before dying. Instead, I felt comfort and joy while reading Young-ju's poems anthology, as if conversing with the poet over a cup of tea.

사람의 언어

우리에게 말만 있을까?
눈길 손길 발길
마음길까지

닿는 곳 어디든
따뜻하게
안을 수 있어

그대를 사랑하는
나는 언어다

(Hwang, 2019. p. 98)

Language of People
Translated by GS

Do we possess words alone?
The paths of eyes, hands, feet,
And even that of the heart

Anywhere they may reach,
Warmly,
Embracing all

I, who love you,
Am the language.

WHILE READING THE poem "Language of People," I rose from my bed and headed to the kitchen, where I ground Indian coffee beans to brew a strong cup. The first sip left a lingering sweet taste in my mouth, reminiscent of the emotions stirred by Young-ju's poem. Enjoying coffee transcends the immediate sensation of consumption. The excitement begins with ordering the beans, contemplating their origin, the significant history behind their production, and anticipating the order's arrival. It extends to the thrill of choosing among various beans when the desire for coffee strikes. As the beans are ground and roasted, they release a rich aroma and develop a brownish hue. The crisp sound of the beans being poured into the mixer and the aroma that fills the air during grinding are essential parts of the experience. Watching the hot liquid flow into the paper filter captures the essence of coffee enjoyment.

In short, just like drinking coffee is not just about the result, poetry is the same. Poetry can only exist with a poet who can express life in language. Therefore, the essential thing in poetry is ultimately human. As the poet said, "For I, who loves thee / Am a language itself: I am the language that loves you," "I" is the poet, and "language" is what allows readers to feel warm.

After reading the poem, I finally understood Hwang Young-ju's verse properly after reading the explanation titled "Reading Poetry in Verbs as Adjectives" by Ms. Sim Myung-ok on the back of the book of poems. It was indeed a well-written commentary.

At this point, I applaud Young-ju for her first collection of poetry. Initially, the first novel or the first poetry collection is bound to contain the highest essence of a writer. The writer's highest achievement is to pour all the energy they lived and thought into a book. So, producing a second and third piece of literature becomes increasingly tricky. However, this worry mainly applies to young people. Just as the moon naturally tilts when complete, everyone needs time to recharge. If you put everything into it at an early age and rush to look at the work without waiting for that time, something is bound to be sloppy. People may remember them as bright young writers, but they will soon forget them.

At 40, late debutants such as novelist Park Wan-Suh, who lived as a respected Korean novelist, have a high probability of producing tight works, even when they publish numerous pieces due to the experience they have gained in life. Therefore, I highly expect my sister Young-ju's following anthology of poems and essays.

I am proud to see Young-ju always one step ahead of me. Even though I have chosen 360 pieces from my writings to be published first, I need help finding the right direction. I mainly divided the topics into travel, contemplation, memories, and education-related essays. I am only thinking about whether to publish them separately or mix them, so I am still waiting to make progress. I am determined to publish it in English in the US, making it even more difficult.

Caption: My daughter MJ baked cookies shaped like two cats, symbolizing our family and the feline pets she hopes to have someday.

TIME PASSES BY, but it doesn't fly away. It will be with us as long as we live, so there's no need to rush. A few days ago, my daughter, MJ, made some cookies with two cats, representing our family and the cats she hopes to have in the future despite our son's allergies. It is important to keep dreaming, even if it doesn't become reality! Poet Hwang Young-ju is an excellent example of someone making their dreams come true individually.

Let's keep dreaming because everyone around you can be happy when you desire. When everyone is happy, the world is happy too.

Below is the full text of "The Time of Verbal Rebirth" and "When the Camellia Falls" by Hwang Young-ju.

말을 씻는 시간

옷을 벗듯 말을 벗어
몸을 씻듯 말을 씻는다

하루를 걷으면
허랑하게 겉돌거나
탈탈 털어내고픈
말 한 줌 잡히니

사람을 손으로만 만지랴
마음이 곧 말이니
말을 씻는 일
나를 다시 빚는 일이다

말갛게 헹궈
볕살 담뿍 담으면
내일은 마음껏 내어줘도 좋으리

(Hwang, 2019. p. 89)

The Time of Verbal Rebirth
Translated by GS

As one sheds their clothes, so do words
Bathing the body, words are cleansed

After a day's walk,
Useless words flit about,
Eager to be shaken free,
A handful grasped

Can one touch others with hands alone?
The heart speaks through words,
To cleanse them
Is to reshape oneself anew

Gently washed and rinsed,
Filled to the brim with sunlight,
Tomorrow, one may freely share their heart.

동백꽃 지면

꽃잎 지는 걸 한두 해 보나
시들해진 마음
덩이째 떨어진
동백꽃이 흔든다

참 좋은 시절이 오기 전
서둘러 생을 접으며
다 가져갈 테니
너는
잘 살아라
꼭 그래라
겨울을 안고 잠든 아버지

후두둑 떨군
붉은 빛
까맣게 꺼진
아버지 눈 같아서
저리게
아파서

>
동백꽃 지면
찬란한 봄이 오리니

(Hwang, 2019. p. 48)

When Camellia Falls
Translated by GS

Witnessing the petals' fall for years,
A wilted heart,
Dropping in clumps,
The camellia stirs

Before the splendid days arrive,
Hastening to fold its life,
Taking all away,
You,
Live well,
Do just that,
Father, embracing winter's slumber

Thudding down,
A crimson glow,
Resembling father's eyes,
Extinguished in darkness,
Aching,
Painfully so,

>
When the camellia falls,
A radiant spring shall come.

HWANG YOUNG-JU'S POETRY reminds us that careful articulation holds power in a world where people often wield words hastily. Her first collection, "The Time of Verbal Rebirth," captures the echoes of her personal journey and the universal resonances of love, loss, and the enduring human spirit. Her poems, seamlessly translated, serve as both a balm and a bridge — connecting hearts across languages, borders, and experiences.

Reading her work is akin to a slow, mindful sip of well-brewed coffee: it lingers, warms, and brings clarity. Young-ju's voice, interwoven with familial anecdotes and life's complexities, rises above mere words on paper. It is the voice of a resilient heart, teaching us that even when the camellia falls, heralding the end of one chapter, it signals the blossoming of another.

The poems invite us not just to read but to feel — to savor each line, each sentiment, much like the rich aroma of freshly ground coffee beans. This is not poetry for the sake of decorative language; it is poetry that resonates with the raw, unadulterated beats of life. And much like the best things in life, her poetry doesn't demand to be understood quickly. It asks for time, presence, and the willingness to journey through its depths.

In the golden twilight of our years, let us learn from the artistry of Young-ju's words that it is never too late for renewal. The life stories we carry, the trials we overcome, are the very substance of our rebirth — nourishing soil for the fresh seeds of dreams yet to be realized. As Young-ju writes, "When the camellia falls, a radiant spring shall come." May we all find the courage to let our camellias fall, to make room for new blossoms in the gardens of our souls. And as we do, may we never forget that we, too, are the language of life, spoken in the dialect of dreams realized, love given, and stories shared.

BELIEVING IN YOURSELF

Penned April 12, 2020

On April 10, 2020, a heartfelt post, "Yonsei Forest #67450th Shout," appeared on Facebook's anonymous bulletin board, 'Yonsei University Bamboo Forest.' The post received an overwhelming response in just two days, garnering 41K likes, 11K comments, and 4.1K shares. The reason for translating and sharing this story is not merely the touching tale of a young woman.

The author bares her soul, recounting her journey through poverty and her path to success on an anonymous forum since her mother died in childhood. Despite the sacrifices and challenges faced by her sister and father to support her, she persevered and triumphed. Her message of hope aims to inspire others.

With challenging work and excellent grades, the author's future seemed bright. But her dreams of attending university disappeared when her father suffered an injury. However, through the sacrifices and resilience of her family, she finally became a medical student at Yonsei University — a prestigious institution with the highest passing score among all significant departments and universities in South Korea. The story reaches its emotional peak when the family savors a festive meal at Outback Steakhouse, symbolizing their hard-won success. The author pledges to make her family's life a place to enjoy such meals without worry. This story is one of perseverance, effort, and hope, teaching readers the value of making tough decisions in demanding situations and unlocking the potential for success.

The author mentions government support for study materials in her story. While South Korea is a developed country, poverty and social welfare challenges persist. Significant government spending may be necessary to provide more robust social protection for low-income families, potentially increasing the budget. Additionally, competitive demands for resources, such as infrastructure development and defense, can limit funding for social welfare programs. Political or ideological factors may also hinder the passage of bills or the implementation of policies addressing poverty and inequality. Moreover, some needy families may be unaware of or unable to access existing social welfare programs. Thus, practical volunteer activities and communication efforts are vital.

OPTIMISM IS CRUCIAL despite these challenges. There are numerous ways to combat poverty and promote social welfare, including building a robust social safety net, implementing job training programs, and investing in education. Encouraging dialogue between government officials, community leaders, and individuals with firsthand experiences of poverty can lead to solutions for a more equitable society. Recognizing poverty as a systemic issue requiring collective action, not an individual's fault, is essential. We must work together to create a community where everyone can access opportunities for success and happiness, regardless of their background.

Countless stories worldwide feature individuals who overcame poverty and adversity to achieve enormous success. For example, Oprah Winfrey, born into poverty in rural Mississippi, faced numerous challenges during her childhood, including sexual abuse and violence. Yet, through arduous work in school, she became a successful television host, media mogul, and advocate for social justice. Additionally, she is a prominent philanthropist,

supporting education and healthcare. Oprah's story parallels the author's —
both faced significant obstacles and challenges but overcame them through
determination, effort, and self-belief.

I experienced severe hunger in my late teens, going without food for
over a week. I collaborated with my friend Soon-il, delivering newspapers
and preparing for my high school equivalency exam. When our money ran
out, Soon-il left to find his father, promising to return in three days. A week
passed, and he did not return. On the verge of death, I found solace in soup
from a food truck operated by a familiar couple. That was the first time I
experienced extreme hunger.

In contrast to the protagonist of this story, I was fortunate to have healthy
parents in my impoverished rural hometown and family members who could
save me from dire situations if I reached out. Unwilling to follow my siblings'
despairing path, I left for Seoul after middle school graduation to forge my
destiny. I encountered numerous obstacles that the author never faced, obstacles I had to overcome to grow and flourish. Nonetheless, this story resonates with many because the author dedicated all her energy to excel in areas
where she could shine the most without squandering her family's sacrifices.
Consequently, her family found hope, people beautifully depicted, and their
story through the heartwarming setting of Outback Steakhouse. Although the
author aspires to become a doctor to conquer poverty, she also possesses a gift
for writing novels, which could lead her to remarkable success in that realm.

In adversity, remaining optimistic and believing in ourselves is crucial.
The author's story and other triumphant individuals demonstrate that anyone
can surmount challenges and achieve their dreams with determination, hard
work, and self-belief. Remembering that we are not alone is vital — support
is available from family, friends, and other sources. By working collectively, we
can create a better world where everyone can access opportunities for success
and happiness, irrespective of their background.

I TRANSLATED THIS story to preserve the author's intended meaning
as much as possible, allowing readers to connect with the profound emotions and experiences shared (연세대학교 대나무숲 *[Yonsei University
Bamboo Forest]*).

Yonsei University Bamboo Forest (an anonymous online forum)
Yonsei Forest #67450 Shout:

Today, I went to the Outback for the first time in my life. I don't remember my mother's face very well. When I turned five, she passed away. A car had hit her on her way home from working at a restaurant to support our struggling family.

After my mom's death, my dad, a day laborer or so-called "manual worker," raised my sister and me alone. He shed blood and tears to provide for us, but sadly, his efforts could only keep us barely alive.

I started elementary school and became friends with a girl who dressed herself in a pretty dress and princess-like shoes and had a hairstyle that someone had put a lot of effort into. I visited her house and learned many things for the first time — that her walls were mold-free, she could prepare fresh fruits at home, she had placed a slide in the house, and I was poor.

I entered middle school. Because of our financial situation, my sister gave up on college early and went to a vocational school. My Unnie wanted to find a job quickly. I imagined I would become just like her. I had no dreams for my future because I couldn't afford to dream. Maybe because I was bored or didn't have anything else to do, or perhaps because I hoped that my talent, as my elementary school teacher once said, could change my life. I listened attentively to my school lessons. The result was that I ranked first in my school. It was the first moment when the hope that my talent could change my life became a reality.

I entered a well-known high school in my area as an "outstanding student." My grades didn't drop in high school, which was not a cliché. However, in my first high school exam, I ranked second in my school. I was immensely proud. I didn't attend any private lessons and bought workbooks with government support, but I still ranked second.

I continued studying, thinking I could earn much money for my family. But then, my dad had an accident at the construction site.

Fortunately, he survived, but he couldn't work anymore. After that, I realized I couldn't study any longer. If I didn't work, our poverty would worsen, and we wouldn't even be able to afford cheap roasted chicken for our annual New Year's gathering.

I cried a lot. My eyes swelled, and I cried until I couldn't breathe. My sister hugged me and gave me words of salvation. My Unnie told me she would somehow earn money and that I should study hard and make something of myself. I was so grateful and sorry that I learned to the point of death. I bought workbooks with the government's money. I purchased an unlimited online lecture pass with the money my sister gave me.

I didn't allow any time for sadness or struggle during my senior year. I knew this was my only chance, so I dedicated myself to studying intensely. On the day of the college entrance exam, I brought along the kimchi fried rice my dad had prepared, its familiar greasiness a small comfort. After the exam, anxiety gripped me as I awaited the results, worried that the sacrifices made by my Unnie and Dad might have been for nothing. When it came time to grade my paper, I took a deep breath and faced the outcome. Holding the answer sheet, which showed only two minor Korean and Earth Science errors, my family and I cried together. Through his tears, my dad apologized to my sister and me for never being able to fulfill our simple wish of dining at Outback, something we had always hoped for.

A few months later, I became a Yonsei University Medical School student. The six words, "현역 정시 연의: a current student who entered Yonsei University Medical School through the regular entrance exam," carried immense significance. I worked hard as a tutor for almost three months, managed to pay off our overdue rent, and still had four million Won left over. I split the money evenly between my Unnie and my dad, who had both dedicated their lives to me.

Today, my dad took us to Outback Steakhouse, where he ordered the lavish four-person lobster set. As my Unnie and I savored the spaghetti, steak, and lobster, my dad watched us with tears in his eyes, which also moved us to tears. We finished every bit of the meal, crying throughout. It was the first time we had eaten to the point of bursting. Witnessing my dad and Unnie enjoying their meal so entirely was incredibly touching. The joy and newfound hope shining among us were profound, marking a moment of overwhelming happiness.

I made a promise to myself. I would give my dad and Unnie a life where we could go to Outback Steakhouse and order the four-person lobster set, not for a birthday, New Year's Day, or any special occasion, but simply because we felt like it.

I INTRODUCED THE above narrative from a post shared on Yonsei University Bamboo Forest (an anonymous online forum) to maintain the emotional integrity and powerful message it holds for all of us, regardless of our background or circumstances.

The story shared from the Yonsei University Bamboo Forest embodies the dormant strength and resilience within us, which often emerges in the face of adversity. It demonstrates that despite facing challenges like poverty, family sacrifices, or societal pressures, hope, perseverance, and self-belief can prevail.

In a world where cynicism and despair are all too common, such narratives remind us of the remarkable achievements possible when individuals choose to be guided by their dreams and actions rather than their circumstances. This story isn't merely about overcoming poverty; it's a celebration of the human spirit, symbolized by a family meal at Outback Steakhouse — a testament to realized dreams and a boundless future.

However, while individual success stories uplift and inspire, it's crucial to contextualize them within the systemic barriers that persist. Celebrating these victories is essential, but equally so is the commitment to dismantling the barriers that make such stories exceptional rather than ordinary.

So, as you find inspiration in this poignant account, let it motivate you to strive for personal success and remind you of the collective responsibility we share in building a society where each individual has a genuine shot at success, regardless of their starting point in life.

And if you ever find yourself questioning your potential or worth, think back to this tale from the Yonsei University Bamboo Forest. Remember that the most extraordinary accomplishments often have humble beginnings — birthed from a place of challenge, nurtured through arduous work, and realized by an unwavering belief in oneself.

So, believe in yourself, for the world awaits your unique contribution, and you owe it to yourself and everyone who believes in you to realize your full potential.

CHALLENGING
STEREOTYPES

Penned January 14, 2022

For us Koreans, "humility" is undoubtedly a great virtue. If you are not humble or rude, and people may label you as no longer a human being who can no longer get along, I can see you as a brag and show-off person. However, this sense of 'humility' is so deeply rooted in Korean culture that people feel obliged to display it in all situations. In the Joseon Dynasty (1392-1897), when Confucian ideology dominated the entire country for 500 years, Inui Yeji (인의예지 仁義禮智) was one of the core ideologies of Confucianism. However, due to overemphasizing humility in the rites, later generations harshly criticized the illusion of the Yangban society, the ruling class of the time. In those days, noble people pretended not to be hungry even though they were hungry. They desperately wanted something and pretended not to be, and they desperately wanted money but pretended not to be. They used the most basic human desire or pursuit of humanity to dominate the era by creating a fictional image different from reality.

Society began to transition from a Confucian culture to a modern society, starting with the Gabo Reform in 1894, just before the collapse of the Joseon Dynasty, as they soon abolished the class system and the enslavement of people that had existed for thousands of years. As a result, Confucianism advocated by the ruling class collapsed. Still, Confucianism influenced society, even after the Japanese colonial period and the end of the Korean War. However, as Korea rapidly succeeded in industrial reorganization, economic development, and democratization based on it, the influence of Confucianism finally faded. However, among them, "humility" persists and remains one of the subconscious minds that oppresses Korean society for the following reasons. After Joseon changed the country's name and system to the Korean Empire (1897-1910) and the Japanese forcibly destroyed it, Western Christianity and Catholicism quickly spread to confused people. As a result, they translated the Bibles into Korean and widely disseminated them.

However, Bible education is about teaching obedience to God. Therefore, Confucianism still weighed on modern Korean society. In addition to that, Koreans learned the doctrines of Catholicism and Christianity. For example, in the Bible's Proverbs 22:4 (King James Version: KJV), "By humility and the fear of the LORD Are riches, honor, and life." Here, "humility" coincides with the humility of rites emphasized in Confucianism. As of 2021, many Koreans among the Christian (17%) and Catholic (6%) demographics, as well as Buddhists (16%) or nonreligious (60%), still value the virtue of humility (Gallup, 2021). Therefore, as concepts from around the world mixed and became globalized, humility's limitations and side effects became evident in Korea.

People now judge humility as one of Korea's proud intellectual and cultural heritage. In a report dated May 19, 2016, by the POSCO Research Institute (POSRI), Kim argues that elements of distorted Confucian culture in Confucian teachings are holding back corporate innovation. The author pointed out that in Korean education based on the Inui Yejisin (인의예지신 仁義禮智信), etiquette (禮) is called Samganoryun as an etiquette education toward superiors (Kim, 2016). The author argues that "keeping concessions, humility, and manners, which are the teachings of courtesy, is deeply rooted in most Koreans, especially as a basic attitude toward their superiors." It is because it is the core content of teaching concessions and humility. Because of that influence, even Today, in most organizations in Korea, subordinates have excessively deep-rooted obedience to their superiors. It has a tremendous impact not only on organizations but also on relationships with individuals in general.

Caption: Lisa Son's book cover published in Korean in 2022.

I WATCHED A YouTube video titled "Barnard Professor Lisa Son Discusses the Psychology of Activism" (YouTube, 2021). Professor Son recounts her perspective on her transition to activism after participating in her rally to Stop Asian Hate in May 2021 (BC, 2021). Professor Son, born and raised in the United States by parents who immigrated from South Korea, notes that she grew up experiencing cultural conflicts and differences in cultural values as a child of immigrants. She recently published a provocative book for 21st Century Books called "IMPOSTER: Masked Parents Make Masked Children." Introducing the book in her Kyobo online bookstore is as follows (Kyobobook, n.d.).

"Parents let their children know they are perfect even when they remove their masks." 《Metacognitive Learning Method》 is a good way of thinking taught by Professor Lisa Son to parents who live with masks.

"You always have to be perfect," "You must do well from the beginning," "Do not pretend to be good "...... From childhood, we wore masks that come with these thoughts: a mask that looks perfect, a genius mask, a good boy mask. In particular, in Korea, where studying and learning hold the highest priority, children take masks for granted. So many Koreans grow up to be 'impostors (meaning impostors, impersonators, scammers)' who suffer from anxiety after losing themselves and wearing masks, that is, mask syndrome. Even when they become adults, they cannot quickly eliminate this anxiety and sometimes pass on the same cover to their children.

Professor Lisa Son, a metacognitive psychology expert, confesses that she also wore the mask of being a good daughter, student, perfect mother after adulthood, and a great professor. Professor Son was only able to find herself sincere while studying metacognition. Like her, to help parents and children struggling with learning and growth, the new book "Imposter" contains metacognitive practices that can be free from masks.

Professor Lisa Son introduces metacognitive practices throughout her book to free yourself from the mask. For example, when your child has received good grades, "My child must be a genius!" "My child knows nothing!" Instead of saying, "What was difficult about this exam?" "What are you more curious about here?" She also recommends that you dare to wait for your child after reflecting on your thoughts, "Let's do a little more," rather than giving up quickly because your child does not know well. It is invisible to parents' eyes, but numerous thoughts are undoubtedly happening in the child's head. To learn, you must think alone and wait to express yourself. Prof. Son emphasizes that by putting metacognition into action in everyday life, they can grow into parents and children who are not afraid of mistakes, do not dwell on results, and achieve learning effects independently.

I have yet to read her book, but I have heard her lecture on a channel related to her publication, and it is consistent with the summary above (ST, 2022). An experience she had as a child motivated her to become a psychologist later. Below is a piece of the confessions made on the above channel.

LIKE MANY KOREAN Americans, I attended a Korean language school every Saturday as an elementary student. Once, I had to give a speech like this in front of people, but my Korean was challenging, so I was extremely nervous and anxious. But I still have to do it. That is right. So, I prepared hard. I first laid out the overall frame and completed the speech with the help of my father for the details. But again, I wanted to receive recognition like "You speak Korean well" somewhere. So, I memorized all the speeches and practiced more than one hundred times.

A week before the presentation, I had an opportunity to practice in front of my classmates at the Korean language school. I was really nervous that day, too, but I did well because I practiced. I also got compliments from my teacher. And a friend compliments me. Like, "Lisa, you did an excellent speech. You speak Korean well."

Caption: Lisa Son's book cover published in Korean in 2019.

So, I answered. "Thank you. I practiced really hard. I think I will do well next week."

I answered so confidently.

But do you know what that friend said? "Lisa, you don't have to show off, do you?" That is what my friend said. To be honest, I was so surprised at that moment. I was initially a kid who thought it was too important to live humbly, so I tried to live that way. But at that time, I prepared a lot for the presentation, practiced, and received compliments, so I just told the truth about myself and my feelings, but is that such a boast?

I was really shocked when I thought of this. And now that I remember, ah, I felt so. "Lisa, why aren't you so humble? Live more modestly from now on." After that day, I worked hard on something, and even though I got satisfactory results, I think I did not show my true feelings well to others.

I, too, have been living through this clash of values for humility. When someone compliments me, I often pretend it does not matter. "Well, it's nothing, ha ha ha," scratching my head or saying, "It just happened somehow. It is something anyone can do," and step back. And then inside, 'I could get it because I worked hard.' I used to take a double-minded attitude. However, when this humility goes too far, it becomes servile. They blame the environment rather than themselves by saying that what they did was possible because people were lucky or they received help from those around them.

When you see someone who humbles themselves like that, it may seem that a person's character is high. However, if everything is like that, you will not be able to understand the person's thoughts properly. Whether the other person's expression is because of humility or nature is ambiguous. In the past, people living together as neighbors in a village could easily understand the other person's intentions. Still, now we live in a completely different world. If a misunderstanding occurs in one meeting, there is no second chance. We live in a world so busy that there is no possibility that the other person is our neighbor. Therefore, there is no reason to meet to resolve a misunderstanding that has arisen deliberately.

Therefore, if we tremble with humility as much as we can, saying that one day we will know who we really are, the loss is only with ourselves. Therefore, it is essential not to go too far, remove the mask of humility, and confidently convey our thoughts to others. Prof. Lisa Son thinks it would be better to converse, "Thank you for your compliments. I really worked hard to achieve this. If you ever need me, I think I can help out with my experience and knowledge."

I KNEW LITTLE about her, but after some research, in 2019, she published "Metacognitive Learning: Thinking Parents Create Thinking Children" (Son, 2019). After graduating with a degree in psychology from the University of

Pennsylvania (UPenn) and a Ph.D. in Psychology from Columbia University, she served as Assistant Professor at Barnard College for eight years from 2002 and then as Associate Professor for nine years from 2011. She has been a full-time professor since 2020 (Son, n.d.).

By chance, I learned a little about Professor Lisa Son. I thought about the humility that has settled in my perception. People who know me are likely to feel that I am not humble. Among the articles I wrote on my blog, I sometimes share them with close people around me. Among them, there may be writings that do not fit humility. Some were genuinely outstanding achievements for me, and those who received my report were stingy at praising them. If I had changed my position and heard such news from someone I knew, I would not have been stingy with compliments. I could feel what they would think of me from their icy silence. Maybe they will think of me as an arrogant person. I have expressed my thoughts through the medium of writing. Still, depending on the person, it may be a modest expression, at least in Korean society.

Like most Koreans, I practiced humility when I lived in Korea. Otherwise, it is challenging to establish proper human relationships in Korean society. If you are not modest, in the words of Professor Son, if you do not wear a mask, the tendency to see you as rude still seems to be in Korean society. However, I have a slightly fresh point of view living in the United States, and there is no need to be humble. Expressing one's feelings honestly rather than being humble is a more transparent, productive, and conflict-free way of building relationships.

As I watched my children go from preschool to college in the United States up close, I understand the importance of expressing one's thoughts well, sometimes in writing, sometimes as a work of art, and sometimes verbally. Humility is gagging a person's ability or expression. I do not know about psychology, but it seems that when we put limits on our abilities, they lock us in that mold at that moment. As Professor Son gave an example, if you hear "You can't do that" from essential people around you or "You don't have the natural talent to do that!" it will significantly influence them. Therefore, you should not use words that rob someone of hope. Then why is hope so important?

When we encounter someone who appears to have lost all motivation for life, as if they have reached the end of the world, we do not see hope in them. Conversely, even in challenging situations, we feel hope from those who long for something with their sparkling eyes. But theoretically, hope is just a stream of the mind, and there is no evidence that it will give any physical benefit. That is why people say it cynically. "Hope is just a fleeting thing; more importantly, it is the reality we face." But is that really the case?

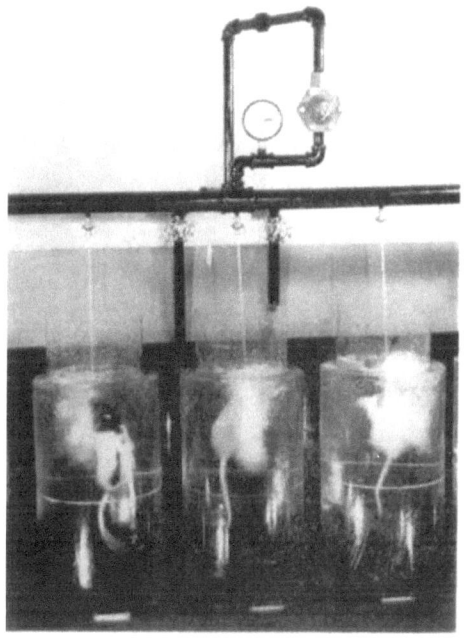

Caption: Glass swimming jars, water jets, cold and hot water faucets, pressure gauge, and pressure regulator.

LET US TAKE A moment to tell the story of Curt Richter, a Harvard-educated Johns Hopkins University scientist who, in the 1950s, performed startling experiments with both domesticated and untamed mice (Encyclopedia, n.d.). These experiments conclusively demonstrated hope's vital role in living beings' lives. The title of Professor Richter's 1957 paper, published in Psychosomatic Medicine, is 'On the Phenomenon of Sudden Death in Animals and Man' (Richter, 1957, Volume 19, Issue 3, pp. 191-198). Figure 1 illustrates a 20 cm in diameter and 76 cm deep glass bottle that they could fill with water at temperatures varying from 17 to 40 degrees Celsius. They specifically designed the bottle to prevent mice from escaping from the outside. In an article for Psychology Today, Joseph Hallinan provides an accessible explanation of Richter's findings.

In one experiment, researchers placed twelve domesticated lab mice in water, where two died within minutes, and the rest survived for several days. In contrast, thirty-four wild mice perished within 1 to 15 minutes when introduced to the water. Wild, more ferocious, and aggressive than domesticated lab rats, they gave up quickly in a desperate state. After repeatedly biting and taking out other wild mice, the experiment showed that they survived for several days when placed in a glass bottle (Richter, 1957).

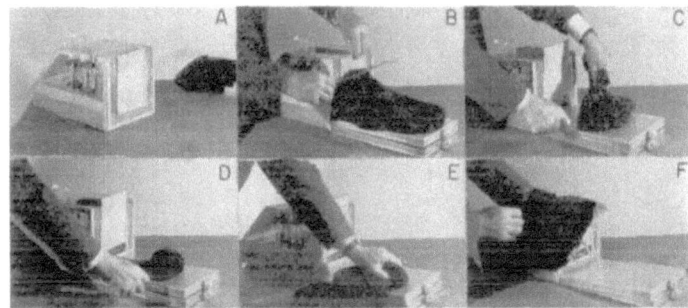

Caption: Various steps involved in transferring wild rat from holding cage to black bag.

The wild mice, known for their fierce and aggressive nature compared to their laboratory-bred counterparts, quickly fell into despair. Richter's research team reported capturing over 2,000 wild rats for their study. As depicted in Figure 3, they restrained the rats to prevent resistance and hand-caught them to avoid bites, yet some of them died on the spot, a clear sign of their desperate state. The team noticed that even minor stressors, such as cutting a rat's long whiskers, could have a fatal impact when the animals were placed in water jars. This phenomenon highlights how the rats, feeling a loss of hope, were quick to give up their lives.

In contrast, when the researchers rescued the same wild rats just before they died, allowed them to rest for a few minutes, and then placed them in a glass bottle, the rats repeatedly survived for several days. This experiment, which took place 70 years ago, clearly demonstrated that the driving force behind the rats' survival was "hope."

A society without hope has no future. So, what should we do in a community with no end in sight? Shouldn't we boldly pull out and throw away the stereotypes that are deeply rooted in our hearts? It is time to throw away the illusion that humility is good. Recognizing that we have only one life, with no alternate world or second chance, it's essential to live authentically, holding high our self-esteem and expressing our thoughts with confidence. We only have one life; no other world or new life awaits us. We cannot afford to spend the rest of our lives pretending to be okay and lowering our self-esteem. Instead, we should have the courage to express our thoughts more confidently. It can start by breaking the vast, centuries-old shell of humility.

CULTURE CLASH

Penned July 5, 2022

Today's top news in South Korea features Professor June Huh, the first Korean recipient of the Fields Medal, often likened to the Nobel Prize in Mathematics. In particular, if you look at only a few news titles, it is as follows.

'고교 중퇴 수포자', 수학계의 노벨상 받다 ›

"한국 학생 수학 수준 의외로 낮고 스트레스
심해... 입시 수학의 병폐"

2022.01.01(토) 김미리 기자

수학자들 두손 든 '리드추측' 45년만에
해결… 난제 11개나 풀어

🕐 4시간 전 이영완 과학전문기자

대학때 F학점 수두룩... 허준이 "시작하기에
늦은 건 없어"

🕐 9시간 전 이영완 과학전문기자, 김은경 기자

Caption: News from Korea covering Professor Huh's
Fields Medal award.

The titles of major news related to this are translated and introduced as
follows:

- High School Dropout Who Struggled with Math Wins 'Nobel Prize in
  Mathematics'... Multiple F Grades in College: "It's Never Too Late to Start"
- From Math Struggler to Late-Blooming Genius: Professor June Huh Wins
  Fields Medal... Solves Ten Unsolved Problems, High School Dropout,
  and GED Holder... Dreamt of Being a Poet and Science Journalist in
  Childhood... Professor Hasegawa of Japan Marks Turning Point
- First Korean to Win 'Nobel Prize in Mathematics' Fields Medal... He
  Was a High School Dropout in Korea

- High School Dropout Who Dreamt of Being a Poet Embraces 'Nobel Prize of Mathematics'
- "Advanced Korean Mathematics by 50 Years"... Academic Community Cheers for Professor June Huh's Fields Medal Achievement
- 'Harder Than a Nobel Prize'... What is the Fields Medal Received by Professor June Huh?
- [Breaking News] Professor June Huh Honored with Fields Medal... First Korean Mathematician to Win the Award
- First Korean to Win 'Nobel Prize in Mathematics' Fields Medal... He Was a High School Dropout in Korea

The Korean media frenzy would have been intense had it been a Nobel Prize. However, the response was more subdued, possibly because the award was in mathematics, a field often overlooked by the general public. Koreans have long been looking forward to the Nobel Prize (although there was a Korean Peace Nobel Prize winner).

The four Fields medal winners, clockwise from top left: Maryna Viazovska, James Maynard, June Huh and Hugo Duminil-Copin
Mattern Fieri/Ryan Cowan/Lance Murphy

Image Source: New Scientist. 2022 Fields Medal: Award in Mathematics for studying prime numbers and spheres (sets of points equidistant from a given point in three-dimensional space).

New Scientist announced, "Mathematicians who have studied the most efficient way to pack spheres in eight-dimensional space and the spacing of prime numbers are among this year's recipients of the highest award in mathematics, the Fields medal" (Sparkes, 2022). Of course, it is not easy to understand even three dimensions. Still, their talent to study the eighth dimension makes me suffocate. When Professor June Huh received the Fields Medal, the Korean media poured various articles. Among them, the business edition of the Chosun Ilbo introduces it as follows (M. Kim, 2022).

PROFESSOR HUH WAS born in California in 1983, while his father, Myung-hoe Huh, professor emeritus of statistics at Korea University, and mother, In-young Lee, professor emeritus of Russian language and literature at Seoul National University, were studying in the United States. He is an American citizen, but he is a domestic student. June Huh came to Korea with his parents when Hur was two years old and attended elementary and middle school in Korea. His unique anecdote about taking the GED after dropping out of high school when he wanted to be a poet is already famous within the math community.

I met Professor In-young Lee, June Huh's mother when I was working for a copyright agency company in Yeonhui-dong, Seoul. It would have been in 1989. I visited her lab to introduce an English book called The Reunification of the Korean Peninsula. I found out this time that Professor June Huh was her son.

Challenges Solved by Professor June Huh	Year Presented
Read's conjecture	1968
Hogger conjecture	1974
Mason-Welsh conjecture	1971
Rota-Heron-Welsh conjecture	1971
strong Mason conjecture	1972
Dowling-Wilson conjecture	1974
Brylawski conjecture	1982
Dawson-Colbourn conjecture	1984
Okounkov conjecture	2003
Dimca-Papadima conjecture	2003
Elias-Proudfoot-Wakefield conjecture	2016

Chart: Challenges Solved by Professor June Huh and Year Presented.

Among the words mentioned by Professor Huh, there is something we need to engrave. In an interview with Chosun Ilbo, he made the following meaningful comments (M. Kim, 2022).

In an interview with Chosun Ilbo regarding the fact that all Koreans suffer from mathematical trauma, he said, "Math is not a problem, but the structure of the entrance examination is a problem." He joked, "If the Ministry of Education says it will not include math in the entrance exam next year, wouldn't math stress be solved right away?" He continued, "I saw that in the U.S., Korean students who had studied mathematics a lot had an unexpectedly low depth of mathematics. However, Korean students experience severe math stress, a symptom of the entrance exam-focused mathematics education system.

I think Korean textbook writers, test questionnaires, and people who plan and insist on it from the beginning are ruining Korea's education. For example, some say that the level of high school mathematics in Korea is similar to that of American universities. It is well-known that among the English questions on the Korean College Scholastic Ability Test, the SAT level in Korea is so high that students from prestigious universities in the U.S. and Britain sometimes give wrong answers. Consequently, the approach of officials associated with the Korean SAT seems fundamentally flawed.

Korean Nationalists want to boast about how outstanding Koreans are, citing such a phenomenon. But they need to learn how much sacrifice is behind it. If I had the authority to overhaul Korea's education, I must change it.

Let seventh to ninth graders study the current fifth to seventh-grade math course.

Let 10th-12th graders study the current eighth-10th grade math course.

Mathematically gifted students can learn high-level mathematics through expert math courses.

For reference, the school system in Korea is 6 (1~6)-3 (7~9)-3 (10~12), and in the U.S., it is 5 (1~5)-3 (6~8)-4 (9~12) or 6 (1~6)-2 (7~8)-4 (9~12), the high school course is three years in Korea but four years in the U.S.

In this way, if it significantly lowered the level of mathematics in Korea than it is now, the number of students who give up learning mathematics would dramatically decrease. If Korean students study as they did, they can solve problems with closed eyes to get high marks in math. The majority of students maintain average grades in subjects other than math. Thus, a reduction in the intensity of math studies could be beneficial. Students will love math if it is at a mediocre level. If the math test is simple, the ability to discriminate against math subjects will decrease, but what is the big deal? If you study hard and get 95 or 100 points, it is fair enough. It is bizarre logic to have students learn to challenge levels and make exam questions difficult to avoid getting high marks. They can recognize the score gained by studying hard regardless of discrimination.

THE SAME GOES for English subjects. The current Korean way of asking tough questions so that even native speakers who have graduated from prestigious universities cannot get one hundred points is idiotic. Everyone should get one hundred grades with a little effort. Korean students must have basic conversational, writing, and reading skills in the English course. It should eliminate the current curriculum management guidelines that Korean students spend too much time on English and math subjects. To do that, adjust the level much more quickly than now. Then, students can devote little time to English. Current high school students only need to master the middle school level. Therefore, there will be no English learners giving up.

Also, math and English are only some of the critical subjects. The other topics in Korea will also require more structure. Therefore, we should drastically lower that level. Everyone should work hard to achieve good grades.

It is vital to build confidence in students from elementary school to high school. The school test should confirm what students have learned, not rank their grades from first place to last. I also took a math course at an American university, at the level of high school 11th-grade math in Korea. Therefore, Korea should consider lowering the difficulty level of its high school mathematics curriculum.

Students who like real math, like Professor June Huh, start by going to graduate school. Among the students who flock to graduate schools worldwide to study mathematics for the first time, people from Asian countries say that they feel low level. However, as time goes by, the skill gap widens. The tasks used to solve are no longer skilled problem-solving ones. Still, it reveals the ability to encounter "strange problems" you have never seen or experienced. So, it is common among those who majored in mathematics in the United States that there will come a slump when students who say they flew around with mathematics in Korea want to give up. There is a substantial difference in the Ph.D. program. Ultimately, it is also why there must be more Koreans among those who shine as mathematicians worldwide.

This time, Professor June Huh, whom we can call Korean, won the award. Everyone's outrage erupted because he finally broke the field ceiling where Koreans had felt the limit. But, of course, he was born in the United States and had American citizenship, so Professor Huh is American. Still, he returned to Korea when he was two years old and received everything from kindergarten to university in Korea, so it is not strange that we call him Korean. It is what Koo Ja-Kyung, an emeritus professor of mathematical sciences at KAIST, spoke about in a talk with the Kyunghyang Shinmun, a Korean daily newspaper.

"As a mathematician, I am pleased," Koo said. "Japan has over 100 years of history in modern mathematics and has produced several Fields Medal winners, but Korea's history of participating in modern mathematics is not as long as 50 to 60 years," he said. "I thought it would take another 50 years to follow Japan, but Dr. Huh's award is 'big news' in Korean mathematics, advancing our wish by 50 years.

However, even Professor Koo could not address such problems in the Korean education system and only applauded the emergence of a genius. So, is it not surprising that Professor Koo expressed his surprise that in Korea, the level of mathematics in high schools across the country is the same as that of universities in the United States?

The Korean mathematics community has yet to achieve outstanding achievements in the international mathematics world because the educational system has not produced many students who really enjoy mathematics. Relying on a genius like this is just a coincidence. There are no international stars in Korean figure skating where a genius named Yuna Kim has been working. Many young children want to become figure skaters after Kim Yuna's fantastic success in figure skating as a model. However, due to the underdeveloped environment for figure skating in Korea, the sport continues to be less popular. Therefore, there is no figure comparable to Yuna Kim because there is only a tiny group of trains as figure skaters.

THERE IS ONE theory I always advocate for this. To excel in a field, the greater the number of people challenging that field, the higher the chances of success. Because it is a matter of probability and, simultaneously, of competitiveness, Korean female players are achieving excellent results in the current international golf tournament because many mothers and fathers have given their daughters golf lessons after seeing Se-ri Pak's success. The larger the pool of people entering the field, the higher the chance that a successful player will emerge.

Korean K-pop has many successful idols worldwide, but remembering that they had to overcome tremendous effort and competition to get there is worth remembering. The key is to pursue something out of passion rather than merely as a means to a livelihood, as the latter often results in lower chances of success.

However, even Professor Koo could not address such problems in the Korean education system and only applauded the emergence of a genius. Isn't it surprising and puzzling that, in Korea, the level of mathematics in high schools nationwide is the same as that of universities in the United States? People like Professor Gu need to point out why there are no outstanding mathematicians like Professor Huh. Most people who do professorships at Korean universities are directly people who designed the Korean education system, so it is right to say that most people like Professor Koo are ignorant of the problem.

Similarly, rekindling interest in the subject becomes challenging if someone dislikes studying mathematics. Like Professor June Huh, he was actually a potential math genius. Still, looking at his life story, I see that he once gave up on math — what a dizzying moment not only in his personal life but also in the world of mathematics. Therefore, the millions of people who live ordinary lives around us could be people who, if it had not happened in their youthful days, could have made a genius reputation in a specific field and led our lives in a better direction.

THE EDUCATION SYSTEM in Korea is full of problems. School education should not determine the level of self-esteem, nor should we adjust the level of questions to improve discrimination in the exam.

I remember a student when I was doing private tutoring in Junggye-dong, Nowon-gu, Seoul. I mentioned she was a high school girl in my article "Breaking Free: A Story of Resilience and Redemption" long ago. After I taught her how to memorize the periodic table of chemistry in her first class, she got good grades on her school test. I remember her liking the result like a child. However, she quickly became depressed when she no longer got good grades on her school exams. As learning progresses, many questions arise about obtaining a chemical concentration in chemistry subjects. You can solve these questions through calculations, much like in mathematics. I remember watching the pretty girl find math and science difficult. As time passed, her hope of going to a good university diminished.

Mathematics professors at Korean universities overlook critical aspects of their teaching approach. They want all students to have fun with math as they do or at least have sufficient math skills. I often remember reading interviews with media professors who said they had to teach new basics to students entering Seoul National University because they lacked math skills. I am sorry, but it is not too late to start something like that after graduate school. Doesn't Professor June Huh show it well? We must create an environment where high school students do not give up math, English, and other subjects.

We must streamline the learning process to help students tackle issues relevant to their daily lives. It's essential to focus on practical knowledge that remains useful beyond exams. There is still time to find a future university or graduate school major. The education system must evolve to allow students to achieve desirable grades through reasonable study hours, such as until 9 or 10 pm, rather than unsustainable late-night sessions extending to 2 am. We should shift from a relative grading system to an absolute one, focusing on individual achievement rather than comparative performance. We shouldn't view a high volume of perfect exam scores as unusual but as a testament to the examinees' hard work. Universities should have complete autonomy in selecting students through entrance exams, free from external influences. The Ministry of Education should refrain from interfering fully with the details as it is now.

THE ARTICLE WAS published in an interview with Professor June Huh titled "From 'Math Struggler' to 'Genius Mathematician'... "Don't Rush to Conclusions in Life or Mathematics" stands out for its depth. This conversation, held on January 1, 2022, occurred well before Professor Huh won the Fields Medal (M. Kim, 2022). Twenty years after abandoning mathematics for poetry, this young man carved a name for himself in the mathematical arena. I want to transfer some of the interview content.

- The Math Struggler Who Dreamed of Being a Poet
  "I really enjoy talking to people. Moreover, having lived abroad for over ten years, I rarely have the chance to speak with Koreans. Therefore, I find these conversations incredibly enjoyable." Professor Huh, on the screen, smiled innocently, like a child. It was a stark contrast

to the image of a genius mathematician immersed in their own world in a secluded room.

- You seem to use the adverb 'incredibly' a lot habitually.

  "Ah! That is a great, big, and disappointing aspect. Vocabulary needs to flow in and out like waves to be maintained, but my Korean keeps slipping away. I cannot make sophisticated word choices. It is not like I can freeze the language to preserve it." It felt like I was talking to a linguist rather than a mathematician.

- I heard you dreamed of being a poet when you were young.

  "I fell in love with poetry during middle and high school. I especially loved the works of the poet Gi Hyeong-do. When I read poetry, I could feel a different kind of communication that I could not experience in everyday conversations. The poetic expressions were ambiguous, making it difficult to know exactly what the author intended, but that led to some special experiences of deep connection and empathy."

- A mathematician who dreamed of being a poet, the connection seems obscure.

  "In fact, they share common ground. Poetry, by nature, is a paradoxical medium. It is an attempt to communicate the inexpressible through language, which creates poetic ambiguity. Conversely, mathematics is about expressing and sharing abstract concepts that are difficult to bring down to earth through numbers and logic. Both highly condense their subjects and create powerful symbols."

- Did people call you a genius from an early age?

  "Not at all. I started at a private elementary school but could not adapt, so I transferred to a local elementary school. In high school, I skipped school to write poetry. I thought I would quickly become a published poet if I wrote poetry instead of attending school. I suffered from a severe case of 'high school freshman syndrome.' In the end, I wasted my time. I did not go to school, but I would wait for my friends to finish and then go to the PC room with them."

- Does that mean you did not like math?

"Initially, I was drawn to math, but linking it with college entrance exams dampened my enthusiasm. In my third year of middle school, I considered participating in a math competition or going to a science high school, so I talked to my teacher. They said it was too late to start. That made me think, 'I'm not good at math.' Looking back now as a mathematician, it does not make sense. Koreans say 'it's too late to do something' too often and harshly to others and themselves. Isn't it never too late to start anything?"

As mentioned, the Korean perspective often tends toward definitiveness, drawing stark lines between 'yes' and 'no.' I, too, have had a similar experience. When I was only 27 or 28, a classical music academy was across the street from my company. One day, I stopped by at lunchtime and talked with the manager. I told her, "I want to learn the violin." She said, "Your fingers are already too stiff to learn. Why not try learning the cello instead?" A few weeks later, I got my paycheck. I went to Sampoong Department Store, Gangnam's most luxurious department store. I bought a cello instrument and had to pay my monthly salary. I went there on the day the academy closed. So, I lost the opportunity to gain experience with the violin or cello. Some so many people talk about other people's future carelessly. If I had played the violin at that age, would I not have been a person with over 30 years of experience now? You do not know if I won a prize in any local contest.

• What kind of childhood did you have?

"I think I was pretty lucky. My parents were busy, but they were available to take evening walks with me every day and go to the movies on weekends. They created a predictable routine that gave me a sense of psychological stability. I believe that allowed me to be interested in abstract subjects like math. It is challenging to pursue pure academics without having peace of mind."

As a father of two young children, aged one and eight, Professor Huh strives to offer them a stable daily routine, just like his parents did. His wife is a graduate school classmate from Seoul National University's Mathematics Department. At first, they both walked the path of mathematicians, but after having children, his wife stopped studying. Professor Huh laughed, saying, "It's all because of my poor participation in parenting."

So, what about math education for the children of a mathematician? "Our kids have no interest in math. Instead, they are like K-pop geniuses. They can correctly identify whether a song is by BTS or BLACKPINK just by hearing the drumbeat once!"

- In 2009, you applied to twelve overseas doctoral programs but only got accepted at the University of Illinois, right?

"The outcome was foreseeable. My undergraduate journey spanned six years with less-than-stellar grades. I think the University of Illinois took a gamble on me, thanks to Professor Hironaka's recommendation letter (laughs)." The gamble paid off as a jackpot. In his first year of the doctoral program, he solved the Reid Conjecture. A year earlier, the University of Michigan had rejected him. Still, later, they reached out to him with a 'love call,' where he eventually completed his Ph.D.

He had poor undergraduate grades, so the graduate schools he wanted to study could not accept him. However, although the University of Illinois is not one of the top universities in the United States, he solved one of the most challenging math problems in the first year of his Ph.D. there. And the University of Michigan, which had not received him a year earlier, sent him a love call. Other than that university, I wonder if the universities that dropped him should pick him up. Just solving one unsolved riddle in the world of mathematics is an outstanding achievement.

- The phenomenon of national math trauma appears to be uniquely prevalent in Korea.

"It is not the math itself that is the problem, but the Korean college entrance exam structure. There is a quite straightforward way to eliminate math stress. Although it is not something a mathematician should say, if we decide not to include math in the college entrance exams starting next year, wouldn't the problem be solved immediately (laughs)?"

As mentioned above, his joke about solving a Korean math problem hit the core. Currently, the level of high school mathematics in Korea is extremely high, and the proportion of scores in the entrance exam is exceptionally high. In this situation, is it typical for education to divide students into those who are good at math and those who aren't (actually, people who have given up on learning math) so that their lives make an enormous difference? You must ensure that anyone studying hard can get 95 or 100 points. The percentage of scores in mathematics must also be less severe than in general subjects so that students can avoid risking their lives in mathematics as it is now. That way, the number of people who dislike math will drop dramatically. Some of them, like Professor Huh, may eventually become brilliant mathematicians. If math looks easy, many students will apply for science. But then, how good would it be to have a large talent pool to lead a technological powerhouse?

- Do you still write poetry these days?

  "I do not write, but I read a lot. Lately, I have been enjoying the works of poet David Whyte. I highly recommend his prose piece 'Consolations'! He uses language very delicately, and savoring his words as you read is a pleasure."

- You seem to have a strong background in the humanities.

  "I view mathematics as an integral part of the humanities. Unlike astronomy and physics, which delve into nature's creations, mathematics navigates the realms of human invention. In that sense, it has a similar essence to philosophy and literature."

Many Koreans will have mixed emotions when they hear the news of Professor Huh's award for Field Award. It is me, too. I remember the math class I took in middle school. The person in charge of us was a teacher who looked like over sixty, whether it was the vice principal or someone about to retire. He always taught by biting a matchstick. After some time, it was interesting to watch the red sulfur of the match finally melt into the saliva and suck into his lips. Then, perhaps bragging to the students that he was memorizing, he would solve all the math problems and solutions from the left edge of the blackboard to the bottom right without saying a word when class started. In short, he taught the answer rather than the concept of mathematics.

Unfortunately, I have never been to high school, so at first, I self-taught high school math the way I learned in middle school, but that did not help me at all. Then, I entered Jongno Academy, Korea's most challenging college entrance academy, and met good math teachers. At that time, about one-third of the first-year students at Seoul National University were from Jongno Academy. Three math teachers were in charge of me, but they all taught different fields. I am a preliminary humanities major, so there are at least three. Still, the science and engineering class students probably had more math teachers in charge. I remember the old gentleman in charge of the logic part among them. At the time, he was in his mid-seventies. His class, dealing with propositions and arguments, felt like a clear and coherent philosophy class. Whenever he argued and proved the truth and falsehood of propositions through his lessons, I used to feel the beauty. At that time, I liked the logic class so much that I almost majored in mathematics or philosophy.

Countless individuals, myself included, encountered teachers who inadvertently steered our lives in unexpected directions. Decades have passed, but such a problem continues in school settings. Studying at school should be a place to understand how the world works, not to do well on exams. That way, step by step, is life and can be truly precious moments. No one may frustrate and subdue young people who know nothing.

OPINION FROM AN MIT MATHEMATICIAN

I previously wanted to reference an article in this discussion but initially couldn't locate it online. However, I finally discovered it after a renewed search effort this morning. However, I need help to see the original text in the first place. Throughout my search, I noticed numerous instances where people used the original author's work without proper source attribution. For-profit study abroad agencies and personal blogs manipulated and used them for their purposes. Most people need to be aware of the problem in such a section, which is a serious matter; even if it is not their writing, they must show the source or get permission from the original author. I found the article I was looking for in several places, but I needed help to figure out where the original was. It did not disclose the source anywhere, so I did not know the year who wrote the original text. And since the contents posted on the Internet did not match all of them, I had to search for the original text more tenaciously.

Caption: A view of MIT that I drew by Midjourney.

So, after persistent tracing, I finally found the source on the Korean Federation of Scientists and Engineers homepage, which someone uploaded on July 17, 2003 (Depressedmode, 2003). The person who wrote the article's nickname is '우울모드 Depressed Mode' the article, "Perspectives on Prestigious American and Korean Universities — Part 1 (Envious of MIT)" offers insightful views. The nickname' Depressed Mode' reminded me of Dr. Yang Shin-kyu, who died in Boston from depression in 2005. In 2003, he was a professor at the NYU Stern School of Business and a visiting professor at MIT after earning a master's and Ph.D. degrees at MIT.

TITLE: PERSPECTIVES ON PRESTIGIOUS AMERICAN UNIVERSITIES AND KOREAN UNIVERSITIES — PART 1 (ENVIOUS OF MIT)

My journey to the United States began six years ago when I started my doctoral program at MIT. I've since earned my degree and am now working here. During my first year of studying here, I had a sense of pride in the college education I had received in Korea. Many Korean international students around me were top graduates from Seoul National University or even the top students in the entire university. Interestingly, over 80% of Korean graduate students at MIT hailed from Seoul National University. So, when looking at American students, I even thought, "Let's see how great you guys really are." In addition, Korean students in the United States tended to perform very well on exams as they did in Korea.

Since the math level taught in Korean middle and high schools is much higher than in the United States, engineering students benefit from that background. As a result, Korean international students usually ranked high in exam scores. Of course, some Korean students even went as far as exchanging cheat sheets to study among themselves. Once, I casually asked an American student about their opinion on cheat sheets. They frowned and said that what matters is how much you learn, not how well you score by cheating, which embarrassed me. (Of course, not all Americans are honest when taking exams.)

Before I knew it, a year had passed, focusing solely on exams. It was time to start my research and consult with my advisor on which direction to take in my doctoral research. Naturally, the professors at a prestigious university like MIT were top-notch. Meeting the very authors I had wondered about in Korea when professors asked students to translate foreign books was an incredible experience. Indeed, such people were different. For the first time in my life, I felt what a genius was like. I had an intuitive sense of admiration for their imagination and creativity. I had resolved the mysteries. I realized that to reach the level of creating those fascinating theories

I had seen only in textbooks and winning Nobel Prizes; one must be such a genius. From then on, I started worrying. How well can I do? What is the secret? What kind of education did these people receive? Of course, I had confidence in my life as an international student. I am attending classes diligently and doing well in exams.

However, I had no confidence in this aspect. However, I consoled myself, thinking that it was natural for the world's best engineering college to have such professors and that they were on a different level from me. Seeing the American students, I initially thought my Korean education, especially the advanced math, would make me outperform them. However, as time passed, chilling events kept happening. Over time, several American students gradually stood out, surprising me, solving increasingly complex problems and finding their way through obstacles. For example, the American student who initially explained differential geometry to me now explains theories I cannot understand. At first, I thought that it was possible. I believed they had chosen the right field for themselves. However, as I saw increased cases like this and watched their progress, I thought: Some of these people might become professors like the geniuses I admired. That is right. It was those students who became such professors.

From that point on, I began to feel a sense of sadness. I realized there seemed to be an invisible barrier that most Korean students studying abroad, including myself, could not overcome. Despite our country's population and passion for education, which should have already produced several Nobel laureates and world-class scientists and engineers, I could not understand why Korean students who received a first-class education in Korea were struggling at MIT. I could not find the answer by reading books in the school library. However, as time passed and I made friends with Americans and observed their lifestyles, I gradually gained some understanding of education in the United States.

The contrast between Korean and American educational approaches starts from early childhood. In Korea, parents often discipline their children emotionally and sometimes physically. Meanwhile, in the United States, explanations are logical and straightforward. Parents provide a detailed description when a child asks why they cannot do something. If the child throws a tantrum, they employ various creative strategies to divert the child's attention. Parents consistently engage their children in conversation and strive to pass on the wisdom of life they inherited from their parents. It contrasted greatly with the minimal conversation found in many Korean households. I have a child myself, but I cannot raise them the same way as Americans do, as most Koreans and I lack the deeply ingrained experience passed down through generations. This difference in upbringing concerns me about whether I can effectively raise my child in America.

The gap widens further when children attend school. While Korean students focus on memorization, critical thinking skills, and comprehension, American students develop creativity, imagination, and social skills. These qualities are a foundation for the geniuses who later stand out in graduate schools. While Korean students absorb prepackaged knowledge created by others, American students learn how to think. They engage in initiative-taking learning and discussions, exploring independently, and prioritizing writing, presentation, and logical thinking skills. Although they may learn calculus later than Korean students, by the time they reach their twenties, when creativity is at its peak, the thinking skills they acquired during their childhood enable them to absorb knowledge like a sponge and create something new.

Upon arriving here, one more thing that surprised me was the curiosity of Americans. Their zeal for learning and exploring new concepts vastly exceeds that commonly seen in our country. While we invented movable metal type (1377), water clocks (1434), and sundials (1437) in Korea but failed to develop them further, the West discovered the laws of universal gravitation. It evolved into today's science and technology. Automatons, perhaps dismissed as childish in our country, gained fame in Europe centuries ago. Many ingenious inventions emerged, such as self-playing pianos, swimming swans flapping their wings, and writing dolls. These developments ultimately led to the creation of machines that automatically calculate, in other words, computers. When I invited American friends to my home and showed them something even slightly fascinating, they would ask a barrage of questions about how somebody made it and the principles behind its operation. There was even an instance when an American fixing a sewer showed the same interest and insisted that I make one for his son, offering money in return.

In contrast, Korean doctoral students at MIT barely glance at such items for over a second, show no interest, and only focus on drinking alcohol. It begs the question: can we truly aspire to be world leaders in science and technology? While we reluctantly engage in science and technology research to become an advanced country or win a Nobel Prize, many people here conduct scientific and technological research out of pure love, fascination, and desire to know. The passion of those who enjoy their work is unmatched.

WHY CURIOSITY MATTERS

Caption: An image of a Korean landscape painting I drew with Midjourney.

Written nearly two decades ago by Depressed Mode, this article highlights the stark contrasts between Korean education and more advanced educational systems. While not explicitly stated, Depressed Mode likely completed his undergraduate and master's degrees in mathematics at Seoul National University. He said he felt elated when he first started his Ph.D. at MIT. Subsequently, he observed American students, initially trailing, gradually surpassing him. His graduation marked a pivotal realization of the disparities between Korean and American educational approaches. As he said, it was because he could not find it in the books in the library.

He said, "One more thing that surprised me when I came here is the curiosity of Americans." It is what I am experiencing. When hosting guests who grew up in America, I've noticed they often prefer exploring the room rather than immediately sitting down, even when offered a seat. Instead, they walk around the living room, etc., paying close attention to the furniture in the house and the pictures and artwork on the walls. Then, if they have any questions, they ask questions first.

In contrast, Korean guests typically sit immediately upon being offered a chair. And they do not get up except to go to the bathroom. "Conversely, Korean students in the Ph.D. program at MIT don't look at them for more than a second, show no interest at all, and drink only," says Depressed Mode. This behavior exemplifies a significant difference in the innate curiosity between Americans and Koreans. This raises the question: does the result-oriented focus of Korean education stifle natural curiosity? It prompts us to ponder the importance of the educational process. Is the obsession with results so deeply ingrained in our psyche that we overlook the journey's value?

BEYOND WHITE

Penned January 24, 2023

[My Question to the ChatGPT]

"Anyone who thinks they are a superior race because they are "white" is a racist. In humans, skin colors are just one form of diverse genes, which does not mean which skin color is superior. Insist on the thesis that humans are equal regardless of skin color, based on 500 words or fewer)."

[ChatGPT's Answer]

Humans are all equal regardless of skin color. Skin color is just one aspect of human diversity, and there is no scientific basis to support the idea that one skin color is superior to another. Everyone has their own unique traits and qualities, and no one should be judged or discriminated against based on their skin color.

Skin color is determined by genetic traits passed down from one generation to the next. This means that skin color is not a sign of superiority, but rather a reflection of the diversity of the human race.

Every culture has its own unique values and beliefs, and no one should be judged or discriminated against because of their heritage or skin color.

In addition to skin color, people are also diverse in other ways. We come in different shapes, sizes, and even genders. We have distinct cultures and beliefs, and each person is unique in their own way. No one can be considered superior because of their skin color, because each person is an individual with their own set of unique experiences and perspectives.

The idea that one race is superior to another is not only offensive, but it is also dangerous. It fosters a sense of superiority and entitlement, which can lead to discrimination and even violence towards people of other races. This is why it is so important to emphasize the idea of equality among all humans, regardless of skin color.

The idea of equality is something that everyone should strive for. We should respect each other's differences and celebrate the uniqueness of the human race. Every person has the right to be treated fairly and to live their life without fear of discrimination based on their skin color. We should strive to create a world where everyone can be accepted, respected, and celebrated for who they are.

[My Same Question again]

[ChatGPT's Answer]

No matter what skin color, humans are all equal and should be treated equally. Anthropologists have found that there is no single race that is superior to another; instead, there is a diversity of cultures, each with its own unique values and beliefs. The notion of racial superiority is based upon a false assumption that one's skin color determines their worth and value as a person, when in reality, it is simply one form of diverse genes.

Our individual backgrounds and experiences shape who we are as individuals, but this should not be seen as a barrier to equality. Everyone should be judged on their own merits, not on their skin color. To suggest otherwise is to deny the basic principles of human rights and equality.

No one can deny that racism and prejudice still exist in our society. We must strive to create a world where everyone is treated equally and with respect, no matter their skin color. This begins with a commitment to understanding and respecting diverse cultures and beliefs. We should strive to increase our knowledge and understanding of the complexities of identity and how it shapes our lives.

We should also recognize that we all have privileges and disadvantages based on our identities. We must recognize and challenge any form of racism or discrimination in order to create an inclusive, equitable society. We must use education and dialogue to create an understanding of why racism and prejudice exist, and how we can combat them.

In conclusion, it is important to remember that skin color is just one form of diverse genes and has no bearing on one's worth or value as a person. We must strive to create an equitable society that recognizes and celebrates our differences while also recognizing our shared humanity. This can only be achieved by working together to challenge prejudice and discrimination and to ensure that everyone is treated with respect and dignity.

I requested the following from ChatGPT. "Summarize the below article in 100 words.

https://www.aljazeera.com/opinions/2021/7/23/white–is–not–a–colour–white–is–an–ideology"
[*ChatGPT's Answer*]

This article by Jumana Abdel–Razzaq argues that white is not merely a colour, but an ideology that has been used to oppress people of colour. She discusses how power, privilege, and authority are all tied to whiteness and are used to oppress non–white people. She explains how colonialism and imperialism have perpetuated white supremacy and how it continues to shape global politics, economics, and culture. She also mentions how white supremacy has been used to justify horrific acts of violence and genocide. Ultimately, Abdel–Razzaq argues that white is not an innocent colour, but a powerful ideology that has been used to oppress people of colour for centuries.

[My Rebuttal]

"Hamid Dabashi authored this article, not Jumana Abdel–Razzaq. So why do you think she is?

ChatGPT wrote someone else. So, I refuted."

[ChatGPT's Answer]

This was an error. The article was written by Hamid Dabashi, not Jumana Abdel–Razzaq. In the article, Dabashi argues that white is not just a colour, but an ideology that has been used to oppress people of colour. He explains how colonialism and imperialism have perpetuated white supremacy and how it continues to shape global politics, economics, and culture. He also mentions how white supremacy has been used to justify horrific acts of violence and genocide. Ultimately, Dabashi argues that white is not an innocent colour, but a powerful ideology that has been used to oppress people of colour for centuries.

IN MY RECENT exchange with ChatGPT (3.5), I explored the capabilities of artificial intelligence in producing coherent writing. This artificial intelligence is setting an example of coherent writing. However, as seen above, ChatGPT also misquotes authors. So, if I go over it without knowing it, the utterly wrong information is correct. Like the above, my next article is about human skin color. There's a prevalent belief that Koreans are fixated on the pale skin often associated with Caucasians. As a result, white people look at such Koreans strangely. In addition, Koreans do not have a proper logic to respond to such stinging gazes from the outside. So, this article will be about both the attacking and defending camps. This article argues that the attacking base needs to resolve misunderstandings, and the defending center needs to become more confident.

It is common knowledge that all Koreans are interested in their skin. People are very interested in how clear and clean the skin tone is, whether there are blemishes or wrinkles on the face. However, they do not limit it only to celebrities who need widespread popularity. The desire for flawless skin, often equated with youth and health, is widespread among Koreans. Therefore, it is common for celebrities and the public to maintain very fair skin in Korea. It is also true that Korea's beauty industry has had a significant impact following the rapid rise of K-culture worldwide. Here, it created people who attacked Koreans' preference for being like white skin. The core of their argument is that Koreans' skin differs from that of Caucasians, so why do they apply makeup like Caucasians' skin?

The Korean preference for fair skin predates significant interactions with Caucasians. Since they didn't even exist on the Korean Peninsula, Koreans already had the average Korean's preference for skin these days. Historically, even centuries ago, Koreans idealized beauty as having "white jade-like skin." The National Institute of the Korean Language's Standard Korean Language Dictionary lists "White Jade" as "white jade in color" (Wordrow, 2022). For example, the novel "Land" by Park Gyeong-ni includes the quote, "Gyu-su, a noble figure like white jade, and the beautiful Choi Seo-hee..." There is no way that women from noble families do manual labor in the fields and mountains like ordinary people. Farmers and servants had no choice but to have rough skin with dark faces because they exposed their skin to the hot sunlight and lived with harmful rays for the rest of their lives. And the skin on their faces is also tanned and wrinkled, making them look older than they really are.

On the other hand, the noble women who always spent time embroidering, reading books, and drawing pictures in their rooms used various methods to block the sunlight even when they went out. Hence, their skin color was clearly different from that of ordinary people. Their skin was as delicate as white jade. Those who didn't engage in outdoor labor naturally maintained lighter skin, untouched by the sun. Therefore, it was natural for those who did not envy their position. And one thing that best reveals the difference between the faces exposed to the outside is the skin.

Caption: Sin Yun-bok's paintings offer a window into daily life during the Joseon Dynasty.

The subjects Sin Yun-bok drew were mostly Kisaeng rather than women of the Yangban class. Kisaeng of the Joseon Dynasty made it their profession to arouse excitement at entertainment venues, etc. They were good at dancing, singing, and poetry (Bae, 2020). They were celebrities like the artists of today. Sin Yun-bok's paintings from the Joseon Dynasty illustrate the meticulous attention women paid to their appearance, such as wearing makeup to enhance and protect their faces from solid sunlight as much as possible.

IN AARTFACT, DATED November 2, 2017, Rachel Garner explains in an article titled 'Why do South Koreans want white skin?' (Garner, 2017). Rachel Garner asserts that historically, across cultures, tan skin was often associated with the lower class. People with tanned skin worked hours in the sun outdoors to earn money, completing manual labor. Then, she said, when the Industrial Revolution broke out in the 19th century, the Western world changed 360 degrees. The lower classes started to work inside factories, and the lack of sunlight made them pale. In contrast, the upper classes began to travel abroad. So, people considered darker, more radiant complexions and golden skin tones more desirable.

Garner (2017) asserts, "In the East, however, fair skin was — and remains still, a sign of wealth and beauty." Next, she focuses on skin lightening for Koreans, saying that her craze for pale skin, in particular, has become somewhat of an obsession. Many have even turned to skin-lightening products and procedures to achieve their ideal complexion. As Garner (2017) stated, historically, people agreed that the ruling class, who could live without work, had fair skin. However, she can't provide a proper basis for why people want white skin in Korea and explains it as an 'obsession.'

Oh5sarah, who introduces herself as a digital creator, wrote in an article titled "My Trouble With Korea's Obsession With White Skin," "I've been living in Korea for almost 5 years, and I still can't get over the fact that most all beauty commercials and ads push the idea that light skin is more beautiful than let's say tan skin," (Oh, n.d.). From her statements, she believes that tan skin is more beautiful and healthier. However, skin color preferences are subjective and not a matter of right or wrong. And not all Koreans have the same skin color. Some people will have fairer skin if not exposed to the sun for a while, while others will have darker skin. However, most Koreans turn white or light skin overall if they live without sunlight for a few months or a year. IN MY VIEW, Koreans, like others in East Asia, have a naturally lighter skin tone, distinct from Caucasian skin, as seen through Korean dramas and K-pop singers. In preparing this article, I focused on the Susan-ri tomb mural in North Korea, a World Cultural Heritage site, as pivotal evidence. As I was doing my research while writing this article, I came across an article written about it. On December 24, 2021, Yoon Min-sik delved into historical perspectives on Korean beauty standards in his article 'Tracing the Root of Koreans' 'white skin obsession' in The Korea Herald (Yoon, 2021). Yun Min-sik spotlights aristocrats by highlighting typical era elements, such as the World Heritage-listed murals in Goguryeo tombs like the Susan-ri Tomb (A.D. 37-668) in North Korea. From a 2014 article in 'Love of Cultural Heritage,' a monthly magazine of the Cultural Heritage Administration, "White and glossy skin symbolized high class, which motivated people — men and women alike — to make their skin white. Our ancestors' preference for bathing and using cosmetic products made from natural ingredients demonstrates this."

Caption: Successfully preserved through a UNESCO/Republic of Korea project since 2000, the Yaksu-ri and Susan-ri tombs stand as remarkable relics of the Koguryo kingdom.

The preservation of the Yaksu-ri and Susan-ri tombs, which exemplify the Koguryo kingdom's civilization, was made possible by a collaborative UNE-SCO/Republic of Korea Funds-in-Trust project, "Safeguarding of Koguryo Tombs in the Democratic People's Republic of Korea (DPRK)," coordinated by UNESCO in 1992 and implemented since 2000 in three consecutive phases (UWHC, 2019).

The mural in the Susin-ri tomb from the late fifth century is critical evidence in addressing misconceptions and debates regarding Korean beauty standards. It was about 1,500 years ago. But first, let's look at what part of this mural is its basis.

Caption: West mural paintings in Susan-ri Tomb, conserved by UNESCO/DPRK national team (UWHC, 2012).

They listed it as a World Cultural Heritage site in 2004 through a trust fund between UNESCO and the Republic of Korea in 2001. A decade-long effort, adhering to international standards, was initiated in 2008 to preserve the Susan-ri tomb's cultural heritage. UNESCO said, "The mural is considered one of Northeast Asia's most important and excellent murals."

Caption: An overview of the Susan-ri Ancient Tombs of the Northeast Asian History
Foundation is as follows (NAHF, n.d.).

Ancient Susan-ri Tombs are earthen masonry stone barrier tombs built
around the late fifth century in Susan-ri, Gangseo-gu, Nampo-si, and
Pyeongannam-do. In 1971, researchers excavated and investigated this
tomb, damaging many murals and only finding a few relics. The tomb has a
single-room structure, and the murals depict the couple's lifestyle. The north
wall, the grave's main wall, shows the spouses' indoor life, while the left and
right walls depict their outdoor activities. The Susan-ri tomb murals vividly
portray the daily life of Goguryeo's nobility, including attire, decorations, and
leisure activities, offering invaluable insights into the era's upper-class culture.
In addition, the portraits in the murals are distinguished by their mature,
refined strokes and soft color palette, showcasing exceptional artistic quality.
In particular, depicting a woman in a colored pleated skirt and Jeogori in the
murals mirrors similar imagery found in Japan's Takamatsu tomb murals,
offering a cultural influence.

Caption: The mural depicts a high-status married couple, noted for their fair-skin symbol of nobility, as they didn't engage in manual labor, setting them apart from the working class.

As depicted in the mural, the tomb likely belongs to a married couple. The high-status women, including the wife, are portrayed with finely made-up faces. One can see that this is the white skin that Koreans prefer. Since the ruling class did not have to go out to the fields and do manual labor like bond servants or ordinary people, they could naturally maintain their skin color differentiated from theirs. Therefore, people with outwardly fair skin would have been regarded as belonging to the ruling class and naturally became the preferred skin color.

Thus, the notion that Koreans' preference for bright makeup tones stems from a desire to emulate white people is mistaken. In other words, they falsely claim that non-white Koreans generally tend to prefer white skin. Yoon Min-sik says, "While people of European origin are often described as white, including in modern Korea, records show that the Far East Asians did not perceive them as having white skin (Yoon, 2021). During the Yuan Dynasty — founded by the Mongolians and occupied most of what is China — the Westerners were called "saekmok-in," which is directly translated into "people of colored eyes" but in practice meant "assorted categories." It mostly referred to the Semu people, from Central and Western Asia." He continues to argue, "Dutchman Hendrick Hamel, one of the few Westerners known to have landed on the Korean Peninsula, spent 13 years in 17th century Joseon and wrote a detailed account of the country. He said Westerners were called "myeon-cheol," which directly translates as "iron face" and in practice used to refer to a reddish, rusty complexion." It is a widespread misconception that white people, including Koreans, identify themselves primarily by their skin color. At the beginning of this article, you will notice that I asked ChatGPT to summarize an article written by Hamid Dabasi, Professor of Iranian Studies and Comparative Literature at Columbia University.

IN A JULY 23, 2021, Aljazeera article, "White is not a colour — white is an ideology," Professor Hamid Dabasi writes, "Precisely in that sense, the word "white" is a signifier of that racism, its ideological register, its coded symbol (Dabashi, 2021). That is all. No human being at birth is "white," "Black," "brown," "red," "yellow" or any other colour. They are all eventually coded with these colours to divide and rule them better. East Asians are called "yellow," West Asians and Latinx "brown," Native Americans "red," Africans "Black," all of them set against the fictive centrality of the Caucasian "white," which Europeans have racialized and reserved for themselves and gave to their settler colonial extensions in North America or Australia as a signifier of superiority. The historical origin of all such racist designations comes to full "scientific" blooming during the period Europeans call — without the slightest sense of irony — their "Enlightenment," he points out.

"What is white? White-skinned people? In fact, East Asians often have whiter complexions. That's exactly what Japanese immigrant Takao Ozawa made in the U.S. Supreme Court in 1922 when he challenged discrimination and demanded citizenship." Dr. Park Seong-chun refutes a historical case through "The position and choice of Asians in the racist system," (Park, 2021) — In the Ozawa vs. United States case, the U.S. Supreme Court legally classified Japanese individuals as non-white, despite scientific considerations (Wikipedia contributors, 2022).

Consequently, Ozawa faced defeat. In less than a year, the U.S. Supreme Court held an inconsistent ruling in United States v. Bhagat Singh Thind, stating that despite Indians being scientifically deemed white, Asian Indians are not legally classified as such. Thus, it becomes evident that the standard for whiteness relied on skin color and appearance. It is undeniable that the notion of white supremacy, prevalent over centuries, has evolved into a deeply ingrained ideology. Thus, Koreans who used white skin as their standard of beauty thousands of years ago suddenly turned into wannabes that Koreans want to imitate.

So perhaps the most significant criterion for racism is skin color? Among them, white is mistaken for having the most robust power. But Bideaux (2021) said, 'Is white skin really pink? 'Europeans' skin color is flesh and has been described as close to light pink in literature, such as paintings and novels. In this article, Kévin Bideaux writes, "I determine the shades associated with the idea of a unique flesh color, retracing its history and highlighting its inclusion in the field of pink. I do this analysis in a transhistorical and surreal way. Medieval texts, works of literature, artist's texts, paintings, abstract works, and other cultural works such as fashion, cartoons, or animation. Based on this overview, I question the hegemonic position that draws the enduring association of the color pink with complexion. I would also question this pervasive association with the racial system because the use of pink refers only to white skin, which is generally understood as skin color," the abstract states.

The belief that skin color can determine superiority or inferiority is fundamentally false, akin to the erroneous ideology of white supremacy, which falsely asserts that white people are physically and mentally superior to other races. Adhering to white supremacy aligns one with the Ku Klux Klan (KKK) or its sympathizers. However, today, very few white people are members or supporters of the KKK. This indicates a widespread rejection of white supremacy among white individuals. The idea that a race is inferior solely because its skin color is different from that of Europeans is deeply flawed. The persistence of racial conflicts underscores the unfortunate reality that some white individuals still harbor such beliefs. While most are not KKK members, discrimination and hatred based on skin color remain prevalent, leading to acts of violence and prejudice in broad daylight, such as Asians being attacked on subways in America. The spread of racial conflict and hatred from offline to online platforms highlights the significant number of individuals who judge others based solely on skin color, considering them inferior or superior. This mindset parallels the ideologies promoted by the KKK, posing a dangerous threat to society.

The preference for lighter skin in modern Korean society does not stem from a desire to imitate European skin tones. Historically, Koreans have favored fair skin long before contact with white or Black populations, driven by a preference independent of external influences. This historical preference for healthy and beautiful skin, avoiding UV rays, and using cosmetics to prevent aging or fatigue mirrors the desires of modern individuals. Thus, Koreans' keen interest in skincare is not a result of Western domination or influence as Europeans began their global conquests but rather a continuation of long-standing cultural values.

Those misinformed should acknowledge this fact and cease their misguided criticism. On the contrary, Koreans who cannot express their opinions clearly when receiving hateful questions or reading articles will take this opportunity to see that the beautiful skin they prefer is not simply a preference for Western skin but a human being in our DNA from birth. Therefore, you should not be ashamed to know that it is one of the most basic needs.

Koreans need to break free from the constraints of European-centered thinking and its resulting fantasy. While Europeans have historically identified their skin color as white, other cultures encountering them for the first time often described them as having a reddish complexion. Skin color experts do not consider white skin as genuinely white. In fact, it is nearly impossible to find someone with white skin without being affected by albinism. Although white people have genetic and racial differences, their skin tone is generally light and relatively thin compared to Asians and other groups. This results in the exposure of blood vessels and a tendency for the skin to appear red. Thus, it's understandable that those first encountering Europeans might have perceived them as 'red-skinned' rather than white.

Despite this, Korean skincare practices have gained popularity worldwide. The skin tone of K-drama actors and K-pop singers has become a symbol of health and vitality. Often compared to white skin, their untanned complexion may evoke envy in some white individuals due to their radiant glow. Nonetheless, Nonetheless, we must reject the absurd notion that skin color dictates racial superiority or inferiority. Professor Hamid Dabasi argues that we cannot define race and that it should only be considered a human characteristic (Dabasi, 2021).

The term "White" should also be abolished from our vocabulary. In the United States, this term is used in various fields, including medicine, education, business, and government. However, using skin color as a criterion for classification or discrimination is no different from the language used to refer to enslaved Black people during colonial times. It is crucial for all, including those identified as white, to reject ideologies of white supremacy and embrace the equality of all humans. If someone feels inferior in front of white people, they should immediately let go of that feeling.

On the other hand, if someone feels an unexplained hatred or resentment toward white people, they should deeply reflect on themselves and examine their beliefs. Skin color should not be a racial discrimination or superiority criterion. Instead, we must strive to create a world where everyone is recognized as unique and valuable, regardless of skin tone.

In a world ever more interconnected, the prejudices and stereotypes anchored in our collective past are more than just outdated; they are dangerous and divisive. The desire for lighter skin in Korean culture is often misunderstood and misinterpreted as a yearning to 'be white' when it has roots far beyond Western influence. This is not just a matter of correcting a historical inaccuracy. It is about reclaiming the narrative and correcting the misinformation that serves to perpetuate divisions based on skin color — a false metric of human worth.

To foster greater unity, we must critically examine our understanding of other cultures and the beliefs underpinning our identities. By doing so, we gain a deeper understanding of ourselves and remove one more brick from the wall of racial misunderstanding and discrimination that still divides humanity.

Therefore, let us strive to create a world that evaluates a human's worth not by the shade of their skin but by the content of their character, the extent of their kindness, and the depth of their understanding. For in the end, our shared humanity is the one currency that holds intrinsic value. Recognizing this truth is imperative, and we must embody this understanding in our daily interactions with all individuals.

INDEX

PART ONE

Allimex, (n.d.). Company profile. Allimex.

Bowser, K. (1991). AIVF guide to international film & video festivals. Foundation for Independent Video and Film. https://searchworks.stanford.edu/view/3301587

Hwang, Y. (2019). 말을 씻는 시간 *[The time of verbal rebirth]*. Puleunhyanggi Publishing. https://m.blog.naver.com/hyj4340

Kaufman, A. (2006, June 14). IndieWire. IndieWire. https://www.indiewire.com/2006/06/closed-association-for-independent-video-filmmakers-134978

KINEKO International Film Festival. (2023, March 1). FilmFreeway. https://filmfreeway.com/KINEKOInternationalChildrensFilmFestival

Readers News. (n.d.). Compnay intro. Readers News. https://www.readersnews.com/com/com-1.html

Ryu, J.B. (2018, July 3). 최영미 "괴물, 10년 전에 썼어야할 시. . .' 괴물 주니어' 넘쳐난다" [Choi Youngmi "the monster, a poem that should have been written 10 years ago. . . 'monster junior' is overflowing"]. Yonhap News TV. https://m.yonhapnewstv.co.kr/news/MYH20180703020100038

Sim, J., Park, J., Lee, Y., & Park, W. (Directors). (2014, October). 과외교사 등 근로자 외의 직종에 대한 직업소개 실태조사 및 법 적용방안 연구 [Investigation of actual conditions of job introduction to occupations other than workers such as private tutors and research on law application methods] (By 숙명여자대학교 산학협력단 [Sookmyung Women's University Industry-University Cooperation Foundation]). KISTI. https://scienceon. kisti.re.kr/commons/util/originalView.do?cn=TRKO201600016687&dbt =TRKO&rn=

Son, D. (2023, March 7). 사교육비 26조, 2년 연속 역대 최대...교육부 " 상반기 중 대책 발표" [Private education expenditure of 26 trillion, the highest ever for 2 consecutive years... Ministry of Education "announcement of countermeasures during the first half of the year"]. Chosun Biz. https://biz. chosun.com/topics/topics_social/2023/03/07/EZXTHUNTT5GBLHIG-ZZJN232X3U/

The Nikkan Kogyo Shimbun. (n.d.). Corporate profile. The Nikkan Kogyo Shimbun. https://corp.nikkan.co.jp/p/english/index

Wikipedia contributors. (2022a, March 11). List of newspapers in South Korea. Wikipedia. https://en.wikipedia.org/wiki/List_of_newspapers_in_South_Korea

PART TWO

Brin, D. (n.d.). David Brin about writing and reading science fiction. (n.d.). David Brin. https://www.davidbrin.com/books_aboutreadingandwriting.html

Chua, A. (2007). Day of empire: How hyperpowers rise to global dominance — and why they fall. Doubleday.

CNN. (2012). Fortune 500. CNN. https://money.cnn.com/magazines/fortune/fortune500/2012/full_list/

Drucker, P. F. (2001). The essential Drucker: The best of sixty years of Peter Drucker's essential writings on management.

Goodreads. (n.d.). A quote by Robert Frost. Goodreads. https://www.goodreads.com/quotes/200-no-tears-in-the-writer-no-tears-in-the-reader

Hindle, T. (2008). Guide to management ideas and gurus. John Wiley & Sons.

Joseph, A. (2017, June 15). WATCH: Joyce Carol Oates reveals a writer's secret: "Nobody wants perfection". Salon. https://www.salon.com/2017/06/25/watch-joyce-carol-oates-reveals-a-writers-secret-nobody-wants-perfection/

Krugman, P. R. (1991). The age of diminished expectations: U.S. economic policy in the 1990s. MIT Press.

Library of Congress, (n.d.). Destitute pea pickers in California. mother of seven children. age thirty-two. Library of Congress. https://www.loc.gov/resource/fsa.8b29516/

Literati Pulp. (2016, October 9). Great quotes from 100 years of Noble Prize For Literature winners. Literati Pulp. https://literatipulp.com/2016/10/09/great-quotes-from-100-years-of-noble-prize-for-literature-winners/

New York Squash. (n.d.). New York Squash. https://www.nysquash.com/

Poore, Ch. (1954, October 29). Hemingway's quality built on a stern apprenticeship. New York Times. https://archive.nytimes.com/www.nytimes.com/books/99/07/04/specials/hemingway-quality.html

Pucci, C. (2011, January 22). Surprise! Sea-tac hotel at top of TripAdvisor ratings. Seattle Times. https://www.seattletimes.com/life/travel/surprise-sea-tac-hotel-at-top-of-tripadvisor-ratings/

Quote Investigator. (n.d.). Writing is easy; You just open a vein and bleed. Quote Investigator. https://quoteinvestigator.com/2011/09/14/writing-bleed/

The Metropolitan Museum of Art, (n.d.). Robert Capa: The falling soldier. The Metropolitan Museum of Art. https://www.metmuseum.org/art/collection/search/283315

PART THREE

Bacic, R. (2017, December 3). His class is famously tough. 'The Dark Knight' and 'Westworld' wouldn't exist without it. Washington Post. https://www.washingtonpost.com/lifestyle/style/meet-the-tough-professor-who-inspired-jonathan-nolan-and-john-mulaney/2017/11/30/5f94d35c-be52-11e7-959c-fe2b598d8c00_story.html

Wikipedia contributors. (2018). Michael Schur. Wikipedia. https://en.wikipedia.org/wiki/Michael_Schur

PART FOUR

Ambler, P., Behal, A., Ramirez, E., Shakirah Mohd Muslimin, A., C Simms, J., II, Wang, Y., Christopher Wong, I., & Yin, D. (2019). 30 under 30 Asia 2019. Forbes. https://www.forbes.com/under30/list/2019/asia/#22f1ec647572

Bae, H. (2020, April 9). Shin Yun-bok, the weed-like figure, opens the Joseon Renaissance. Maeil Business Newspaper. https://www.mk.co.kr/news/culture/9288851

Barnard College. (2021, September 1). Barnard professor Lisa Son discusses the psychology of activism [Video]. YouTube. https://www.youtube.com/watch?v=H9_7rwzIWck

Bideaux, K. (2021, November 1). Is white skin really pink? Le Centre pour la Communication Scientifique Directe. https://doi.org/10.23738/ccsj.130205

Centers for Disease Prevention and Control. (2022, August 11). Coronavirus Disease 2019. Centers for Disease Control and Prevention. https://www.cdc.gov/media/releases/2022/p0811-covid-guidance.html

Dabashi, H. (2021, July 23). White is not a colour — white is an ideology. Al Jazeera. https://www.aljazeera.com/opinions/2021/7/23/white-is-not-a-colour-white-is-an-ideology

Depressedmode. (2003, July 17). 미국유명대와 한국대학에 대한 시각 [Perspectives on famous American universities and Korean universities]. Scieng. http://scieng.net/now/19996

Edward Family. (n.d.). Edward Weston & Cole Weston Family. Edward Family. https://edward-weston.com/

Encyclopedia. (n.d.). Richter, Curt P. Encyclopedia. https://www.encyclopedia.com/science/dictionaries-thesauruses-pictures-and-press-releases/richter-curt-p

Gallup. (2021, April 7). 한국인의 종교 1984−2021 (1) 종교 현황 [Religion of Koreans 1984-2021 (1) status of religion]. Gallup. https://www.gallup.co.kr/gallupdb/reportContent.asp?seqNo=1208

Garner, R. (2017, November 1). Why do South Koreans want white skin? Artefact. https://www.artefactmagazine.com/2017/11/02/why-do-south-koreans-want-white-skin/

Giordano, R. (n.d.). Portraits of Edgar Allan Poe. PoeStories.com. https://poestories.com/gallery/portraits-of-poe

Harvard University. (2023, March 8). Harvard University athletics. Harvard University. https://www.harvard.edu/campus/athletics/

Henni, J., & Schonfeld, A. (2023, March 6). Women changing the usic industry today: 'I deserve the spotlight.' Peoplemag. https://people.com/music/women-changing-music-industry-today/#d812a098-d619-4ccb-932e-becfdb9d1222

Hostetler, L. (n.d.). Alfred Stieglitz (1864–1946) and American photography. The Met's Heilbrunn Timeline of Art History. https://www.metmuseum.org/toah/hd/stgp/hd_stgp.htm

Hwang, Y. (2019). 말을 씻는 시간 [The Time of Verbal Rebirth]. Pluenhyanggi Publishing. https://m.blog.naver.com/hyj4340

International Center of Photography. (n.d.-a.) Artist Eugène Atget (1857 - 1927) French. International Center of Photography. https://www.icp.org/browse/archive/constituents/eug%C3%A8ne-atget?all/all/all/all/0

International Center of Photography. (n.d.-b.) Artist Paul Strand (1890 - 1976) American. International Center of Photography. https://www.icp.org/browse/archive/constituents/paul-strand?all/all/all/all/0

Kim, M. (2022, January 1). "인생도, 수학도 성급히 결론 내지 마세요." ["Neither life nor math, don't jump to conclusions"]. Chosun Ilbo. https://www.chosun.com/national/weekend/2022/01/01/ASP3UHRZTBD3VC7X-N3LGQCIS2A/

Kyobobook. (n.d.). 임포스터 | 리사 손[Imposter | Lisa Son]. Kyobobook. https://product.kyobobook.co.kr/detail/S000000711553

Laura Letinsky. (n.d.). Laura Letinsky. https://lauraletinsky.com/

Laurent, O. (2017, June 30). Why we do it: Photographers and photo editors on the passion that drives their work. Time. https://time.com/4839246/photographers-passion/

Lewis Center for the Arts, Princeton University. (2014, October 24). Visiting artist lecture series: Laura Letinsky — Lewis Center for the Arts. Lewis Center for the Arts. https://arts.princeton.edu/events/visiting-artist-lecture-series-laura-letinsky/

Mathews, J. (2011, Juyy 7). How many high schools are there?. Washington Post. https://www.washingtonpost.com/blogs/class-struggle/post/how-many-high-schools-are-there/2011/07/06/gIQAaaN10H_blog.html

National Archives. (2021, September 30). The Civil War as photographed by Mathew Brady. National Archives. https://www.archives.gov/education/lessons/brady-photos

Northeast Asian History Foundation. (n.d.). 수산리고분 [Susan-ri Ancient Tomb]. NAHF. http://contents.nahf.or.kr/english/item/level.do?levelId=kk.e_0004

Oh, S. (n.d.). My trouble with Korea's obsession with white skin. Oh My Gloss Blog. https://www.ohmyglossblog.com/my-trouble-with-koreas-obsession-with-white-skin/

Park, S. (2008, October 3). 44% of Korean Ivy league students quit course halfway. Korea Times. https://www.koreatimes.co.kr/www/news/nation/2008/10/117_32124.html

Park, S. (2021, May 15). 과연 무엇이 '백인' 인가. . .인종은 사회적으로 구성됐다 [What is 'white'? race is socially constructed]. Pressian. https://www.pressian.com/pages/articles/2021051423014971135

Poemuseum(2018, July 25). Poe and the early development of photography. Poemuseum. https://poemuseum.org/poe-and-the-early-development-of-photography/

Richter, C. P. (1957). On the phenomenon of sudden death in animals and man. Psychosomatic Medicine. https://journals.lww.com/psychosomaticmedicine/abstract/1957/05000/

Ryu, J.B. (2018, July 3). 최영미 "괴물, 10년 전에 썼어야할 시. . .' 괴물 주니어' 넘쳐난다" [Choi Youngmi "the monster, a poem that should have been written 10 years ago. . . 'monster junior' is overflowing"]. Yonhap News TV. https://m.yonhapnewstv.co.kr/news/MYH20180703020100038

Sally Mann. (n.d.). Sally Mann. https://www.sallymann.com/

Sebasi Talk. (2022, January 14). 겸손이라는 가면을 벗어 던지세요: 리사 손 "임포스터" 저자, 콜롬비아대학교 바너드칼리지 심리학과 교수 | 메타인지 성장 공부 [Throw off the mask of humility: Lisa Son, author of "The imposter," professor of psychology, Barnard College, Columbia University | metacognitive growth study]. [Video]. YouTube. https://www.youtube.com/watch?v=fjre3LBFV8M

Son, L. (2019, June 26). 메타인지 학습법 [Metacognitive learning method]. Yes24. https://www.yes24.com/Product/Goods/74602725

Son, L. (n.d.). Lisa Son. LinkedIn. https://www.linkedin.com/in/lisa-son-a1ba144/

Sparkes, M. (2022, July 5). Fields medal 2022: Work on prime numbers and spheres wins maths prize [Video]. New Scientist. https://www.newscientist.com/article/2327304-fields-medal-2022-work-on-prime-numbers-and-spheres-wins-maths-prize/

Student Life Athletics. (n.d.). Harvard students life: Athletics. Harvard College. https://college.harvard.edu/student-life/athletics

The Ansel Adams Gallery (2023, March 10). Welcome to the world of fine arts. The Ansel Adams Gallery. https://www.anseladams.com/

The Harvard Crimson. (n.d.). Nominate fifteen minutes' 15 hottest freshmen. The Harvard Crimson. https://www.thecrimson.com/flyby/article/2014/1/25/15-hottest-nominations-2017/

The J. Paul Getty Museum Collection. (n.d.). Timothy H. O'Sullivan Ameican about 1840. Getty Museum. https://www.getty.edu/art/collection/artists/1892/timothy-h-o'sullivan-american-about-1840-1882/

U.S. Department of the Interior. (n.d.). Historic photographs by Alexander Gardner. Antietam National Battlefield. https://www.nps.gov/anti/learn/photos-multimedia/gardnerphotos.htm

UNESCO World Heritage Centre. (2012, October 12). Photo exhibition for the preservation of the World Heritage Site of the Koguryo tombs and mural paintings of the Democratic People's Republic of Korea. UNESCO. https://whc.unesco.org/en/events/960/

UNESCO World Heritage Centre. (2019, June 4). UNESCO and Democratic People's Republic of Korea launch new phase of project to safeguard Koguryo Heritage. UNESCO. https://whc.unesco.org/en/news/1992/

Wikipedia contributors. (2022, December 24). Ozawa v. United States. Wikipedia. https://en.wikipedia.org/wiki/Ozawa_v._United_States

Wikipedia contributors. (2022b, November 8). Jangdokdae. Wikipedia. https://en.wikipedia.org/wiki/Jangdokdae

Wikipedia contributors. (2023a, March 1). Alexander Gardner (photographer). Wikipedia. https://en.m.wikipedia.org/wiki/Alexander_Gardner_(photographer)

Wikipedia contributors. (2023c, March 13). Harvard University. Wikipedia. https://en.wikipedia.org/wiki/Harvard_University

Wordrow. (2022, September 23). 백옥[白玉]의 의미: 빛깔이 하얀 옥 ['Bae-kok': a jade that is white in color]. Wordrow. https://tinyurl.com/y44ruya7

Yoon, M.S. (2021, December 27). Tracing the root of Koreans' 'white skin obsession'. The Korea Herald. https://www.koreaherald.com/view.php?ud=20211223000883

AUTHOR BIO

Great Summer is a multifaceted pioneer with a background in technology, entrepreneurship, and the arts whose work has reached across the globe. He has contributed significantly as an entrepreneur, educator, and film industry advocate. Summer is the author of "Between Two Worlds," a memoir that explores themes of culture, identity, and the pursuit of meaning in a changing world.

Educated at notable institutions, including MIT Sloan and Columbia Business School, Great has founded several successful businesses in diverse locations, including the United States, Europe, and Korea. He has received various accolades, including being recognized as an MIT Emeritus Scholar.

Beyond his professional achievements, Summer has a keen interest in film and the arts, initiating film festivals and educational programs and contributing to over 100 multimedia projects. His dedication to creative storytelling is evident in his memoir, "Between Two Worlds," where he shares personal and cultural reflections, offering insights into the experiences that shape our understanding of the world. This work reveals Great Summer as a thoughtful individual deeply exploring the nuances of human knowledge and cultural exchange.

www.ingramcontent.com/pod-product-compliance
Lightning Source LLC
Chambersburg PA
CBHW030351130626
46549CB00004B/1451